LILIES OF THE HEARTH

LILIES
of the Hearth

THE HISTORICAL RELATIONSHIP
BETWEEN WOMEN & PLANTS

JENNIFER BENNETT   CAMDEN HOUSE

Canadian Cataloguing in Publication Data

Bennett, Jennifer
    Lilies of the hearth

ISBN 0-921820-27-5

1. Plants - Folklore.   2. Plants - Mythology.
3. Plants - Social aspects.   4. Women.   I. Title.

GR780.B46 1991   398.24'2'082   C91-093131-3

Trade distribution by
Firefly Books
250 Sparks Avenue
Willowdale, Ontario
Canada M2H 2S4

Printed and bound in Canada by
D.W. Friesen & Sons Ltd.
Altona, Manitoba, for
Camden House Publishing
(a division of Telemedia Publishing Inc.)
7 Queen Victoria Road
Camden East, Ontario
K0K 1J0

Design by
Linda J. Menyes

Cover etchings by
Marta Scythes

Colour separations by
Hadwen Graphics
Ottawa, Ontario

Printed on acid-free paper

Acknowledgements

Acknowledgement is gratefully extended
to the following for permission to reprint from
their works: Lines from "Matter: How We
Know" in *Women and Nature: The Roaring Inside
Her* by Susan Griffin, ©1978 Susan
Griffin, Harper & Row, New York. Quotation
from *The Englishwoman's Garden* reprinted
by permission of Rosemary Verey. Quotations
and poetry by Vita Sackville-West reprinted
by permission of Nigel Nicolson. Quotation
from *The Return to Cosmology* reprinted
by permission of Stephen Toulmin.
I would also like to thank Wayne Grady for his
graceful translation of the excerpt from
Christine de Pizan's *Le Livre du dit de Poissy*.
Mary Patton, my editor, has been wonderfully
encouraging and enthusiastic since she
first heard about this project. I thank her for
her support, patience and expertise
and also thank the many people involved at
Camden House: art director Linda Menyes,
artist Marta Scythes, who prepared the
cover art and the illustrations; former associate
publisher Frank B. Edwards; editor Tracy C.
Read; photo researcher Jane Good; publishing
coordinator Mirielle Keeling; production
manager Susan Dickinson; production
coordinator Charlotte DuChene; copy editor
Lois Casselman; typesetter Patricia
Denard-Hinch; and associates Catherine
DeLury, Laura Elston, Christine Kulyk
and Ellen Brooks Mortfield.

To my mother and sisters, who have been
with me since the beginning, and to my father,
the family gardener.

"O, a woman is then like a delicate garden . . ."
—Ben Jonson, *Epicene*,
or The Silent Woman, 1609

"Now, fare forth into all the lands, thou noble
and beautiful garden, thou delight of the
healthy, thou comfort and life of the sick.
There is no man living who can fully
declare and use thy fruit. I thank thee,
O creator of heaven and earth, who has given
power to the plants . . . contained in
this book that thou hast granted me the grace
to reveal this treasure, which until now has lain
buried and hid from the sight of common men."
—*Gart der Gesundheit*, 1485

Contents

Introduction

A couple of years ago, I was asked to speak
to a group of university women about
gardening. I decided to talk to them about this
book, which was partly researched at the
time, and I wore a flowered skirt that I used as
my "show and tell" for the evening.
"Flowers," I said, holding out my skirt, "are
considered suitable decorations for women's
clothing but less so for men's." I explained how
my flowery skirt was just one example
of a many-faceted relationship so ancient, so
subtle and so pervasive that we scarcely
notice it: the relationship between women and
plants. The women were obviously interested,
listening intently and asking thoughtful
and stimulating questions, even though (I later
learned) they had expected a talk on "Plants to
Choose for Your Perennial Garden."

∽

If those women did not receive exactly
what they had bargained for, neither did I in
working on this book. The idea for it

Ladies of the Victorian era were identified with flowers: delicate, passive and fleetingly beautiful.

~

germinated as I researched various horticultural subjects as the author of one gardening book, the editor of five more and the gardening editor of Canada's *Harrowsmith* magazine. Not frequently but often enough to impress me, I came upon references to women and plants that suggested a partnership of unexplored depth and complexity. I began to pursue the subject in its own right and discovered that woman was sometimes the ancient fertility goddess, sometimes the creator of helpful or dangerous herbal concoctions, sometimes the Victorian botany student getting a little recommended fresh air, sometimes a saint associated with roses or lilies and sometimes even the namesake of a flower or plant: Heather, Daisy, Rose, Iris, Myrtle. How many men have names like

Violet or Fern? Woman was the flower, the plant or, occasionally, the entire garden.

It seemed to be a subject worth pursuing, so I applied for and received a Canada Council grant to cover the six months I planned to spend researching and writing. That was six years ago, and except for the odd hiatus created by life's inevitable small crises, I have been working on the book ever since. The more I explored, the more satisfying the search became. I was discovering not only an interesting historical perspective but also a new way of looking at women, even modern women. Woman-as-flower was delicate, sexually passive, fleetingly beautiful and cherished, while woman-as-plant was earthy and powerful and either nurturing and creative or poisonous and destructive. Of course, little girls are associated with the colour pink — the colour of flower petals and sunsets, of things that change — while boys take for themselves the colours of the constants, such as the sea and the sky. But still, the entire picture eluded me. Just what was it that bound all these woman-plant images together?

And what of men as gardeners, cooks and plant breeders? When I was first talking about this book, many people said that, in reality, it was not their mothers but their fathers who were the family gardeners — as was the case with my own parents. The truth is that men have been involved in almost every human activity imaginable (except, of course, childbearing and breast-feeding), including all of those described at length in this book — botany, herbal medicine, witchcraft, embroidery and flower gardening — and often quite eminently so. It is they who have written most of the books on these subjects, formed the guilds to make the activities profitable and made names for themselves as experts and craftsmen. And their stories have been told.

On the other hand, Mother Nature and Mother Earth are decidedly and forever female, and disproportionately large numbers

*Mother Nature and Mother Earth are forever
female, though they, like the Roman goddess Flora,
have altered through time.*

~~~

~~~

of women have been involved, usually far more quietly, in the same plant-related activities as those concerning men. About 85 percent of the people executed for witchcraft were women ("as women in all ages have beene counted most apt to conceive witchcraft," according to Reginald Scot in the 16th century). In the early 19th century, more than half of the botanists in New England were female, a remarkable statistic for a scientific pursuit at the time. And so unnoticed that they did not rate statistics at all were the majority of women who prepared home herbal medicines and foods, embroidered tea towels and handkerchiefs and tended kitchen gardens. Even people not directly associated with plants (whom I find difficult to imagine) were influenced throughout the centuries, I believe, by various plant-related ideas of femaleness, ideas that have their roots in prehistory, in the ancient goddesses of fertility and vegetation.

Unfortunately, women's work, though "never done," was seldom documented. Women have maintained a silence and an invisibility that are frustrating to the historian. Illiteracy, modesty, fear and custom kept most of them away from pen and paper until only about two centuries ago, and then for another century, they tended to remain anonymous as authors. Meanwhile, in the writings of men, only noblewomen or notorious women made much of an appearance, and common women were seldom described in more than a facile way. Most remarkably, not a single woman is mentioned in most of the books about the history of botany, not even in those on the history of herbal medicine. I must thank the Public Archives of Canada and the librarians at the Hunt Institute, Cornell University, Agriculture Canada, Queen's University at Kingston, the University of Guelph and the British Museum for making my research considerably easier than it might otherwise have been. I wish, also, to thank the many women who talked to or wrote to me and to express my appreciation for the thousands of uncelebrated women, many long returned to the earth, whose work with plants I have come to value.

I finally realized, by the time I had gathered countless bits of information about Mother Earth, witchcraft, botany, flower gardening and the like, that the prehistoric association of women with useful plants, fertility, nurturing and the earth is so deeply ingrained in humanity, it has never really been lost, whatever changes societies have endured and however separate from nature the modern world may seem to be. Throughout the centuries, this relationship has been manifested in different ways, but always, it has simultaneously limited, defined and freed women. That long, floral, sweetly scented, dangerous, romantic path women share with plants is expressed at the end of the 20th century in the environmental movement, with its renewed appreciation of Mother Nature as both creator and destroyer.

In writing this book, my aim has been to produce not an encyclopaedia of women in horticulture but a general overview of what became, for me, a fascinating perspective on the history of women. Not as relevant to my subject and therefore excluded from the book are modern agriculture and forestry, two garden-related fields in which women have had less influence and less interest. The plants with which women have been most closely associated in this millennium are all those once loosely defined as "herbs," including shrubs, flowers and the species we still call herbs, both culinary and medicinal. To keep the text uncluttered, I have omitted footnotes and have instead compiled a bibliography for each chapter. There, interested readers will find further avenues of discovery.

May those avenues be fruitful, floral and as endlessly interesting as Nature herself.

I

"They Were the Earth Itself"

Of goddesses, moons and maypoles

Not long ago, a television commercial for
canned fruit featured the weighty line,
"It's not nice to fool Mother Nature," and
Mother Nature, not about to be fooled gladly,
let loose an animated lightning bolt
to show her disapproval of chemical additives.
It is the kind of image that sets one to
thinking. Just who is this creature, Mother
Nature, who has enough clout to send
viewers after unadulterated peaches?
Advertisers spend thousands of dollars for
every second of television time. They don't
waste their efforts on nonentities. Whoever this
character is, she commands respect.

To understand the changing face and social
position of the disembodied force called Mother
Nature, defender of purity in canned
fruit, is, I discovered, to understand something
of the changing role of mortal women and
their ties with the earth and plants. These ties
are so subtly interwoven in the tapestry

of women's history that they are scarcely noticed, yet the silent partnership between
women and plants has affected all aspects of
society, including business, science, religion,
art and medicine. The first manifestation of
those ties can be found, significantly enough,
in the earth—in small, buried icons created
in the darkness of prehistory.

If Mother Nature is now employed in advertising, she was once the most powerful of
deities, a goddess remembered in bone, stone
and ivory statues described as the most per-
sistent archaeological finds from the ancient
world. Many of the statues, which appear in
human burial sites from India to Great Britain, date back to the Neolithic, which began
around 7000 or 6500 B.C., but others are scattered among remains at least 20,000 years
older. The figures lack a distinctive face or
even head and are usually fat (although some
are slender, suggesting virgins), often with ex-
aggerated sexual features and torsos. Except
for their sexuality, some of these "fat Venuses," as they have been called, are almost
unrecognizable as human. Aside from cave
paintings, they are the earliest works of art
known in Europe and the Middle East. In
The Fear of Women, Wolfgang Lederer writes
of the statues: "These women were goddesses,
and for a period five times as long as recorded
history—far longer than any other deities—
they alone were worshipped, and in their
own peculiar manner." Mostly, the figures
have no feet, "suggesting that they stuck in
the earth, as if emerging from it. They were
of the earth—they were the earth itself . . . ."

The statues are so numerous, clearly so
important, they are assumed to be representations of goddesses. Marija Gimbutas, professor of archaeology and author of *The
Goddesses and Gods of Old Europe* (entitled
Gods and Goddesses in its first edition because "the editors did not allow me to say
goddesses first"), writes that new discoveries
"have served only to strengthen and support

*The most powerful prehistoric deities
worldwide were goddesses.*

the view that the culture called Old Europe
was characterized by a dominance of woman
in society and worship of a Goddess incar-
nating the creative spirit as Source and
Giver of All."

Long before the birth of the modern
religions, their foundations seem to have
been laid in goddess worship, in the venera-
tion of a Tellus Mater—a great Earth Mother,
controller of fertility and birth and, by extension, of infertility and death. She is entwined
in the roots of the relationship between
women and plants and shows up even now
in important places.

Although the earth goddess was worshipped mostly during a dim expanse of aeons defined by a lack of written information, shadows of a probable link between the earth and woman remain in many languages. Both nature and earth are still called "Mother" in English and the other Germanic languages, and in the Romance languages, they have retained feminine grammatical gender. The words "matter" and "matrix" themselves come from the same root as the Latin *mater*, mother.

In primal symbolism, woman as mother is the earth: life grows within her, separates from her and, like all the living products of the earth, is nourished by the milk of her own body. Mysteriously, like the earth with its springs of water, she sometimes bleeds but does not die. In her predictable, rhythmic fertility cycles and her less predictable pregnancies, woman is like various aspects of nature that became associated with her: the trees, which lose their leaves in fall and regrow them in spring; the snake, which sheds its skin and grows a new one; the moon, which waxes and wanes. Woman is also like the cow, which has a similar gestation period and whose horns, when seen head-on, resemble the shape of the crescent moon — as does the hook, precursor of the sickle, which was used and revered at least 14,000 years ago. While every one of these things, along with bees, honey and flowers, fell within the domain of many later goddesses, each was ultimately like the earth, which yields all life and takes all life. According to Shakespeare, "The earth that's nature's mother is her tomb/What is her burying grave, that is her womb."

Fortunately, the earth goddess survived long enough to be written about, when she emerged in the pantheons of early religions and in legends, albeit in different guises, as the mother of food crops, the source of knowledge about cultivation, the personification of the moon and vegetation, the embodiment of the principle of generation

A Mediterranean stone figure has the features typical of the goddess statues.

and procreation and sometimes as the patron of sexual love and prostitutes. One of these goddesses was Ishtar, or Artemis, who, under many similar names, was a preeminent figure throughout the Middle East. Mother of the gods in the last centuries before the birth of Christ, she was the overseer of vegetation and fertility and guarded maternity and childbirth.

Out of the chaos before the creation of the world, according to the Greeks, there came, on the one hand, the goddess Gaia (the earth) and Eros (love) and, on the other hand, Erebus (darkness) and Nyx (night). Young male partners often accompanied later manifestations of the earth goddess, typically a brother or son who was also her lover. Gaia, for instance, and her son Uranus (the heavens) together gave birth to numerous other gods, goddesses and such fantastic creatures as the Cyclopes. Gaia was the grain mother, goddess of vegetation and of domestic animals. Although she was not particularly important in later Greek worship, the earth goddess was the first one to exist, according to the poet Hesiod, and Plutarch said that worshipping her was "a custom handed down to us by our fathers."

The belief that the earth was female was cross-cultural. In Peru, the Earth Mother was Pachamama, and various North American tribes had female earth and plant deities. In the *Atharvaveda*, a collection of East Indian hymns that probably dates from before 600 B.C., is a hymn addressed to the earth goddess: "Upon the firm broad earth, the all-begetting Mother of the Plants, that is supported by divine law, upon her, propitious and kind, may we ever pass our lives." In Africa, the Ashanti praise their Earth Mother, Asase Yaa, at ploughing and harvest times. The Ibo worship the earth spirit Ala, who is portrayed in temples as a madonna with a child in her lap.

Gods and goddesses change with the needs of people. One century's fierce warrior god becomes another's peaceful, fatherly god. The same god may be asked to come to the aid of both soldiers and peacemakers. But what of goddesses? Today, of course, Westerners have no real goddesses to speak of, even though the Virgin Mary is the object of the prayers of some Christians, and such "sex goddesses" as Marilyn Monroe, Elizabeth Taylor and, more recently, Madonna, satisfy a lingering social hunger. The female principle, once held in high regard, has endured some tough times.

In tracing the history of the goddess from granter of fertility to advertising gimmick and movie star, I found that one period emerged as especially important. From about 4000 to 3000 B.C., the invasion by northern tribes with male gods influenced Mediterranean societies already undergoing fundamental changes as cultivation gradually changed from a job done largely by women with hand tools to a mechanized, male occupation. Controlling women and their relationships with men — hence keeping track of paternity and inheritance — became a high priority. Women became property, much like the domesticated animals whose fertility was also monitored. Powerful women now threatened the entire structure of society. Mother Nature had to be fenced.

The story of the Garden of Eden is pivotal in this process of change, for it marks (in metaphorical or historical terms, depending upon one's point of view) an important stage in the emerging dominance of the patriarchal religions. Sentiments like those expressed in an ancient Irish prayer — "I am Eve who brought sin into the world; there would be no grief, there would be no terror but for me" — are part of Western cultural heritage. Eden, paradise until the fall — the word "paradise," derived from the Persian *pairi-daeza*, literally means a garden or park containing trees — is a place where the first woman (and therefore all women) was shamed because of her own weakness. She was exploited by a snake and tempted by a plant, both ancient symbols of female power.

Snakes would seem to be the ultimate phallic symbol, and indeed, they have often been perceived that way; but in Egypt, the cobra was the hieroglyph for the word "goddess." Hecate, the moon goddess, was depicted either as partly snake in form or with snakes in her hair. Ishtar was said to be covered with snakelike scales, and at Delphi, Pythia, the priestess who brought forth the oracles of divine wisdom, was portrayed with a python coiled about her stool. Snakes themselves

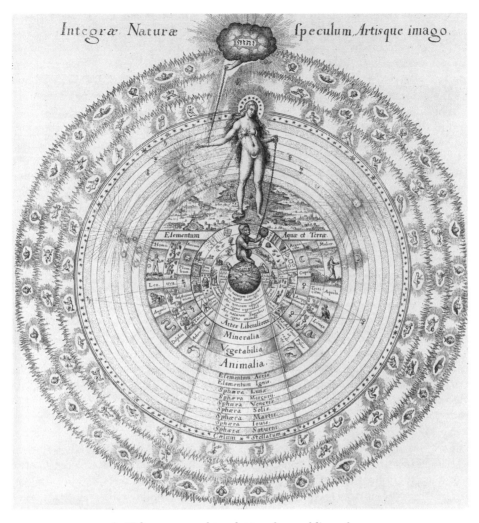

A 17th-century etching depicts the world's soul as a woman, with the female aspects on her left.

were also thought to be able to counsel, as did the serpent in the Garden of Eden.

The entire biblical account of the creation of humanity, some scholars have pointed out, can be explained in terms of the beginning of the dominion of males. Eve's creation from Adam's rib, for instance, is typical of the new era: "Unnatural symbols and hostility to the nature symbol . . . are characteristic of the patriarchal spirit," writes Erich Neumann in *The Great Mother.*

The cultural evolution from female to male deities has been interpreted as part of a wide-ranging social and psychological shift from the age of moon, matriarch and unconsciousness to that of sun, patriarch and consciousness. In Chinese terms, the age of yin, the dark, receptive female principle, the earth, gave way to the age of yang, the light, intellectual, male principle, the sky. The dominion of intuition faded, to be replaced by the dominion of logic, industry, mechanization and computers.

In a male-dominated world, a male god is seen to be an appropriate leader and model. By about 3000 B.C., government by male deities was well established in most cultures. The principal god, such as the Greek Zeus, who had been born of the mother goddess, now assumed a dominant role, while the Earth Mother retreated into the background, chastened and subdued, her responsibilities often divided among several goddesses and gods. In his treatise on agriculture written in the first century B.C., for instance, Varro thanks several gods and the goddesses Ceres, Flora, Minerva and Venus, saying of the latter two, "One protects the olive yard and the other the garden."

In ancient Rome, the prehistoric earth goddess, writes James George Frazer in *The Worship of Nature*, "would seem to have been pushed into the background by other and more popular deities, above all by the sky god Jupiter and by the corn goddess Ceres, with whom she was often confounded." Virgil advised his readers to "worship the gods, paying your yearly tribute to the corn goddess." (Corn, in this case, means Eurasian grains such as wheat and barley. Maize, a New World plant, had not yet reached European shores.) According to Ovid, the corn goddess made the seeds grow, while the earth goddess gave them a place in which to grow.

Similar to Ceres was the Greek Demeter — the last two syllables of her name mean mother — vegetation goddess, source of wise counsel and the mother of Kore, later called Persephone, the Roman Proserpine or Proserpina. Persephone's symbol was the pomegranate, because as a result of eating its seeds, she was committed to an eternal marriage with Hades in the underworld. (The pomegranate is an emblem of red, womblike, seed-filled fertility and, like the apple, recurs throughout the history of women and plants. It is interesting that the pomegranate has recently been found to contain small quantities of the female hormone progesterone.) Demeter was in such despair as she searched for her daughter that she allowed the world to become barren. Eventually, foreseeing the death of humanity in the death of plants, Zeus worked out a bargain with Hades: Hades could keep Persephone for four months of each year, but she would return to her mother for the remaining eight. In Greece, the fields were ploughed and sown after the October rains, when Persephone's return to the upper world allowed the crops to grow again. Her reappearance was celebrated in the three-day October festival of Thesmophoria, which was one of the most important in ancient Greece and was performed entirely by women.

Demeter was one of several goddesses responsible for teaching the skills of agriculture — a curious reminder of earlier times, considering that agriculture was by then an essentially masculine endeavour, its symbol the phallic plough working the female furrow. In fact, the beginning of the domestication of plants, which can be traced back at least as far as 8000 B.C. in some areas, may coincide with the birth of the vegetation goddess. The association of women with agriculture arises from an early era of smallholdings and hand tools, subjects explored in the next chapter.

The Roman goddess Ceres gave her name to the cereals she supposedly offered humankind. In a popular 15th-century book, *The City of Ladies*, Christine de Pizan wrote that in her imaginary community of women, "the noble queen Seres found a plow and showed them how they should cleve apart the earth and all the labour thereto pertaineth, how to cast the seed upon the earth and to cover it, and when the seed was grown

Ceres holds the key to the secrets of agriculture.

and multiplied, she showed them how they should reap the corn."

In Mesopotamia, the goddess Ninlil was responsible for teaching people about planting and harvesting. And half a world away, the Apinaye Indians, southeast of the Amazon River, believed that corn originated when a widower fell in love with a star, which came to him in several guises, including that of a woman. She introduced him to corn growing on a hardwood tree and taught him and his tribe how to plant it. According to another tribe nearby, corn and cassava sprang from the grave of an old woman who had instructed a man about growing food plants and then had herself buried in what subsequently became a lavish garden. An Indonesian belief has a woman's corpse giving birth to rice: a virgin raped by a god dies, and 40 days after she is buried, a variety of foods arise from her grave, including rice from her navel, a coconut tree from her head and corn from her teeth.

In one Southeast Asian story, rice existed from the beginning of time, but it did not produce grain until the goddess Kuan Yin, seeing that people were almost starving, resolved to help them by squeezing her breasts so that milk flowed into the ears of the rice plants, filling them with grain. To complete her task, she had to squeeze so hard that blood flowed from her breasts, creating two different types of rice: white from the milk and red from the mixture of milk and blood.

The idea that a woman's body can grow crops was fairly common in early cultures and not far removed from the idea of the goddess as agricultural instructor. In New Guinea, the Arapesh tell the tale of a woman, Sherok, who, by climbing a coco palm, is spared when her entire village is drowned by rain. When the earth becomes dry enough for her to descend, she puts yams into openings in her toes, fingers, feet and hair, where they appear as boils. Although men find Sherok repulsive, she is given work as a servant in a village where the people make soup from wood chips. But she can make soup from yams removed from her body, and the people find it so delicious that Sherok instructs them in the cultivation of the vegetables.

Sherok saved herself and was able to spread her knowledge because she climbed a tree — trees, like field crops, were often associated with the great mother. Paracelsus wrote in the 16th century: "Woman is like the earth and all the elements, and in this sense, she may be considered a matrix; she is the tree which grows in the earth, and the child is like the

The tree of knowledge is entwined with a serpent-woman in a blend of symbols.

fruit born of the tree. . . . Woman is the image of the tree."

One of the best-known mythical trees is the tree of knowledge, the one bearing the fruit which tempted Eve in that important place, the Garden of Eden. The goddess-as-tree, when she appears under the names Asherah or Ashtoreth in the Old Testament books of Ezekiel, Isaiah and Jeremiah, is described as worthy of fear and censure and as being an object of worship for women in particular.

Other mythological trees involve women. For instance, stories of a wonderful tree that bears many different fruits are known throughout the world and often have female connotations. In a painting of the Virgin Mary, a tree that is Jesus sprouts from her body. In an Indonesian version, a miraculous tree grows from the breast of a self-sacrificing mother and blooms and produces all sorts of valuables, among them a chest in the treetop that contains, paradoxically, the mother herself. In London's Victoria and Albert Museum is a sandstone statue of a tree spirit of North India, a Yakshi, that dates from the second century. It depicts a sensuous, bare-breasted woman who appears to be part of a tree trunk. The goddess as a sycamore or date palm that nourishes souls is a principal figure in Egyptian art; the sycamore goddess Hathor bears the sun on her head at the tip of the tree. And the heavenly tree of rebirth that shines with stars by night is the origin of today's winter solstice companion, the Christmas tree.

Besides the tree of knowledge, there was another symbolic tree in paradise, the tree of life, which would have given Adam and Eve immortality had they eaten from it. This legendary tree, which also has female aspects, recurs throughout the world's mythologies — it was a date palm in the Near East, an oak to the Druids, a cedar to the Hebrews — and it is often portrayed as penetrating three zones: heaven, earth and underworld. It draws its power from the earth and, like other trees, shelters, protects and nourishes humankind and other creatures. One of the best-known trees of life was the Scandinavian Yggdrasil, a gargantuan, evergreen, immortal ash watered by the three goddesses of fate, the Norns, who had their parallels in Greek and Roman mythology and who represent three phases of the moon — waxing, fullness and waning. As well as caring for the tree, the Norns passed the cosmic shuttle among themselves, weaving the fates of people and the world. The third of the Norns cut the thread of life. For the Greeks, it was Atropos who did this, and her name was given to atropa, deadly nightshade, a favourite plant of witches.

When stripped of its foliage, the tree's changeless centre is revealed — the essential woman beneath the more changeable exterior. The maypole, one such stripped tree, may be a remnant of goddess worship in which the season of rebirth was especially important. E.O. James describes the origins of May Day in terms of Hera, the official wife of Zeus, head of the Greek pantheon. Hera, who had been transformed into a cow, was the deity of marriage and female sexuality. When her milk fell on the ground, lilies sprang forth, and she was worshipped as the goddess of flowers. Girls in her service were known as flower bearers, and the spring festival in her honour celebrated by Peloponnesian women "might be described as the prototype of our later May Day revels." The Floralia, the festivals of the Roman goddess of flowers, Flora, took place between April 28 and May 3 and so also encompass the original May Day, May 1. (In many English-speaking countries, May Day celebrations are now held on the weekend of Queen Victoria's birthday, May 24.) The eve of May Day, Walpurgis Night, is an ancient pagan festival, supposedly the night when witches meet with their chief, the devil.

May Day revels, especially those of former centuries, recall ancient fertility rites, some of which may have their roots in the era of the goddesses. Englishman Phillip Stubbes described with disgust the festival in Elizabethan times when the maypole was brought home: "They have twentie or fortie yoke of oxen, every oxe having a sweet nosegay of floures placed on the tip of his hornes, and these oxen drawe home this maypole (this stinkyng ydol, rather), which is covered all over with floures and herbs, bound round about with strings, from the top to the bottom, and sometime painted with variable colours, with two or three hundred men,

*A sentimental picture of spring in female form
recalls more powerful goddesses of the past.*

～

women and children following it with great devotion. And thus being reared up, with handkercheefs and flags hovering on the top, they straw the ground rounde about, binde green boughs about it, set up sommer haules, bowers, and arbors hard by it. And then fall they to dance about it, like as the heathen people did at the dedication of the Idols, whereof this is a perfect pattern, or rather the thing itself. I have heard it credibly reported (and that *viva voce*) by men of great gravitie and reputation, that of fortie, threescore, or a hundred maides going to the wood over night, there have scaresly the third part of them returned home again undefiled."

The revelry has since toned down considerably and has, in many places, entirely disappeared. In the 19th century, Catharine Parr Traill recorded her memories of being "Queen of May" as a child in England, "my crown a circlet of flowers, my sceptre a flower-wreathed wand of hazel, and my throne a mound of daisy-sprinkled turf . . . ."

As a child of this century, I was a maypole dancer myself, a privilege granted all the girls in my primary school in a Canadian community of predominantly British background. We learned the dance that made the red, white and blue ribbons we held form a net-like braided pattern around the pole. (M. Es-

～

ther Harding writes that the ribbons of the maypole are interwoven "to represent the decking of the bare tree with bright-coloured leaves and flowers and fruits, all gifts of the moon goddess, giver of fertility." The weaving of the ribbons on the maypole also recalls the role of goddesses spinning the threads of fate and creating the fabric of life, the body's "tissues." Plaiting, weaving and knotting are generally women's activities, while the crossing of the weft and warp are symbolic of sexual union—people still refer to "crossing" plants and animals.) On May Day, we wore white, and the prettiest girl in the 12th grade was elected May Queen. We were as oblivious as our parents behind their cameras to our reenactment of the ancient ritual of weaving the cosmos around the tree of life, coaxing the mother goddess to ensure the fertility of the ground, the fertility of dozens of little virgins and the continuation of life for another season.

But if we children were unaware of maypole dancing as a fertility rite, we were soon to become part of another rhythmic and far more primal dance as puberty brought us under the dominion of the moon, another face of the great goddess. In most mythologies, the moon has been deemed female—Ishtar, Hecate, Diana—its 28-day cycle of waxing and waning remarkably similar to the average woman's cycle of fertility. The word "moon" has the same root, *mens*, as menstruation, month and mental; lunacy, too, was long considered to be moon-influenced.

The similarity between women's rhythms and those of the moon also has significance for plants. Moon, woman and plant were once seen as forming a sort of circle, each element linked to the others. The moon was known to influence the ocean's tides and was also thought to affect the movement of liquid in plants and people. Pliny wrote of mulberry that "if there be broken off at a full moon a branch beginning to bear, it must not

Flora, Roman ruler of vineyards, was transformed by artistic romanticism.

touch the ground, as it is specially useful when tied on the upper arm of a woman to prevent excessive menstruation." So closely linked were the moon and plants that sowing seeds, transplanting and harvesting according to the phases of the moon were generally accepted until the last century and were the priorities of Thomas Hill, the author of England's first gardening book, published in 1577. Gardeners knew the proper moon phase for the appropriate activity as well as they knew the depth and spacing for planting their seeds. People still plant by the moon in many places; instructional calendars can still be bought, and the advice within them is touted by such modern authorities as *The Farmer's Almanac*. In general, the waxing of the moon is the recommended time for sowing seeds, as the plants will supposedly grow along with the moon.

While the moon's supremacy in horticultural matters persisted through the centuries, women did not always fare so well. Around the fourth century B.C., Democritus wrote that a girl in her first menstruation should be led three times around garden beds so that any caterpillars there would instantly fall and die and that "usually the growth of greenstuff is checked by contact with a woman; indeed, if she is also in the period of menstruation, she will kill the young produce merely by looking at it." About 400 years later, Pliny recorded that "all plants indeed turn yellow when a woman comes near them at her monthly period." And Turner's *Herbal* of 1551 notes: "Let weomen nether touche the younge gourdes nor loke upon them, for the only touchinge and sighte of weomen kille the younge gourdes."

If women, especially those under the influence of the moon, came to be perceived as intrinsically antagonistic to food plants, they were increasingly allied with ornamental ones. As the earth goddesses gave way to a host of minor goddesses, one of the few members of the ancient pantheon to endure was Flora, goddess of flowers, who belongs to the oldest order of the Roman gods, although she was originally a minor deity. Flora presided over individuals transformed into flowers, such as Narcissus, Crocus and Adonis. Flowers fell from her hair when she shook it, and she ruled the blossoms of the grainfields, vineyards and olive yards and procured honey. She was, of course, most closely associated with spring. As I noted earlier, her festivals, the Floralia, were held in late April and early May. She was a sensual goddess, sometimes associated with Venus and sometimes portrayed nursing plants. As decorative gardens became more important in Europe after the mid-16th century, Flora became better known, a common model for painters and sculptors, who liked to portray her flirtatiously festooned with flowers and potted plants. But by the Victorian era, she had become a sort of comfortable great-aunt figure, and her name was given to countless baby girls.

Flora's extended reign brought her – her revels and erotica left behind – into an age when she was considered decorative but useless. She is, for instance, maligned in a 14th-century narrative poem, *The Floure and the Leafe*, attributed to Geoffrey Chaucer, which divides people into two groups: those associated with the leaf and those associated with the flower. The latter group is led by Flora. The leaf is the symbol of the chivalric values of endurance, wisdom, virtue and purity, while the flower signifies idleness, inconstancy and frivolity. The leaf group wears white, the followers of Flora green:

And as for her that crowned is in greene,
It is Flora, of these floures goddesse.
And all that here on her awaiting beene,
It are such that loved idlenes
And not delite of no business
But for to hunt and hauke and pley in medes,
And many other such idle dedes.

The followers of the flower, the poem declares later, "no greevance may endure." And thus were women, assigned to being both lovely and useless, increasingly portrayed. As brides began to carry bouquets of flowers to the altar, rather than the sheaves of wheat they used to bear, so too, for better or worse, a goddess of quiet passivity and mere prettiness replaced the substantial earlier goddesses of fertility and power. But woman's connection with plants endured, however changed it might be. Mother Nature would not be forgotten.

II

"Tyme for a Wyfe to Make Her Garden"

Woman as horticulturist

The heritage of Mother Nature is a humble
one, manifested in dirty fingernails,
sunburned skin and muddy feet. The great
vegetation goddess had not just a
mythical or symbolic association with plants
but a much more tangible one as
well: her mortal counterpart was a gardener.

Although worship of the great goddess
has been traced back 20,000 years, the goddess
of vegetation is probably much more
recent, her appearance coinciding with the
beginning of an agrarian way of life
around 6000 B.C. The consignment of
agriculture to a goddess rather than to a
god came about naturally: the first gardeners
—that is, the first people who tended
seeds, plants and roots and moved them to
more convenient places for caretaking
—were mostly women. Certainly, studies of
various tribes worldwide disclose
a trend of women working the soil, and even

27

recent statistics suggest that a majority of gardeners and seed buyers are women.

William Strachey observed of Indians in 17th-century Virginia that "the women, as the weaker sort, be put to the easier workes, to sow their corne, to seed and cleanse the same of the orabauke, doder and choak weed, and such like . . . ." Cherokee women raised thousands of bushels of maize every year, and the Huron Indians, who occupied a small stretch of land between Lake Simcoe and Georgian Bay in what is now Ontario, had, when first visited by Europeans, developed a prosperous culture in which tasks were clearly divided according to sex. The men hunted, fished and cleared land, while the women wove, prepared food and gardened. Using small wooden spades, they tended maize, beans and squash, supplying about three-quarters of all the food eaten by perhaps 20,000 people.

No more delightful telling of women's horticultural history can be found than the recently republished *Buffalo Bird Woman's Garden*, in which the narrator, a Hidatsa woman born more than 150 years ago in what is now North Dakota, describes to an anthropologist how she and her grandmothers raised their corn, beans, squash and sunflowers. In her tribe, each woman raised food for her own family, using tools made from wood and bone. "I remember seeing my grandmother digging along the edges of the garden with her digging stick to enlarge the field and make the edges even and straight." The squashes did double duty as dolls: "Each little girl carried her squash about in her arms and sang for it as for a babe."

These stories are not atypical. As Norman Scott Brien Gras writes in *A History of Agriculture*, "While men were engaged in herding livestock and in carrying on war, women were busy cultivating the fields with more continuous labour than had been required of them in the nomadic stage. Sometimes,

A Sioux woman demonstrates the use of a bone hoe to till squash, a native crop.

indeed, the men cut or burned down the trees on a plot of ground, leaving the actual cultivation solely to the women. Sometimes they aided the women in planting and harvesting also, but not in the care of the crops. Plant cultivation was primarily a woman's occupation."

Archaeologist Joseph R. Caldwell adds, "I would expect most of the earlier agricultural innovations to have been made by women. Most primitive societies contain two economies: men's work and women's work. Women, collectors par excellence, could cultivate a few plants without disturbing either the fabric of society or their own self-esteem." Only in the highest latitudes, poleward of 60 degrees, was meat a more important source of nutrients than plants, gathered or cultivated. Elsewhere, women's dominion in gardens gave them a powerful social position as providers of foods and medicines.

Nevertheless, it was more or less by default, or, more accurately, by biology, that women became living versions—fat, thin, tall and short—of the "fat Venuses," the prehistoric statues found throughout Eurasia. Slowed by pregnancy and bound to small children by the breast, women tended to stay close to the hearth, where food gathering and preparation, the use of medicines and the creation of household goods usually took place. All of these activities, as it happened, were likely to depend upon plants.

As well as gardening, Huron women cooked, wove mats from reeds or corn leaves, wove baskets from reeds or birch bark, made bowls from birch bark and gathered wild foods such as berries, acorns, walnuts, grapes and chives. The men, meanwhile, might stay away for days or weeks at a time, hunting, fishing, fighting or trading—not the sorts of activities that blend well with the ongoing care required by food plants (or babies). Masculinity meant being able not only to eat and run but to mate and run as well.

Carl Ortwin Sauer writes in *Land and Life* that because a mother had to care for her children, "hers was the greater necessity to learn the use of tools, digging stick, handstone and club." Indeed, "We speak of mankind as masculine collectively, but the great innovation [of controlling fire] and its elaboration was mainly done by woman, keeper of the hearth and provider of food." Being a woman meant staying put, more or less "stuck in the earth," as Wolfgang Lederer described the fat Venus statues. It is in part because women have been similarly "rooted" that they have been so frequently compared with plants and flowers.

But the fact that gardening was an essen-

Deities aside, the reality of Mother Earth lies in women growing food.

tially stationary activity did not make it unimportant or passive. Very likely, woman's role as gardener also made her the earliest plant breeder, implementing the process of selection over countless generations. At each harvest, women saved seed from only the best plants—the biggest, the most pest-resistant, the fastest-maturing, whatever—thereby ensuring the gradual development of superior crops. Even by the time Europeans visited the Americas, native New World plants such as tomatoes and corn had come so far from their wild origins that they were much more like the modern domesticated versions than the original species. Wild tomatoes, for instance, are tiny, seedy berries that still grow on Andean slopes, while the ancestors of maize are unremarkable grasses so far removed from their domesticated kin, they could not be identified positively until the 1980s, and then only by sophisticated genetic analysis.

The actual gardens that women cultivated were, in many cases, communal. Others, such as those of the Hurons, were individual family plots. Inheritance was of little import,

Aided by sun and moon, the mistress of the garden follows ancient rituals.

～

however, because the ancient system of slash and burn meant that when soil fertility in one area declined, new plots were wrested from virgin territory.

Within the gardens, crops were seldom planted in straight rows, which are concessions to agricultural machinery, but were grown instead in patches or hills conveniently spaced to allow pathways where necessary. The Iroquois women of New York grew corn, beans, squashes and sunflowers on ridges or mounds made with digging sticks and with hoes that had wood, bone or shell blades. The Hagen women of New Guinea kept individual family plots in which sweet potatoes, yams, corn, green vegetables and taro were also tended with wooden digging sticks. Such sticks could become more sophisticated, writes G.E. Fussell in *Farming Technique from Prehistoric to Modern Times*, if the woman "added a crosspiece to her stick or selected a suitable branch so that she could exert foot pressure, a possible origin for a spade."

Charles Darwin assumed that men were the gardeners and plant breeders, which would not have raised an eyebrow in the Victorian era: "The savage inhabitants of each land, having found out by many and hard trials what plants were useful or could be rendered useful by various cooking processes, would, after a time, take the first step in cultivation by planting them near their usual abodes. . . . The next step in cultivation, and this would require but little forethought, would be to sow the seeds of useful plants; and as the soil near the hovels of natives would often be in some degree manured, improved varieties would sooner or later arise. Or a wild and unusually good variety of a native plant might attract the attention of some wise old savage, and he would transplant it or sow its seed."

If the pronoun in the last sentence were "she" instead of "he," Darwin's observation would be more in keeping with the findings of modern anthropology. Unfortunately, the early accomplishments of women did not rate the attention of historians, partly because their achievements were so commonplace as to seem unremarkable. The improvement of crops was a gradual, ongoing process—there was no "discovery" of the beefsteak tomato, for instance, although occasional sports, or genetic mutations, did speed the process of crop development if they were noticed by gardeners alert to improvements.

If modern anthropological studies have placed prehistoric woman firmly in the garden, early authors were not so forthcoming. The first books about plants describe what was grown in gardens and why—and sometimes how and when—but very seldom by whom. It seems a case of not seeing the forest for the trees or, in this case, of not seeing the plantswoman for the plants, although an Egyptian poem of the 10th century B.C. does refer to "the little sycamore which she hath planted with her hand."

In their treatises on agriculture and husbandry, which range from the third century

Small household plots in which many different useful plants are tended with hand tools are the traditional responsibility of women.

B.C. until the first century A.D., the Romans Cato, Varro, Columella and Pliny the Elder record grape growing, tree pruning and farm buying in detail, but they make almost no mention of women's roles. The 35-volume *Natural History* of Pliny the Elder describes at great length all the plants to be grown in a kitchen garden and refers to nature, the earth and the moon as "she" but never says who actually did the gardening. Cato tells us only that a housewife must keep the farmstead neat and clean, raise hens, have plenty of dried and preserved foods and know how to make good flour.

Over the next centuries, books about kitchen-garden plants largely evaded the subject of who was out there in the garden. Most of the books were herbals—dictionaries of the medicinal uses of plants—which are covered in the next chapter. Some nonscientific writing is a little more helpful. For instance, in the 14th-century *Tale of Beryn*, possibly by Geoffrey Chaucer, a tavern keeper's wife describes her garden as "right a sportful sight."

Over the next two centuries, as literacy became more widespread, a clearer picture emerged. Books about gardening, although written by men, were addressed either to men or to women, depending upon the activity described. Women now came to light as the

If the garden of a married woman was unkempt,
"the wyfe of the house was no good huswyfe."

people in charge of vegetables and herbs, while the culture of grains, forage crops and fruit trees was more frequently the province of men. Agriculture and horticulture had come to be separate disciplines, their practitioners determined by gender. Agriculture (from the Latin *ager*, field) is now perceived as heavy work that may require machinery or animals and involves relatively large tracts of land devoted to a single crop, while horticulture (from the Latin *hortus*, garden) usually requires only hand implements and involves growing several different plant species together. Although the distinction between the two practices is not always clear, it could

be said, in general, that horticulture serves the needs of the family, while agriculture serves livestock and the community at large.

The division between the two practices has been widening for thousands of years. Many researchers of prehistoric gardening have considered the words agriculture and horticulture to be synonymous. But the use of draft animals and machinery made a difference, as reflected to some extent in Peter Farb's comment on North American Indians before industrialization: "As the primary food producers, women tend the gardens, collaborate in processing the food, have common storage places and sometimes even cook together. Irrigation somewhat changes the picture, as the responsibility for the success of agriculture then depends upon the men, who must cooperate to keep the water flowing."

As the tools of agriculture became increasingly sophisticated, allowing fewer people (and animals) to tend ever larger plots, horticulture came to be confined almost entirely to private family plots. Before the Industrial Revolution, the population of Europe was overwhelmingly rural, so most single-family dwellings could have some kind of garden. Rosetta E. Clarkson writes in *The Golden Age of Herbs and Herbalists*, "In mediaeval England, the garden of the mistress of a castle was limited by walls, while the little plot of the cottage housewife was compassed within the few feet permitted by the huddling of buildings together." As most smallholders owned less than an acre and a good deal of their produce went to paying the rent, as much food as possible had to be grown in as little space as possible. In any case, only one or two plants of some species, especially the medicinal ones, would have been required by a single family —only one plant of, say, rosemary, rue or lovage. More numerous items such as cabbages and carrots could be closely planted and reseeded whenever harvesting left a bare patch of ground. City gardens were not much different from those in the country, although pollution and shade limited what could be grown in most urban plots. Fortunately, gardens were less needed in the cities, where markets, herb sellers and apothecaries could provide goods already harvested and sometimes processed as well.

Early gardening books indicate that during the Middle Ages and Renaissance in Europe, women still cared for the vegetables and herbs which had always been their concern. And still, it was not a matter of choice: somebody had to take care of the household garden, and that job fell within the traditional dowry of skills a wife brought to her marriage.

If she were not *au courant*, her husband encouraged her to take up the trowel. At the end of the 14th century, the Ménagier de Paris, a Frenchman who wrote some rules of gardening and household skills for his young wife, instructed her not only about the seven deadly sins and about being chaste and loving her husband but also about the timing and method of planting and caring for herbs, vegetables, berries and roses. Barnaby Googe noted in his *Foure Bookes of Husbandry* of 1577, "Herein were the olde husbandes very careful and used always to judge that where they founde the Garden out of order, the wyfe of the house (for unto her belonged the charge thereof) was no good huswyfe."

Thus the ability to present a decent-looking garden as well as a neat house was expected of a woman. Dusting and weeding are not particularly interesting jobs, of course, but they were suitable for the large pool of unskilled female labour. La Quintinie, who managed Louis XIV's soup makers, recommended that married men be hired so that their wives could clean out the soup pots and weed. Weeder women were employed by royalty and the wealthy in Renaissance England, and diarist Celia Fiennes wrote that she saw a "figure of stone resembling an old weeder woman used in the garden" at Woburn Abbey in Bedfordshire in the 17th century.

As someone apt to be ill-humoured while performing the necessary but endless job of weeding, I am amused by a story in *The Sexual Life of Savages in North-Western Melanesia*, in which Bronislaw Malinowski describes the natives of the Trobriand Islands. The islanders believed that the women, when carrying out the strictly female task of weeding the gardens, would seize any man who wandered by, rape him and submit him to other indignities. The native men avoided the gardens during weeding season, as did Malinowski himself. In 1656, however, when William Coles published *The Art of Simpling*, all such danger and drudgery were merely wholesome. "Gentlewomen," he wrote, "if the ground be not too wet, may doe themselves much good by kneeling upon a Cushion and weeding." It's all for your own good, dear.

Woman's place in European gardens was not much documented until the 16th century, when books appeared that not only clarified activities previously taught by example and word of mouth but also defined them in such a way that the authors became "experts." (As always, the written word had more authority than the spoken; such is the elitism of literacy.) The authors of these first gardening books were male; not for another 200 years would women address one another in print on the subject of gardening. (One 17th-century author wrote, "The Pen must be forbidden [women] as the Tree of good and evill, and upon their blessing they must not handle it.") Nevertheless, the early gardening books for women, who were just becoming literate in sufficient numbers to make such publishing worthwhile, were often charming, if sometimes patronizing, works that must have been useful for the reader who wanted to learn a few new skills or wanted to find out whether she was doing things in the proper — or popular — manner.

In 1523, Sir Anthony Fitzherbert's *The Boke of Husbandry* spelled out tasks for the wife to do while the men were out caring for animals and crops, mending fences and digging ditches: "In the begynnynge of March, or a lytell afore, is tyme for a wyfe to make her garden, and to gette as many good sedes and herbes as she canne, and specially such as be goode for the potte and to eate: and as ofte as nede shall requyre, it muste be weded, for els the wedes wyl overgrowe the herbes." Fitzherbert also gave his readers the best advice he could gather about cooking and sewing.

No more delightful guide exists, however, than *A Hundreth Good Pointes of Husbandrie*, published in 1557, in which Thomas Tusser,

Like everyone else, women gardeners wanted to know how to work in the proper—or popular—manner.

a farmer and musician, rhymed out in couplets the country duties of both men and women. The chapter entitled "Marches husbandrie" includes these instructions:

In March and in April, from morning to night:
in sowing and setting, good huswives delight,
To have in a garden or other like plot
to turn up their house, and to furnish their pot.

And in a list of things to do in August:

Good huswifes in sommer will save their
*   owne seedes*
against the next year, or occasional needes.
One seede for another, to make an exchange,
with fellowlie neighbourhood seemeth not
*   strange.*

Both authors make it clear that it was the woman's duty to produce plants for food as well as medicine. Tusser listed 42 herbs for the kitchen, including primrose, marigold, tansy and violets; 22 herbs and roots for salads and sauces, including sage, artichokes and asparagus; 11 common vegetables—"Herbs and Roots to Boil or to Butter"—and also plants "to trim up the household." It is interesting to note, however, that Tusser does not mention a flower garden, although he does recommend potted flowers for windows.

Such books were reminders of duties to be done and apparently were written for readers already familiar with the assigned tasks. Gervase Markham, in his 1615 book *The English Housewife* (its counterpart, *The English Husbandman*, had been published two years earlier), wrote of the housewife-gardener: "She shall also know the time of year, month and Moon in which all Herbs are to be grown; and when they are in their best flourishing, that gathering all Herbs in their height of goodness, she may have the prime use of same." For instance, "In June, the Moon new, sow gourds and rad-

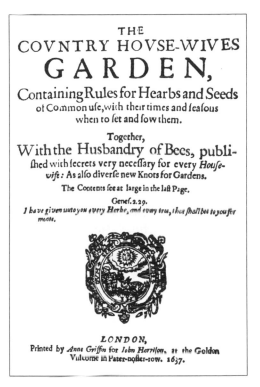

William Lawson's guide recommended that women plant two gardens: one practical and one beautiful, for decorative plants alone.

⌇

ishes, the Moon old, sow Cucumbers, Mellons and Parsnips."

While some books were clearly written for the knowledgeable, some women knew very little about gardening, according to William Lawson's *The Country House-wives Garden . . .* published in 1637. During weeding, for example, that ancient chore for which women have been considered so well suited, "I advise the Mistress either to be present her self or to teach her maides to know herbs from weeds." Furthermore, the housewife should start with a few easy plants, such as peonies, tansy, mint and bachelor's-buttons: "Let her first grow cunning in this, and then she may inlarge her Garden as her skill and ability encreaseth." Lawson listed exactly what plants were to be grown by "the country house-wife" and how.

He also recommended that the reader have two gardens—one practical and one beautiful—which marks an important change in gardening and in women's activities, although the two gardens were as yet not entirely different. There would be "a garden for flowers, and a Kitchin garden; or a Summer Garden; not that we mean so perfect a distinction that we mean the Garden for flowers should or can be without herbs good for the kitchin, or the Kitchin garden should want flowers nor on the contrary; but for the most part, they would be severed . . . ." Indeed, Lawson's "kitchin" garden grew many plants that today's gardener would think more appropriate in the flower garden: "daffadowndillies," roses and lavender, the latter two, which "yield much profit and comfort to the senses," recommended for both gardens. The flower garden, on the other hand, included some plants that we would now classify as pot-herbs—hyssop, sage and thyme—along with the more clearly ornamental cowslips, peonies, daisies, pinks and lilies. Putting plants in different gardens was, said Lawson, "a plain and sure way of Planting, which I have found good by 48 years (and more) experience in the North part of England."

Lawson divided his herbs into three groups—those "of great growth, of middle growth" and "of smaller growth," the sort of classification still useful for gardeners just learning about various plants and wanting to know which should go at the back of the border or bed and which in front. Among the tall species were angelica, tansy, hollyhocks, lovage, elecampane, lilies and poppies. The smallest included pansies, strawberries, saffron crocuses, daffodils, onions and daisies, while among the middle-sized plants were parsley, irises, anise, coriander, "fether-few" (feverfew, *Chrysanthemum parthenium*) and marigolds.

Another of the middle-sized herbs, a must in every garden, was what Lawson called the "Stock-Gilliflower," the clove pink (*Dianthus caryophyllus*), a type of carnation especially valued for its sweet, spicy scent. The species name bears the old word for clove tree, caryophyllon, and the common name came into English via the Old French *girofle*, clove. Lawson wrote that "of all flowers (save the Damask Rose), they are the most pleasant to sight and smell . . . their use is much in ornament and comforting the spirits by the sense of smelling." John Parkinson added in his 17th-century *Paradisi in sole, paradisus terrestris* that the "Stock-Gilloflower" was "almost as common as Wall-flowers [*Cheiranthus cheiri*], especially the single kindes in every womans Garden." Sweet scent was a far more important attribute of flowers then than it is now, and such plants were used in liqueurs, perfumes and potpourris as well as for strewing, an old custom of laying scented plants on floors.

Among the culinary plants, wrote Lawson, "lettice" was "usual in Sallets and the pot"; that is, served cooked as well as fresh. Savory was "good for my House-wifes pot and pye," and other English favourites were leeks, onions, garlic, broad beans and peas. Although Lawson declared that "we are Gardiners, not Physitians"—an indication of the increasing divergence of the two disciplines—he also mentioned a few medicinal uses of plants: "fether-few" should be included in the garden because it was "good against the shaking fever," radish was "sawce for cloyed stomachs," and rue was "too strong for mine House-wifes pot, unless she will brew Ale therewith, against the Plague."

A list of the plants grown by women in the early 18th century, by which time plots for beauty and utility were often quite separate, comes from Charles Evelyn, who wrote that

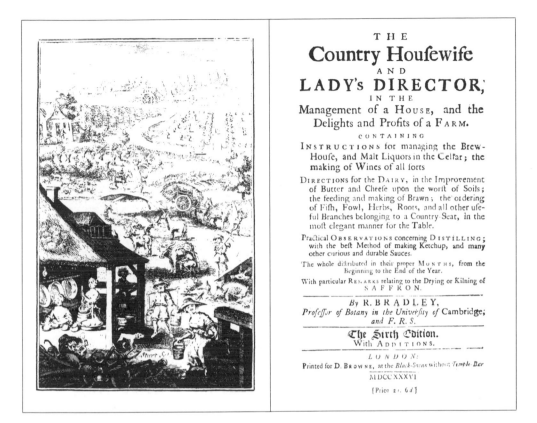

THE
Country Housewife
AND
LADY's DIRECTOR;
IN THE
Management of a HOUSE, and the
Delights and Profits of a FARM.

CONTAINING

INSTRUCTIONS for managing the Brew-
Houfe, and Malt Liquors in the Cellar; the
making of Wines of all forts

DIRECTIONS for the DAIRY, in the Improvement
of Butter and Cheefe upon the worft of Soils;
the feeding and making of Brawn; the ordering
of Fifh, Fowl, Herbs, Roots, and all other ufe-
ful Branches belonging to a Country-Seat, in the
moft elegant manner for the Table.

Practical OBSERVATIONS concerning DISTILLING;
with the beft Method of making Ketchup, and many
other curious and durable Sauces.

The whole diftributed in their proper MONTHS, from the
beginning to the End of the Year.

With particular REMARKS relating to the Drying or Kilning of
SAFFRON.

By R. BRADLEY,
Profeffor of Botany in the Univerfity of Cambridge;
and F. R. S.

The Sixth Edition.
With ADDITIONS.

LONDON:
Printed for D. BROWNE, at the Black-Swan without Temple-Bar
MDCCXXXVI

[Price 2s. 6d]

Richard Bradley's book for women dealt with
household management rather than gardening.

such common flowers as foxgloves, Canterbury bells, monkshood and lupins "almost every Country Dame has in her Garden and knows how to sow, plant and propagate them. Then, for your sweet Herbs, there's Marjoram, Basil, Penny-royal, Mastick, Lavender, Thyme, Sage Gold and Silver, and double flower'd Rosemary, which every Kitchin-Maid is so well acquainted with that I need make no farther Mention of them."

As ornamentation became increasingly important in all areas of life, food gardening for sheer necessity became relegated to poor women, while richer women, who bought their produce or hired gardeners, grew flowers simply for the sake of ornament and fragrance. The decorative garden, like the decorative woman, was put on display, while the homely kitchen garden assumed the backdoor rank of the servant woman. As early as 1629, John Parkinson was advising readers not to place the kitchen garden in front of the house, "for the many different scents that arise from the herbes, as cabbages, onions, etc., are scarce well pleasing to perfume the lodgings of any house." As the traditional roles of women decreased in value, so their homely gardens, judged "a sportful sight" three centuries before, lost value as well.

In the 18th century, Richard Bradley wrote

a trilogy of works that assumed women's place was not in the garden at all but indoors dealing with the fruits of men's labour. The books aimed to "show the complementary nature of domestic economy—the balance between men working outdoors on the land, planting and harvesting crops and husbanding their animals so as to produce food, and women labouring within the house to process it." The first volume of Bradley's trilogy was directed to men in general, the second was on the "science of good husbandry," and the third was *The Country Housewife and Lady's Director*, which was concerned with such female pursuits as preparing raisin wine and pickling "Mary-gold-Flowers."

Around the same time, Charles Evelyn wrote another trilogy, *The Art of Gardening Improved*, which included, along with a book for clergymen and one for gentlemen (both dealing largely with fruit trees), *The Lady's Recreation*, which considered the provinces of women to be flowers, conservatories and greenhouses, including "the Culture and Management of Exotics . . . ." Evelyn wrote that "the curious Part of Gardening in general has been always an Amusement chosen by the greatest of men, for the unbending of their Thoughts, and to retire from the World; so the Management of the Flower-Garden, in particular, is oftentimes the Diversion of the Ladies, where the Gardens are not very extensive, and the Inspection thereof doth not take up too much of their Time." Gardening had by then become an "amusement" for men and a "diversion" for women. So much for necessity, at least among Evelyn's readers.

Tired, perhaps, of millennia of toiling with herbs and vegetables, most women took quite willingly to the less earnest work of growing plants for beauty alone. Certainly, the Industrial Revolution gave privileged people money to spend, time to spend it and less need to be self-sufficient. By the mid-18th century, an unsigned article in *The Univer-sal Magazine of Knowledge and Pleasure* went so far as to insist that women "never contemplate on nature and are insensible to her beauteous works; the barren heath and the verdant lawn are, to them, objects equally indifferent. With vacant eye they pass the pleasing landskips, whose variegated prospects display the evident marks of an all-perfect and all-bountiful Creator." And in 1795, when *The Garden-Companion for Gentlemen and Ladies* appeared, its author assumed virtual imbecility on the part of his female readership: "The ladies, also, who cannot amuse themselves better, and in a way that will more contribute to their health, are here instructed how to dispose their flowers to the best advantage and to procure a general bloom throughout the year."

Today, women have many ways to amuse themselves and, for the most part, have no need to garden at all, yet the female presence in the garden persists. Bonnie Loyd, editor of *Landscape* magazine, estimated that in 1987, 60 to 80 percent of the people who ordered seeds and plants were women, and landscape architect Christopher Grampp reported at the same conference ("Meanings of the Garden") that in more than two-thirds of the average, middle-class California households he visited, the designer and maintainer of the garden was a woman.

Avilde Lees-Milne and Rosemary Verey, who have edited two companion volumes on male and female gardeners, found the two groups essentially different: "Generally speaking, the men are more serious, definite and self-assured. On the other hand, many of the women were agreeably surprised when they found how successful their gardens turned out to be . . . their lives and their gardens proved to be the successful means of expressing their artistic ability." The fat Venus is still alive, even though she may have replaced her digging stick with a set of stainless steel secateurs.

III

"This Most Excellent Art of Physick"

Home herbal medicines, perfumes and cosmetics

In my kitchen cupboard a few years
ago was a box of Keen's mustard powder whose
label bore a recipe for mustard plaster,
a herbal remedy so old that it was
once expected to work because the "hot" plant
would cure a "cold" disease, according to
the second-century alchemy of Galen.
As a child, I was treated with a mustard plaster
—a wet cloth sandwich filled with mustard—
and I remember just how hot it was.
In fact, through the generations, a few of
the countless children whose chests have borne
this weighty treatment have been badly
blistered by practitioners unaccustomed to the
power of the mustard seed. During
the last years that the Keen's box listed
the recipe, it came with the warning "for adults
only." Now, the recipe has disappeared,
a symptom, within my own lifetime, of a decline
in everyday use of herbal remedies that
started about two centuries ago
and has accelerated in the 20th. Before then,

THE
QUEENS CLOSET
OPENED:

Incomparable Secrets in
Physick, Chyrurgery, Preserving, Candying, and Cookery;

As they were presented unto the
QUEEN

By the most Experienced Persons of our
times, many whereof were honoured with her
own Practise, when she pleased to descend to
these more private Recreations.

The Fourth Edition corrected, with many Additions: together with three ex-
act Tables, one of them never before
Printed.

Transcribed from the true Copies of her
MAJESTIES own Receipt Books,
by W. M. one of her late Servants.

Vivit post funera Virtus

London, Printed for Nathaniel Brooks at
the Angel in Cornhill, 1658.

HENRIETTA MARIA REGINA.

G. Faithorne fec:

*Sold by Nat. Brooke,
att y Angell in Cornhill*

*Early household guides included recipes for both
"physick" and "cookery."*

almost any woman would have known how to use a mustard plaster.

Plants such as mustard—not just medicinal herbs but all sorts of useful plants—are so entwined with female history that it is impossible to understand one fully without taking the other into consideration. Plants were dietary staples in all societies except the most Arctic and were also used, chiefly by women, in the home treatment of all sorts of ailments, ranging from the common cold to the plague. But as is the case with home gardening, little information is available on the use of plants in everyday life before the Middle Ages and the Renaissance. Records of the time reveal that housewives lived unremarkable, mostly unremembered lives so closely associated with plants that even women would not have considered the partnership worthy of attention. Unlikely to venture far beyond the nearest town in her lifetime, the housewife created around her a world limited in scope but complex in its own ways by producing just about everything perishable on site and from scratch – or rather, from leaf, root and flower. Some of the plants she grew at home, some she collected from the wild, and others she purchased from apothecaries or herb women. The flavours, fragrances, homeopathic properties and physical characteristics of dozens of plants were as well known to some women as were the characteristics of their friends and families.

This herbal knowledge had been learned, passed on and embellished by conversation and example for countless generations and was eventually collected in herbals, books that typically consist of a list of plants with a paragraph about the medicinal uses of each one. The earliest compilers of herbals were men such as Dioscorides, who recorded in his first-century *De materia medica* the medicinal properties, real and supposed, of about 600 plants. Dioscorides was quoted for more than a thousand years by such herbalists as Elizabeth Blackwell, who wrote, 17 centuries later, of white mustard: "Dioscorides recommends the Juice mixed with Water and Honey as good to gargle the throat with and help Women who are troubled with the Mother." Of course, such "fathers of herbal medicine" as Dioscorides did not simply pull their therapeutic theories out of the air. His herbal was the human, largely female heritage finally recorded by a man interested in the subject and literate enough to be able to write it down. Ironically, the early records of women's knowledge could be read by very few women.

One early herbal was written by a woman (much earlier than Elizabeth Blackwell, which is remarkable enough), and she was, as one might expect, a very unusual person – a mystic recognized as such by Pope Eugenius III, a woman who corresponded with many leading theologians, intellectuals and emperors of her day. Hildegarde, abbess of a convent at Rupertsberg until her death in 1179, produced several books, including *Physica*, the earliest book about natural history written in Germany. In *An Illustrated History of the Herbals*, Frank J. Anderson writes that Hildegarde's book "influenced the 16th-century works of . . . the so-called 'German fathers of botany,' but the fact is that German botany is more indebted to a 'mother.'"

In *Physica*, Hildegarde described the natural world and provided medicinal advice garnered from her own observations, from books and from folk tradition. She listed 230 plants as well as many animal and chemical substances with their supposed therapeutic qualities for both humans and animals. Like other medical treatises of her time, Hildegarde's prescriptions combined the fabulous with the sound. Carrying a dead frog about, she wrote, was good for gout, a decoction of mulberry leaves could remedy skin diseases, hemp seed (marijuana) could soothe a headache, prunes would help a dry cough, and herbal baths might ease various complaints. Using her knowledge and her simples (medicinal herbs used alone), Hildegarde treated the sick so effectively that she was credited by one monk with miraculous powers of healing. She has, in fact, been called Saint Hildegarde, although she was never formally canonized.

In the later Middle Ages, women's increasing literacy meant they had access to widely published herbals they could use as references. John Gerard's *The History of Plants* was especially popular in 17th-century Britain. By that time, women not only could glean information from the herbals for themselves but – more important in terms of their own history – also could exchange their own knowledge and experience in the form of published collections of "receipts." Richard Bradley acknowledged that he had collected the receipts in *The Country Housewife and Lady's Director* from "ingenious Ladies, who had Good-nature enough to admit of a Transcription . . . for public Benefit . . . ."

Bradley's collection was one of a genre known as stillroom books, essentially scrapbooks that were part herbal, part cookbook, part household guide. The typical stillroom book, whose recipes were in the form of short paragraphs rather than lists of ingredients as in modern cookbooks, included directions for food preservation and preparation of such items as spiced bread, "fine Pippin Tartes," pickled oysters and "Haggesse Pudding," as well as instructions on drying apples and other fruits, candying flowers and making almond paste.

In keeping with the education of their readership, the stillroom books were written "in easie termes without affected speech," as Sir Hugh Platt noted of his 1609 *Delightes for Ladies, to Adorn Their Persons, Tables, Closets & Distillatories*. Some of the books were simply published forms of scribbled kitchen journals, such as the 1714 *Collection of Above Three Hundred Receipts in Cookery, Physick and Suergery*, generally attributed to Mary Kettilby. One typical stillroom book was started around 1600, when the Fairfax family of England began to keep a record of their household activities. The book was passed down through several generations, continuing to acquire comments on cookery and cures, sometimes written neatly, sometimes almost illegibly, according to the hand at work. Mrs. E. Smith's 1727 *Compleat Housewife* included a "Collection of about three hundred family receipts of medicines: viz, drinks, syrups, salves, ointments, and various other things of sovereign and approved efficacy in most distempers, pains, aches, wounds, sores, & c."

What became clear as I looked through various stillroom books was that the "compleat housewife" was expected to know not only how to cook with plants—to make soups, "salats," vinegars and cordials—but also how to make snuffs, pomanders and such herbal cosmetics as tooth cleansers from tamarisk bark or pomegranate peels, hand whiteners from oatmeal, and hair dyes from turmeric, barberry bark or rhubarb steeped in white wine and left to sit in the sun. (Elizabethan Englishwomen used those plants to turn their hair fashionably reddish, while Spanish and Arabian women had recipes with gallnuts and mallows that would turn blond hair dark.) Some books also included the occasional bit of gardening advice: how to ripen "musimillions" (muskmelons), for instance, and when to sow seeds according to the phases of the moon.

More important, the books described how to make various herbal medicines. "It is meet," wrote Gervase Markham in *The English Housewife*, first published in 1615, that the housewife "have a physical kind of knowledge, how to minister any wholesome receipts or medicines for the good of [her family's] healths, as well as to prevent the first occasion of sickness, as to take away the effects and evil of the same, when it hath made seisure on the body."

The line separating food from medicine was then a vague one—and rightly enough. Now, although scientists have proved that plant alkaloids affect people in various ways and that vitamins and minerals can cure or harm or simply keep a body well, food is by and large considered to be quite distinct from medicine, which (with the exception of stewed prunes, bran muffins, orange juice and more recently discovered "miracle foods" such as oat bran and broccoli) is something with a meaningless name taken as an anonymous-looking syrup or pill. The gradual division of food and medicine into separate camps helped to allow scurvy, rickets and other nutrition-related diseases to be troublesomely and even fatally common in turn-of-the-century Britain, where a diet based on tea

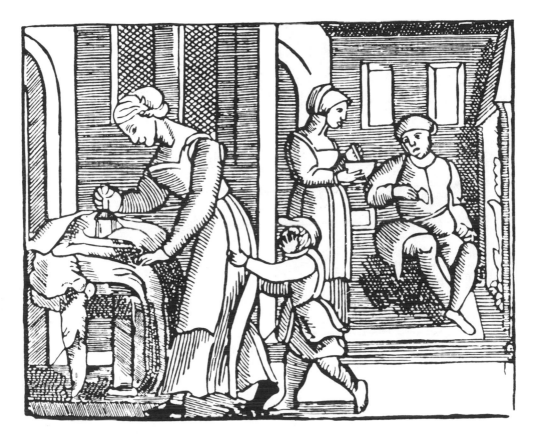

*In centuries past, women's daily duties required an
extensive knowledge of plants.*

～

and white toast with jam created several generations of pale, sickly people with bad teeth.

The truth is, however, that foods and some
medicines can be seen as the same things in
different dosages. Foods which are health-
sustaining may, in larger amounts or different forms, be curative or dangerous, while
substances which are toxic in large amounts
may be edible and even therapeutic in smaller
ones. Until the present century, recipes for
meals and recipes for medicines were quite
naturally found in the same books, and sometimes they were the same recipes. The liqueur
Chartreuse, for instance, was and continues
to be both medicine and beverage.

Chartreuse is a sort of aqua vitae, or *eau de
vie*. Water of life, it has been called, so beneficial has it been considered for spiritual and
physical well-being. While the genuine Chartreuse is made by French monks according
to a closely guarded recipe, similar drafts such
as green usquebaugh (whisky), the heady
Gaelic version, were made at home in past
centuries. One printed recipe for usquebaugh
called for the housewife to infuse a mixture
of anise seeds, fennel seeds and coriander
seeds in a gallon of French brandy for nine
days, "then take of the Spirit of Saffron one
Drachm, distil'd from Spirit of Wine, mix
with the rest; infuse during this time some Li-

The aquavite women prepared water of life in their simple stills.

～

quorice sliced in Spirits, one Pound of Raisins of the Sun, and filter it." Herb women of 15th-century Germany were called *Wasserbrennerinnen*, or aquavite women, in honour of such spirits concocted with their simple stills. Aqua vitae could alleviate almost any ill—or at least help the sufferers forget their pains.

Aqua vitae was medicinal enough alone, but mixed with poppies, gillyflowers, marigolds, rosewater, spices and raisins, it became "surffet water," listed in almost every stillroom book as a tonic to take after overindulging at mealtime. The illnesses addressed in stillroom books included a host of common complaints, ranging from too much dinner to headaches, melancholia, dry skin and constipation. There were also cures for baldness, medicines "to strengthen ye eyes" and, of course, "for a cold in ye head," which, noted Mrs. Ann

Blencowe in her receipt book, was to be treated by rubbing sage leaves and applying them "to ye nostrils in ye morning." Sufferers of colic might be given the most venerable of matronly cures, "a great quantity of Chicken broth, a gallon or more." One could make "a most pleasing and wholesome messe of broth for a sicke body," one author promised.

But there were also prescriptions for less common, more severe disorders. *The Ladies Cabinet Opened* lists recipes to treat such symptoms and diseases as the plague; "canker in the breast"; "bloody flix" (or flux, a heavy flow); "consumption" (the dreaded, all-too-common and at that time deadly tuberculosis); "dropsie" (another killer, an illness in which watery fluid is retained in the body due to heart disease); and "French pox" (syphilis, also known to the English, in the typical manner of blaming one's worst diseases on one's enemies, as Spanish pox). Even though women could not cure everything, they were expected to be familiar with every ailment from the most common to the most deadly and to be able to apply first aid until the physician, or "leech," arrived with his rather malevolent black bag and his often horrendous treatments.

The Fairfax family's stillroom book, published in 1890 under the title *Arcana Fairfaxiana*, points out, as do other such collections, that the home healer recorded "old wives' " recipes as well as those garnered from physicians and that the latter are often considerably less attractive than the old wives'. Early household remedies were largely herbal concoctions, such as a cure for laryngitis that included rosemary, sage and hyssop heated, wrapped in a cloth and laid "about the nape of the neck and the pulses of the arms as whott as it may be suffred daily." Among physician's receipts, however, one is more likely to find excrement, vermin and other ingredients that might have been gathered in a house of horrors. One recipe Henry Fairfax entered in the book—an old formula for treating wounds caused by weapons—called for blood, turpentine, boar fat and moss scraped from a skull. Recipes from three of the physicians who attended the last illness of Charles II appear in *The Lady Sedley Her Receipt Book*. One is Sir Edward Greaves' "Receipt for Convulsion Fitts," which consisted of peony roots, the skull of a dead man, asses' hooves, white amber and bezoar (from the stomach of a ruminant), ingredients that could be purchased from apothecaries—or so they said. One of Gervase Markham's recipes, which, he said, came not from his own knowledge but from physicians, recommended that in treating "the falling-evill," epilepsy, the healer oven-dry a mole of the same sex as the patient, powder it and then give it to the patient morning and evening "for 9 or 10 days together." (Mary Kettilby had her reservations: "I dare say this is an approv'd Receipt, because I had it from a very choice Hand; but I should fear 'twould be impossible to make a young Child take so much of so loathsome a Thing as this Powder must needs be.")

Strange but benign substances such as amber and dried mole added little more than an aura of mystery to the physician's cures, but more common ingredients such as sulphuric acid, lead, copper sulphate and salts of arsenic and mercury either cured dramatically, with a great deal of sweat, saliva, urine and bile, or administered useless suffering and a painful death.

With a steadily changing pharmacopoeia to fuel the newest medicinal fads and fashions, physicians needed to be *au courant* if they were to bring in higher fees and stay competitive with their colleagues. Keeping up to date often meant using remedies so disgusting and so mysterious in origin and purpose, one could take as a compliment to housewives Gervase Markham's condescending comment that they were intrinsically incapable of practising medicine in the fashion of physicians: "Indeed, we must confess that the depths and secrets of this most excellent Art of Physick are far beyond the capacity of the most skilful woman, as lodging only in the brest of learned Professors, yet that our Housewife may from them receive some ordinary rules and medicines, which may avail for the benefit of her family is (in our common experience) no derogation at all to that worthy Art."

In fact, "the most skilful woman" was, according to Robert Burton in his 1621 *The Anatomy of Melancholy*, supplying a service at least as valuable as that of physicians: "Many an old wife or country woman doth often more good with a few known and common garden herbs than our bombast Physicians with all their prodigious, sumptuous, farfetched, rare, conjectural medicines." Burton wrote from experience when he declared, "The country people use kitchen Physick, and all common experience tells us that they live freest from all manner of infirmities that make least use of Apothecaries." His own mother he "knew to have excellent skill in chirurgery, sore eyes, aches, & c., and such experimental medicines, as all the country where she dwelt can witness, to have done many famous and good cures upon diverse poor folks, that were otherwise destitute of help . . . ."

In the 16th century, the famous Swiss physician Paracelsus wrote that "not all things the physician must know are taught in the academies. Now and then, he must turn to old women . . . to elderly country folk and many others who are frequently held in contempt. From them he will gather his knowledge, since these people have more understanding of such things than all the high colleges."

Traces of such medicinal women appeared from time to time in my research and sometimes in contexts showing their knowledge to be at least as useful as the physicians'. In *A Botanical Arrangement of all the Vegetables*

Naturally Growing in Great Britain, Dr. William Withering wrote: "In the year 1775, my opinion was asked concerning a family receipt for the cure of dropsy. I was told that it had long been kept a secret by an old woman in Shropshire who had sometimes made cures after the more regular practitioners had failed. . . . This medicine was composed of 20 or more different herbs . . . ." One was foxglove. Until only about a century ago, dropsy was among the most common fatal diseases of adults. Digitalis, the common foxglove, can, in small doses, relieve dropsy by strengthening the working of the heart. Digoxin, a glycoside obtained from digitalis, is now the most widely prescribed cardiotonic drug in the United States.

And in 1770, concerning another plant, John Hill wrote in *The Virtues of British Herbs*, "A lady of great worth and virtue, the mother of the late Sir William Bowyer, told me that having in the younger part of her life a very terrible and almost constant Head-Ach, fixed in one small spot, and raging at times almost to distraction; and which the neighbouring Dr. Thorold, of Uxbridge, very eminent in his profession, had attempted in vain to remove; she was at length cured by a maid servant, with this Herb." The herb was *Chrysanthemum parthenium*, feverfew, or featherfew, which, according to a recent report in the *British Medical Journal*, is indeed effective in helping to relieve migraine headaches.

Elizabeth, Countess of Kent, said that she, too, had "with God's blessing recovered divers severall Patients," and an 18th-century book credits some of its receipts to "Mrs. Mariamny Packer, the Travelling Doctress," "Mary Burton, a Traveller" and "Madam Sparks's, a great Doctress in Pater Noster Row." In her own collection of "three hundred receipts," Mary Kettilby commended those of the "Fair Sex" who "Kneel down to the Dressing of a Poor Man's Wound" or "walk through Midnight-Frosts to the As-

Pulmonaria, top, was considered lung medicine because of its shape.

sistance of some Poor Neighbouring Woman in her Painful and Perilous Hour."

Such hours were frequent, because married women were almost always pregnant during their childbearing years and birth was risky for both mother and child. Gynaecology and obstetrics were areas of medicine that were, naturally enough, especially attractive to women. Until this century, midwives were more likely than physicians to be involved with childbirth, every stage and possible complication of which was described in all herbal and stillroom books. Indeed, almost every herb had some relationship to fertility, lactation or parturition, "to bring a woman to a Speedy birth." Nicholas Culpeper, a physician with an unusual empathy for women and home remedies, lists in his herbal among the A's alone: all-heal (*Prunella vulgaris*), which "provokes the terms, expels the dead birth"; alkanet (*Anchusa officinalis*), which "draws forth the dead child"; alexander (*Smyrnium olusatrum*), which "is good to move women's courses, to expel the after-birth"; wild or stinking arrach or, significantly, vulvaria or stinking motherwort (*Chenopodium olida*), which is "a universal medicine of the womb. . . . It makes barren women fruitful: it cleanseth the womb if it be foul and strengthens it exceedingly: it provokes the terms if they be stopped and stops them if they flow immoderately; you can desire no good to your womb but this herb will effect it; therefore, if you love children, if you love health, if you love ease, keep a syrup always by you made of the juice of this herb . . . ."

And the A's do not include such significantly named plants as motherwort (*Leonurus cardiaca*), which "makes mothers joyful and settles the womb," or birthwort (*Aristolochia clematitis*), used to induce childbirth. ("Wort" means a useful plant.) Motherwort, like most herbs of particular usefulness in "women's complaints," was said by Culpeper to be under the dominion of Venus, the only planet in the solar system judged female by early astrologers; its symbol is the universal sign of woman, a circle with a cross.

In 1737, Elizabeth Blackwell wrote in *A Curious Herbal* that motherwort would not only "expediate the birth" but would also soothe "hysteric fits," the next most common female complaint after obstetrical matters. Also called "the hysteric disease," "vapours," "fits of the mother" or simply "the mother" in herbals and stillroom books, this illness was peculiar to women. (Hysteric means "pertaining to the womb"; the Greek for uterus is *hystera*. Ancient Greek physicians believed that the symptoms of hysteria were the result of the wanderings of the uterus within the body.) During the time of the stillroom books and herbals, hysteria was quite common, judging from the frequency with which it was mentioned. Sometimes classed with hypochondriacal ailments, its symptoms included weeping, fainting, weakness, hypersensitivity, anaesthesia and a gamut of symptoms we might now call a nervous breakdown or simply the effects of exhaustion, an inadequate diet and too many pregnancies. Culpeper wrote that motherwort "is of use for the trembling of the heart, fainting and swooning," symptoms of hysteria. The plant does, in fact, have sedative properties and is still considered beneficial for menstrual disorders.

As the therapeutic use of herbs declined, cures for the still prevalent hysteria became less pleasant and less compassionate. In 1873, Marie Bashkirtseff wrote in her journal that her mother had had "a very bad fit of hysteria, worse than any she has had. The whole family is in despair. . . . Those brutes of doctors have applied a blister which has made her suffer horribly. The best remedy is cold water or tea; that's simple and natural." Certainly tea seems preferable to a cure that appeared a year later in *The Illustrated Annual Register of Rural Affairs*: "Let the patient lie on a couch, and then continue to pour cold water on the head till relieved." Hysteria became an important area of study for Sigmund Freud, whose teacher, Jean Martin Charcot, used hypnosis in the 19th century in an attempt to find an organic basis for the condition.

Freud, born in 1856, investigated the psychological reasons for hysteria in an era of many medical advances, such as the development of safe anaesthesia and sterile surgery. His attempts to link the health of the body and the mind were not new, however. Centuries earlier, even the lowliest, most illiterate peasant woman was influenced by the doctrine of the four humours, the foundation of the medicine of her day. In the fifth and fourth centuries B.C., Hippocrates, the "father of medicine," had put into organized form the ancient system in which the four elements of fire, water, earth and air corresponded with four humours, substances of the human body: blood (like air, hot and wet); phlegm (like water, cold and wet); yellow bile, or choler (like fire, hot and dry); and black bile (like earth, cold and dry). There were, then, hot humours and cold humours. A balance of all four in a patient contributed to "good humour," whereas an imbalance produced a personality that might be sanguine, phlegmatic, choleric or melancholy. "And if cold humours be her complaint," reads one prescription in a mediaeval gynaecology text, "let her bathe in a bath of hot herbs. And when she comes out of the bath, give her a draft of wine that cumin and ginger are boiled in."

Cumin and ginger are among the hot herbs that could help counterbalance an excess of cold humours, which caused such ailments as rheumatism and head colds. Not only is our word for the latter affliction a remnant of an old belief, but a poultice of hot, dry mustard is still considered a remedy for a cold. Galen, in the second century, added to the theory of the four humours to establish a rigid system of hotness and coldness in plants and diseases that would be the cornerstone of medicine for 1,500 years. Elizabeth Blackwell, like many other herbalists, referred frequently to these qualities. Lady's mantle was deemed "drying and binding"; the love apple (tomato) "cooling and moistening." While a yellow flower like that of mustard was often produced on a "hot" plant, blue flowers such as those of violet and borage were likely to be "cold," so that, according to *The Ladies Cabinet Opened*, "Oyle of Violets . . . if it be rubbed about the Temples of the head, doth remove the extreme heat, asswageth the head-ach, provoketh sleepe and moisteneth the Braine. It is good against melancholy,

dulnesse and heavinesse of the Spirits and against swellings and sores that be overhot." Thomas Tusser recommended that

Good huswives provide, ere an sickness
  doo come,
of sundrie good things in hir house to
  have some.
Good Aqua composita, Vinegar tart,
Rose water and treakle, to comfort the hart.
Cold herbs in her garden, for agues that burn,
that over strong heat to good temper may turn.

Complicating the theoretical basis of herbal medicine at the time was the Doctrine of Signatures, another ancient system of belief but one of minor importance until it was promoted by Paracelsus in the early 16th century. According to this system, a plant part resembling a part of the human body was useful in treating that organ: the "signature" of the organ had been written in the shape of the plant. William Coles, an English herbalist who published *The Art of Simpling* in 1656, wrote that God had given plants "particular signatures, whereby a Man may read even in legible Characters the Use of them." This system would have influenced the home herbal practitioner as well. Birthwort, for instance, was assumed to be useful for obstetrical matters because it has womb-shaped leaves. By the same token, lungwort (*Pulmonaria officinalis*) has spotted, lung-shaped leaves that are thought to be good for pulmonary problems. Viper's bugloss (*Echium vulgare*) has brown stems resembling snakeskin and seeds like snake heads, so the plant was considered to be the antidote for snake venom. An emergency supply of bugloss ointment should, according to John Parkinson's *Theatrum botanicum*, be in the house of every "good gentle-woman in the land that would do good."

Such theories might seem cumbersome, and indeed, the Doctrine of Signatures

Various methods of distillation remove the essential oils from herbs.

~

proved to have severe shortcomings, but the modern woman who can identify a few local wildflowers should not underrate the knowledge of her forebears. The number of medicinal plants familiar to the "good gentlewomen" of centuries past, whether they worked with or despite prevailing medical trends, was impressive. Seldom did their recipes call for only one herb, or simple. One early-15th-century recipe called for a pound of pennyroyal and half a pound each of rosemary, costmary, chamomile, lavender, balm, woodruff, hyssop and savory along with smaller amounts of cypress, calamint, feverfew, fennel, wormwood, sage, rue, oregano, southernwood, mugwort, aloes wood, mace, balsam wood, spikenard, galingale, mastic, saffron, cloves, myrrh, camphor and ambergris. There were herb women and apothecaries from whom women could buy many of these ingredients had they the resources and contacts, and they grew many of the plants themselves.

In the Middle Ages and the Renaissance, this pharmacopoeia, the size of which varied with the season, was stored in the kitchen or stillroom, with its bronze, copper and iron cauldrons, its ladles, cooking forks, "warmynge-panne" and gridiron, its fish kettle and a mortar and pestle, tools of primitive simplicity that could blend pastry, powder sugar or grind seeds, roots and dried plants. Rows of glass bottles and earthenware jars of ingredients and finished medicines, waters, powders and oils—the more containers, the better off and more expert the woman was likely to be—lined the shelves and filled the cabinets or the closet. (After it was equipped with running water, the closet became the water closet, the W.C., the equivalent of the North American bathroom, where medicines and cosmetics are still kept.) Inside the closet were the products of an extremely busy woman who was as much chemist as herbalist.

The vials contained plant substances rather than fresh herbs, in part because the recipes often called for processed plants, in part because of the characteristics of the plants themselves. Lacking dependable refrigeration, these women had to rely on other methods to preserve their precious greens. Fresh plants are composed mostly of water, which not only is weighty excess baggage but also permits spoilage. Drying, the easiest method of preservation, removes about 85 percent of the water from leaves and flowers. In the stillroom, bundles of drying plants hung from the walls or ceiling beams, where they could be easily reached. But dried plants would still deteriorate when exposed to air, light and humidity. Salves and unguents, on the other hand, preserved plants by excluding air; in early stillrooms, a mortar-ground plant might be mixed with fat and sometimes with wax and turpentine to create a long-lasting ointment. Sugar, another preservative, could be mixed with herbs to yield a medicinal syrup.

Active herbal ingredients such as alkaloids and oils would occupy even less space in storage, and the essential oils were obtained by various methods: pressing the plant, preparing it in alcohol or distilling it, the process that gave such rooms the names stillroom, stillatory and distillatory. In steam distillation, a layer of pulverized plant was placed over boiling water so that the essential oil – the oil containing the "essence" of the plant – mixed with steam, evaporated and then condensed in a tube or vessel above. The same process could be carried out more slowly by the heat of the sun or even by the heat produced by a manure pile. Lighter than water, the essential oil could be skimmed from the surface of the distillate and saved.

A woman who had a still and was thus able to obtain essential oils might make such prized substances as liqueurs and toilet waters based on that most popular of solvents, alcohol. One recipe for Hungary water (a type of cologne) "from Mrs. Du Pont of Lyons" was prepared by mixing with "every Gallon of Brandy or clean Spirits" a handful each of rosemary and lavender, "and these Herbs must be cut in Pieces, about an Inch long. Put these to infuse in the Spirits, and with them, about an handful of Myrtle, cut as before. When this has stood three Days, distil it, and you will have the finest Hungary-Water that can be."

As it happened, the liquid drawn off after distillation, the combination of essential oil and distilled water known then as the "water," was free of contaminants and therefore suitable for medicinal use in an era when other water might well be tainted with bacteria. Stillroom books list many such waters, including "Raddish water, which is good for the stone; Angelica water good against infection; Celandine water for sore eyes; Vine water for itchings; Rosewater and Eyebright water for dimme sights . . . ." Peppermint water consisted of six handfuls of mint infused for two days in six quarts of "clean spirit," which was then drawn off "in a cold still." The wa-

One critic thought that women's cosmetics were the work of the devil.

ter distilled from strawberries, declared John Parkinson, "is good for the passions of the heart . . . and maketh the heart merry."

The purity and scent of these waters also made them ideal for cosmetics. In 1525, Bancke's herbal recommended rosemary water as a cleanser: "Boyle the leaves in white wine and washe thy face therewith and thy browes and thou shalt have a faire face." Soon after, Turner's herbal breathlessly stated that "some weomen sprinkle ye floures of cowslip with whyte wine and after still it and wash their faces with that water to drive wrinkles away and to make them fayre in the eyes of the worlde rather than in the eyes of God, whom they are not afrayd to offend." Elizabeth Blackwell wrote in her herbal that the water distilled from the flowers of broad beans "is used by many as a Cosmetic . . . ." And Frenchwomen, wrote Parkinson in his *Theatrum botanicum*, "account the distilled water of pimpernell mervailous good to clense the skinne from any roughnesse, deformity or discolouring thereof and to make it

50

smooth, neate and cleere." Italian women, meanwhile, "doe much use the distilled water of the whole plant of Solomon's Seal," which, added Nicholas Culpeper, "is the principal ingredient of most of the cosmetics and beauty washes advertised by perfumers at high price." Queen Victoria preferred lavender water, which she got "direct from a lady who distils it herself."

Rose water—fragrant, colourful and medicinal—was a particular favourite in Middle Eastern and early European kitchens. It had been distilled in Persia for centuries before its virtues, along with the roses themselves, came westward with the Crusaders. Abulcasis, a Muslim physician of the 10th century, included it in many mixtures, such as nutmeg aromatic water, which had a rose-water base. Distilled oil of roses was even more valued: it sold in Paris for twice the price of gold in the mid-18th century and cost an astonishing $2,270 a pound in 1980. While its rarity and value make it most prized as an ingredient in costly perfumes, "oyle of roses and Rose buds," according to The Treasury of Hidden Secrets in 1653, "is good against inflammations, it cooleth the burning and boyling of the stomacke and fretting of the bowels if it be given in glister, and to anoint the teeth, it taketh away the ach."

It is not surprising that housewives used roses in all kinds of goods. Not only were all parts of the plant medicinal—the fruit, or hip, is a rich source of vitamin C—but the flowers also tasted good, and they looked beautiful and smelled pleasant, even when dried. Sweet fragrances were believed to have healing properties in themselves, a theory with a sound basis, according to modern aromatherapy practitioners as well as recent research at Yale and Duke universities. A 17th-century recipe for "odiferous candles against venom and the plague" transcribed by Philibert Guibert, Physician Regent of Paris, called for, among other things, roses, laudanum, frankincense, cloves, citron peel and juniper berries in a gum dissolved in rose water. While it is unlikely they were very effective against the plague, psychologist Susan Schiffman of Duke University has at least found that the scent of peaches can help to alleviate pain.

John Gerard wrote that fresh roses "bringeth sleep . . . through their sweet and pleasant smell." Perhaps it was their healing scent that began the long tradition of giving roses to women, who were seen as especially susceptible to melancholy, an affliction which could be eased with pleasant fragrances, as Robert Burton wrote in The Anatomy of Melancholy. The scent is particularly pronounced in old-fashioned roses, the damasks and centifolias and dog roses these women would have known.

Other scents appear in a recipe for a herbal bath for the treatment of melancholy: "Take Mallowes, pellitory of the wall, of each three handfulls; Camomell flowers, Mellilot flowers, of each one handfull; hollyhocks, two handfulls; Isop one great handfull; senerick seede one ounce, and boil them in nine gallons of Water untill they come to three, then put in a quart of new milke and go into it bloud warme or something warmer." Even the sound of that recipe could soothe a melancholic spirit.

Home-distilled perfumes rendered more bearable for the nose a world without deodorants, mouthwashes, sewers and regular baths. In the 14th century, one rubbed one's hands with perfume after eating, and John Lyly wrote that "ladies had rather be sprinkled with sweet waters than washed." Many mixed their own scents, so perfumes were very personal statements. Some statements were more agreeable than others, of course, especially when animal substances began to replace or augment the floral ones. Some women left entire houses redolent of musk or civet, strong-smelling, oily secretions produced, respectively, by a type of deer and a catlike animal. By the 17th and 18th centuries, human society reeked. Perfumes were used on the hair, on clothes, furniture, beards and gloves, and women carried embroidered bags filled with scented herbs such as violet, lavender, rosemary and bergamot. These little sachets could be carried, placed in chests with clothing or even worn in the bosoms of dresses "to impart a fuller beauty to their defective forms," as one observer slyly noted.

Fragrant plants were also used for strewing, spreading on floors in the manner of renewable carpets that scented the room, covered and warmed dirt or stone floors, kept the feet relatively clean and even repelled fleas and flies, which wormwood, pennyroyal and hyssop were reputed to do. Dozens of plants, from homely rushes to fragrant roses and lilies, might be used in that way. Cleopatra strewed roses on the floor one cubit deep — about a foot and a half of flowers — for one banquet, and Queen Elizabeth I "did more desire meadowsweet than any other sweet herbe to strewe her chambers withall," according to John Parkinson. A Dutch visitor to England wrote that in 1560, "their chambers and parlours strawed over with sweet herbes refreshed me; their nosegays finely intermingled with sundry sorts of fragraunte flowers in their bedchambers and privy rooms with comfortable smell cheered me up, and entirely delighted all my senses." In France, the Comte de Foix found his room "toute jonchée" with new, fresh greenery, the walls covered with green branches to make it fresher and more fragrant. Similarly, Lady Clarendon "hung a closet" with Calamus aromaticus, which "retains the scent very perfectly." (Calamus aromaticus is the sweet flag of Europe, now Acorus calamus or Iris pseudacorus.)

More closely analogous to today's room deodorants were bowls of rose water or potpourris made of roses, Iris florentina and other scented flowers and herbs prepared by either a dry or wet method. The latter called for layering plants with salt and letting them ferment, while the dry method, which was easier but whose results were not as long-lasting, simply asked for ingredients to be prepared in an airy room and then mixed. A woman who knew how to dry plants properly by burying them in sand, however, might "have Rose leaves and other flowers to lay upon your basons, windows & c. all the winter long . . ." promised Sir Hugh Platt.

That could be done only if the housewife had "gathered her rosebuds while she may," to paraphrase Robert Herrick. Like the plants she worked with, the housewife of past centuries was influenced by the season. Throughout the summer, she gathered roses from hedgerows, as many as she could collect or could convince her children to collect for her — a gallon of rose water required about six pounds of petals. As other ingredients became available in the garden or field, they could be dried or distilled, then mixed together later as needed. Thomas Tusser listed 17 herbs the housewife should "still in summer." April, wrote one author, was the time "for sowing or otherwise propagating all medicinal plants . . . ." In England, May was the month for gathering and drying elderberry flowers and making flavoured vinegars, while June was "a proper season for making several sorts of Wine, whether it be that of Goosberries, Currants, Cherries, Apricots, or Rasberries, all of which are very agreeable and worth the trouble," wrote Richard Bradley in 1736 in The Country Housewife and Lady's Director. August was the time for making mead and September the month for gathering mushrooms and pickling.

When the Industrial Revolution introduced mass production of pills, syrups, cosmetics and household goods, the medicinal aspect of the kitchen was largely lost. Floors,

Roses were esteemed because the plant is medicinal, beautiful and perfumed.

~

covered with boards or tiles, could now be washed, making strewing unnecessary. Perfumes and cosmetics were mixed on assembly lines and sold at prices entirely out of line with the cost of their meagre ingredients, thanks to glamorous packaging and flashy advertising which attempted to convince the buyer that these mass-market goods were designed just for her. Herbal ingredients were synthesized so that they could be patented and accurately dispensed. (Acetylsalicylic acid, marketed as aspirin, is a synthetic form of a fever and ache remedy previously derived from willows. The drug can be controlled in a far more profitable way than can the tree.)

Herbal medicine survived, of course, especially away from cities. In *Gardening for Love*, a collection of excerpts from *The Mississippi Market Bulletin*, a magazine founded in 1928, Elizabeth Lawrence gives an account of Dr. R.L. Sanders, a patron of the bulletin and an authority on botanical medicines. Sanders told Lawrence that when he was a little boy, he followed his grandmother, a "root-doctor," as she gathered plants. "All medicines, she said, come out of the earth." Every morning in spring and summer, she prepared a tonic of sassafras and prickly ash for her grandchildren, and she was renowned for her rheumatism medicine made from bark and roots. Before extracting teeth, she rubbed the gums of her patients with a leaf powder so that there was no pain and little bleeding. She kept all her teeth until she was 88, lived to be 93, and, says Sanders, "when she died, it was not from illness. She was just worn out, like an old wagon."

Cures, even those based on the four humours, continued to appear in the cookbooks of the 19th century—Sarah Josepha Hale's *The Good Housekeeper* noted that coffee was "very bad for bilious constitutions. The calm, phlegmatic temperament can bear it." But the fading role of the housewife-as-nurse is apparent in one of the most popular cookbooks of that century (60,000 copies were printed in its first year, 1861)—Isabella Beeton's *The Book of Household Management*, less than a tenth of which includes medicinal information. The proportion in earlier books was about half-and-half.

This paring down brought into greater prominence a plant that had always been important to women for both home medicine and witchcraft: the opium poppy. One of its products, laudanum—tincture of opium in alcohol or wine, sometimes with spices—had been a favoured remedy since at least the 17th century, because it was faster-acting than solid opium. Solid opium was still available in Beeton's day, however, and she wrote that it "is mostly seen in the form of rich brown fattish cakes, with little pieces of leaves sticking on them here and there, and a bitter and slightly warm taste." Fifty-one tons of opium juice were imported into England in 1852, when Sarah Bowdich Lee reported that "we ourselves have known a lady swallow a pint of laudanum every day . . . ." Addicts were, of course, not uncommon.

Isabella Beeton's medicine for thrush in babies called for castor oil, sugar, mucilage, mint water and laudanum, although Beeton warned that "Syrup of Poppies" given to children to help them sleep might prove fatal. Besides powdered opium and laudanum, there were just three other plant substances recommended by Beeton for the medicine chest: linseed oil, myrrh and "aloes pills." The juice of aloe vera (*Aloe barbadensis*), now best known for treating superficial burns, was traditionally used as a purgative.

Certainly, many of the home recipes did work, and their herbal components were often powerful enough to cure on their own without modern mineral additives. Quinine from cinchona bark has saved millions of lives that would otherwise have been lost to malaria; the rosy periwinkle has significantly increased the rate of recovery from infant leukemia and Hodgkin's disease; and reserpine, from the snakeroot (*Rauwolfia serpentina*), is used to control hypertension. Plant materials are still the principal active ingredients of more than 25 percent of the drugs prescribed in the United States. In China, more than 5,000 plants, unrefined and refined, are the mainstays of a pharmacopoeia that has been effective for thousands of years.

"The fact is, herbs do work," says Peter Pang, who is researching Chinese medicinal herbs at the University of Alberta, "but very often, we don't know how and why the herbs work, and as long as the scientific information isn't available, Western scientists will look on the effects of herbal medicine as 'all in the mind.'"

In parts of the Third World, "plants are the sole source of remedies," says Olayiwola Akerele, manager of the World Health Organization's traditional-medicine programme. Yet hundreds of plant species, potential medicines, are being lost through the destruction of natural habitats.

Many of the old European recipes would be useful today too, but their lack of precision, not to mention the work involved in preparing them, is discouraging. Still, herbalists and herbal remedies do linger, and even a conservative American women's magazine, *Family Circle*, included five herbal or plant-based ingredients in a 1986 article entitled "16 Home Remedies You Can Trust." For hiccoughs, the recommendation was a teaspoon of dry sugar or a lemon wedge saturated with angostura bitters (made from the aromatic bark of certain South American trees); for motion sickness, powdered ginger; for a cold, spicy foods or Tabasco sauce (made from chili peppers – Galen would be pleased); and for insect stings, meat tenderizer, whose active ingredient is papain, an enzyme extracted from papaya fruits.

The relegation of the home therapist to tasks no weightier than treating insect stings and motion sickness will seem a good thing to pharmaceutical manufacturers and, indeed, to many homemakers who would not happily return to the self-sufficient life style of a century or two ago. It may be, however, that a vital link between women and plants has been lost – or, more precisely, hidden. The boxes of Keen's mustard in our mothers' kitchens, used for seasoning salad dressings, mayonnaise and soup, affected their families in ways that went beyond its warm, herbal flavour. If a plant is therapeutic, it will be so even if no one appreciates that quality. Similarly, if people will be doctors to their families, they, too, may be so in secret.

IV

"The Deadliest Enemies of Heaven"

*Witchcraft, herbal potions and
the powers of darkness*

"The one outstanding province of women,"
declared Pliny the Elder in the first
century A.D., was the "compelling power of
charms and magic herbs." If women
have but one outstanding province, Pliny's
choice was logical enough for his day,
considering their position at the hearth and in
the garden. But in the centuries
that followed, some of the women who were
especially skilled in their work with
"charms and magic herbs" became known and
feared as witches. Their story is the darkest
one in the history of women and plants.

~

Take, for instance, an otherwise mild
little book of 1616 called *Asylum veneris, or A
Sanctuary for Ladies*. The author, Daniel
Tuvil, used horticultural turns of
phrase to define and describe the virtues of
good women, such as the "right worthy
and vertuous" Lady Alice Colville, to whom the
work is dedicated: "I never eye

~

you, but I think on Eden in the State of Innocence, so richly planted is your Bosome with all variety of Graces and Abilities. Everything growes there in so good order that the searching eye of Malice can finde nothing to be lopt, little to bee pruned. The hand of Heaven hath made it as it were a Nursery, from whence many Virtues & Perfections are oft times transplanted into others." There are shades here of the Virgin Mary, described in the next chapter.

But then, venturing from the verdant delights of the bosom of Lady Colville, the author launched into an armament of rhyming couplets about "foule adulterate brats of Hell whose lunges exhale a worse than Sulphrous smell . . . ." These "brats," whom Tuvil called "the looser sort" of women, were not intended to read his book. In fact, the two types of women scarcely seemed to belong to the same sex, or even to the same species.

As Lady Colville was an example of horticultural wholesomeness, the "brats of Hell" were also associated with plants, but in an entirely different way. These women, Tuvil believed,

seek by Philtres, drugs and charms,
To bring the curl'd-head Youth into your
    armes;
And doe not feare by poyson to remove
A worthy Husband, for a worthless Love.

These women were witches. Tuvil's era, the 17th century, saw not only a growing knightly dedication to genteel (and floral) femininity but also the waning of two centuries of such fanatical hatred directed toward the mysterious herbalists called witches that millions of people, mostly women, were tortured and killed. By 1590, Henri Boguet, Grand Judge of St. Claude, France, a man who alone may have ordered 600 executions of what he called "the deadliest enemies of heaven," wrote in his *Discours exécrable des*

sorciers that "Germany is almost entirely occupied with building fires for them. Switzerland has been compelled to wipe out many of her villages on their account. Travellers in Lorraine may see thousands and thousands of the stakes to which witches are bound . . . there are witches by the thousands everywhere."

What had gone wrong? Since the time of Pliny, these herbal practitioners had been considered "wise women," who could cure or curse as they chose. They were involved in medicine, and in most ways, their work was not very different from that of other early healers. Physicians, too, used plants as well as other materials to produce sometimes unexpected, often apparently magical results. And just as the physician could frequently kill a patient, so could the wise woman frequently heal. One open-minded 16th-century observer noted that "these uncultured women are wise in the virtues of herbs and cure the most difficult diseases . . . ." But between about 1450 and 1650, their therapy was perceived as wholly different from that of physicians and monks, who, unlike witches, worked within approved disciplines in a society which was itself ordered by God, as interpreted by the church and its followers.

And the church stood in judgement of all outsiders, however clever they might be. As Josse Damhouder of Antwerp wrote in 1601, "There are even natural ills—as by poison—incurable by human means, but speedily removable by the aid of demons, whose knowledge of natural secrets is much greater than that of men and is only communicated by them to sorcerers. This is not prohibited by the common law, but it is by the canon law." If someone was too good at healing, then evil might be at work and the church would disapprove.

Followers of a tradition older than canon law, witches could not win. One Spanish

Much of the fear that surrounded witches arose
from their knowledge of powerful plants.

salutadore (healing sorceress) was burned, although she had used her powers only for beneficial purposes. Henri Boguet wrote: "There is always evil in cures affected by witches . . . the cure is only effective for a limited time, or else it is necessary for the sickness to be transferred to someone else; and sometimes we find both these conditions operating at the same time." As witches were perceived to be agents of the devil, usurping the power of God, who "alone doeth great marvels," according to the Psalms, even their good works were suspect. At the end of the 16th century, Boguet described them as "multiplying upon the earth even as worms in a garden."

The image is an interesting one. In the 20th century, the earthworm is appreciated as a source of soil fertility and plant health, but 400 years ago, the image of writhing, multiplying life thriving underground suggested sin, death and hell. Diseases were often attributed to the supposed presence of "worms." At the time, an understandable terror of darkness, mystery and disease was manifested in much mediaeval writing and art—and in the fear of witches. Chaos constantly threatened the most hallowed rules that ignorance had granted science and the church. Could witches fly? Kill with a glance? Could they transform themselves into wolves? Could they "deprive men of their privities," as one man wrote? Did they give birth to cats and dogs? Bouts of bubonic plague, which tormented Europe throughout the worst of the witch-hunting era, shook the foundations of faith and science, neither of which could explain or cure the disease. Perhaps evil, personified by these strong women, was to blame.

In fact, witches were perceived as being both powerful and ungovernable. In 1621, Robert Burton wrote in *The Anatomy of Melancholy*: "They can cause tempests, storms, which is familiarly practised by Witches in Norway, Iceland, as I have proved. They can make friends enemies and enemies friends by philtres . . . hurt and infect men and beasts, vines, corn, cattle, plants, make women abortive, not to conceive, barren, men and women unapt and unable . . . make men feel no pain on the rack, nor any other tortures; they can stanch blood . . . they can, last of all, cure and cause most diseases to such as they love or hate . . . ."

Meanwhile, as the witches were supposedly curing and killing at will, the most respected physicians were fumbling with leeches and purges or accomplishing very little at all with folklore and symbolism. In a time when the workings of bacteria, viruses, sexual fertilization and even blood circulation were unknown—although there were rigid, largely unworkable theories that attempted to explain them—medicine was mostly a hit-and-miss affair compounded of science, tradition and superstition. Reginald Scot, who campaigned against the punishment of witches in 16th-century England, was nevertheless a man of his age, believing that a unicorn's horn had curative powers, that a bone from a carp's head could stop excessive bleeding, that witches could carry water in a sieve and that some medicinal herbs might as well be tied around the neck as eaten. The belief that scrofula could be cured by the Royal Touch (contact with the king) endured in England until the 17th-century reign of William III. And in the same century, the great chemist Robert Boyle believed that a small portion of human skull, grated like ginger and mixed with food, could help prevent fits. So witches were feared not so much because their ingredients were strange, like Shakespeare's three hags' "eye of newt and toe of frog," but because they were female, unruly, unpredictable and possibly unchristian. They were also said to fly and to transform themselves into other creatures, habits bound to unsettle those who wished to attribute all miraculous powers to the church.

In their powerful role of facilitating births, midwives were "especial favourites of the devil," according to Christian Stridtbeckh in the 18th century. Traditionally, women have been midwives and abortionists, concerned with all matters pertaining to fertility and childbirth. Jacoba Felicie, a 14th-century Parisian physician, said that "it is better and more seemly that a wise woman learned in the art should visit a sick woman and inquire into the secrets of her nature and her hidden parts than that a man should do so. . . . Many women and also men have perished of their infirmities, not being willing to have doctors lest these should see their secret parts."

Wise women—locally available, inexpensive, knowledgeable and of the right sex—were usually called upon for gynaecological matters. So it is not surprising that impotence, infertility, deaths before, during or after childbirth or lack of milk in humans or animals, particularly cattle, should all be conveniently blamed on the devil and (the devil being difficult to haul to trial) his agents, even though, as Johann Klein, an 18th-century professor of medicine, noted, it was "most rare" for even a very experienced physician to be able to distinguish between natural disease and that caused by witchcraft. The only proof was the confession of the witch, and that was usually elicited by torture. Proof of guilt, incidentally, consisted not of presented evidence but of confession or accusation. "I have always maintained that a person should always be imprisoned on the accusation of even only a single accomplice," declared Henri Boguet.

This meant, of course, that some people accused of witchcraft were not even effective herbalists but pathetic, mentally unstable or "melancholike" women, as Reginald Scot, author of the 1584 *Discoverie of Witchcraft*, put it. Melancholia was an understandable state at a time when most old women had neither power nor property, and mortality rates were such that they could easily find themselves quite alone in a difficult world: "For as some of these melancholike persons imagine, they are witches and by witchcraft can worke wonders, and doo what they list; so doo other, troubled with this disease, imagine manie strange, incredible and impossible things. Some, that they are monarchs and princes and that all other men are their subjects; some, that they are brute beasts; some, that they be urinals or earthen pots, greatly fearing to be broken; some, that everie one that meeteth them will conveie them to the gallowes; and yet in the end hang themselves."

That some thought they could "worke wonders, and doo what they list" would itself have engendered discontent in an age when the church and medical fraternities were working to concentrate power—and payment—in the hands of only a few accredited men.

Many harrowing tales of the trials, tortures and deaths of witches exist. Anyone interested might read Henry Charles Lea's *Materials Toward a History of Witchcraft*, Henri Boguet's *An Examin of Witches* or almost any other book on the subject. But a less onerous tale—one that at least lacks a tragic ending—is in a small English book called *A Collection of Rare and Curious Tracts Relating to Witchcraft Between 1618 and 1664*. Here,

the story is told of "an old widow-woman of rather singular habits of the name of Scotcher," who, along with her daughter and son-in-law, was found gleaning in a farmer's field at "a much earlier hour than the rest of the inhabitants were accustomed to go out into the fields to glean. On being told that they had no right to be there at that time of the morning and ordered to leave the field, they were much offended, and Scotcher became very abusive." The farmer finally drove the three from the field with a hedge stake and knocked the two women's heads together "with great force, telling Scotcher that she was a witch and that he would have her swam."

This double-edged test of innocence involved throwing an accused person into a pond. If she sank, she was innocent; if she floated, she was guilty. Scotcher, with a rope tied around her waist, was thrown into the water "and—she swam! Although she tried all she could and even 'dived down into the water like a duck,'" an eyewitness was recorded as saying. " 'She could no more sink than a piece of cork!' After she had been worried about in the water for some time, she was taken out and allowed to depart; those assembled being quite satisfied that she was one of those 'slaves of the Devil,' yclept a Witch!"

That witches were generally women—we hear nothing, for instance, of the offending son-in-law in that story—can be seen as the dark side of woman's long tradition of keeping hearth, home and health, her early role as plant gatherer and her powerful position in childbirth and child rearing. Erich Neumann notes in *The Great Mother*, "It is quite evident that the preparation and storage of food taught woman the process of fermentation and the manufacture of intoxicants and that, as a gatherer and later preparer of herbs, plants and fruits, she was the inventor and guardian of the first healing potions, medicines and poisons." Arnaldo Albertini, however, had a different explanation for the preponderance of female witches, which he set forth in 1572 in his *De agnoscendis assertionibus catholicis et haereticis tractatus*: "These illusions mostly are found in women because they are more given to superstitions and these diabolical maleficia than men, and the devil has easier access to them and they are frail and more easily deceived." Like Eve, he might have added.

It is appropriate then, that apples, bane of Eve, were seen as favourite playthings of witches (and even of Esmeralda in Walt Disney's *Snow White*). One writer tells of an American woman, Mary Johnson, accused of witchcraft because she "came to the house of this Informant and gave her child an apple and kissed it; and within a short time after, the said child sickened and died." This took place during North America's 17th-century outbreak of witch fever in and around Salem, Massachusetts, which resulted in the eventual execution of 20 people and the death of another 2 in jail ("a surprisingly good record," according to one modern author).

As far as written documentation goes, the Salem situation seems to have had little connection with herbs. However, in the 1940s, a *Boston Globe* reporter told Marion Starkey, author of *The Devil in Massachusetts*, that after handling jimsonweed, or datura, a favoured plant of European witches, his children had convulsive seizures, falling fits and spasms of pain, leading the reporter to believe that the Salem women, whose symptoms were similar, may have been poisoned by the plant. And in one recorded incident at the Salem trials, Candy, a Barbadian slave, brought into court a handkerchief containing rags, a piece of cheese and a piece of "grass." The woman was forced to swallow the "grass," with the result that "she was burned in her flesh" that night. Another link with herbs was flying, a phenomenon now associated with hallucinogenic plants. Tituba, one of the accused Salem witches, would fly "upon a

Datura stramonium is a poisonous plant mentioned in witch recipes.

~~

stick or pole and Good and Osburn behind me. We ride taking hold of one another; don't know how we go, for I saw no trees nor path but was presently there."

One theory about the Salem episode is that it was caused by ergotism—poisoning from fungus-contaminated grain, especially rye. In 1976, Linnda R. Caporael hypothesized in *Science* magazine that a "witch cake" of rye flour and urine spawned trauma. Ergot, which quite commonly develops on grain in warm, damp conditions, contains several potent pharmacological agents, one of which is lysergic acid amide, an alkaloid with about one-tenth the strength of the hallucinogen

LSD. Symptoms of convulsive ergotism include crawling sensations in the skin, tingling fingers, vertigo, headaches, hallucinations, convulsions, vomiting and diarrhea, "all," says Caporael, "symptoms alluded to in the Salem witchcraft records."

Caporael's argument was soon challenged, however, by Nicholas P. Spanos and Jack Gottlieb, who pointed out, also in *Science*, that the symptoms of convulsive ergotism listed by Caporael were rarely recorded in any of the Salem testimonies. "The symptoms of the afflicted girls and of the other witnesses were not those of convulsive ergotism. And the abrupt ending of the crisis and the remorse and second thoughts of those who judged and testified against the accused can be explained without recourse to the ergotism hypothesis." (Incidentally, midwives in the Middle Ages used ergot to assist with difficult births.)

Unfortunately, our insights into the truth behind the accusations at Salem, as in Europe, are dimmed by evidence not from women speaking or writing freely but mostly from those being interviewed, often in court, and sometimes during or after tortures that would have wrung confessions from a saint. Apparently, no witch has left records of either her recipes or her reasons. The remnants of information we do have about European witches, however, suggest there were herbs in their medical repertoires so dangerous that some of the plants were not used at all by more conventional physicians. Other plants did have therapeutic uses, but physicians would not have mixed them together as the witches did. Datura, belladonna and henbane, all frequently mentioned in witch-ointment recipes, are called "the three most poisonous plants growing freely in Europe" by A.J. Clark in Margaret Murray's *The Witch-Cult in Western Europe*.

The Latin word for witch, *venifica*, has the same root as the word for poison. If it is true that, as Sherlock Holmes once opined, "poison is a woman's weapon," then witches were the best armed of women. Or as Reginald Scot wrote: "Augustine, Livie, Valerius, Diodorus and manie other agree that women were the first inventers and practisers of the art of poisoning," which they are "more naturallie addicted and given thereunto than men."

Witches did work with dangerous plants, but even more intriguing was their aptitude for flying, "transvection," an activity which does not often seem to have been voluntarily mentioned by the witches themselves but which was of great interest to their accusers. Flight, sometimes via broomstick or animal, culminated in the Sabbat, an orgy of dancing, sex and general wickedness. By the ninth century, a European general council decried "certain wicked women" who, "reverting to Satan and seduced by the illusions and phantasms of demons, believe and profess that they ride at night with Diana on certain beasts, with an innumerable multitude of women, passing over immense distances, obeying her commands as their mistress and evoked by her on certain nights."

Although the common modern belief is that only torture and ignorance could account for such tales (Reginald Scot asked, "What an unapt instrument is a toothless . . . impotent and unwieldy old woman to fly in the aier?"), the flights have connections with the very plants with which Diana's riders worked. The witch's preflight ritual included rubbing herself with a greasy herbal ointment, a mixture of soot, plants and fat (the fat of murdered babies, many accused). A 20th-century experiment with a possible flying ointment gave German folklorist Dr. Will-Erich Peuckert and some of his colleagues an experience remarkably similar to reported witches' flights: "We experienced in dreams first wild and yet restricted flights and then chaotic revels like the wild tumult of an annual fairground and finally progressed to erotic licentiousness."

One such flying ointment was described by Scot in 1584 as consisting of "the fat of young children" along with "*Eleoselinum*" (wild parsley), "*Aconitum*" (monkshood), "*Frondes populaes*" (poplar leaves) and "soote." Another recipe included "*Solanum somniferum*" (nightshade). According to Scot, the witches "stampe all these togither, and then they rubbe all parts of their bodys exceedinglie till they looke red and be verie hot, so as the pores may be opened and their flesh soluble and loose." William Coles, in his 1656 *Art of Simpling*, wrote, "the Oyntment that Witches use is reported to be made of the fat of Children digged out of their graves; of the Juices of smallage, Woolfsbaine and Cinquefoyle mingled with the meale of fine Wheat. But some suppose that the soporiferous Medicines are likeliest to doe it, which are Henbane, Hemlock, Mandrake, Nightshade, Tobacco, Opium, Saffron, Poplar Leaves, & c."

In this century, Alfred J. Clark wrote that the three recipes he examined, which included herbal ingredients like parsley, aconite, poplar leaves, water parsnip, sweet flag, cinquefoil and deadly nightshade, would produce such symptoms as mental confusion, impaired movement, irregular action of the heart, dizziness, shortness of breath and excitement. He found the use of aconite and belladonna especially interesting: "Irregular action of the heart in a person falling asleep produces the well-known sensation of suddenly falling through space, and it seems quite possible that the combination of a delirifacient like belladonna with a drug producing irregular action of the heart like aconite might produce the sensation of flying."

In the 16th century, Giovanni Battista Porta paid a well-known witch to answer some of his questions about transvection. Unknown to her, Porta watched her through a crack in the door as she set off on one of her flights by stripping, rubbing herself with ointment and then falling asleep. She could not be awakened for some time, but when she was, she told Porta that she had crossed mountains and seas, a fantasy Porta blamed in part upon poor nutrition and suggestibility. "Their minds dwelling perpetually on these subjects, they are more susceptible, and as they live exclusively on insufficient vegetable food—beets, chestnuts, greens, etc.—they are more easily affected."

Sixteenth-century Spanish court physician Andrés Fernandez de Laguna noted that a pot of green salve, composed, he suspected, of hemlock, nightshade, henbane and mandrake, was found in the home of a witch and a wizard who were executed. A woman in Metz, anointed "from head to toe" with the salve, "suddenly slept such a profound sleep, with her eyes open like a rabbit (she also fittingly looked like a boiled hare), that I could not imagine how to wake her." Thirty-six hours later, the woman reluctantly woke and told of having been "surrounded by all the pleasures and delights in the world" and of having made love to a lusty young man.

Around the same time, a French doctor saw a Bordeaux witch anoint herself with an unguent and fall unconscious for five hours, after which she told the doctor of several incidents that had actually happened around her while she slept. In Nantes, France, seven women fell into a trance lasting three hours, after which they told of a number of verifiable events within 10 miles, a divulgence of real or imaginary talents that had them burned.

De Laguna believed that "most delusions of witches and wizards must be due to the ointments with which they anoint themselves; the excessive coldness of these ointments renders them so unconscious that, during their prolonged sleep, a thousand stray visions so insistently appear in their brains that when they awake, they confess sins they never committed."

According to Henri Boguet, "there have even been cases of persons who were not witches but have, following the example of and at the instigation of witches, rubbed themselves with a certain ointment, and of farmers who have been transported to as much as a hundred or two hundred leagues from their homes so that they have had great difficulty in finding their way back again." Boguet also recorded that a prisoner given witches' ointment was able to jump out of a prison window, climb along a metal bar "on which it was impossible to set foot except by the devilish arts" and, while fleeing, to attain "quite incredible speed" without tiring.

Attempts to re-create the ointments for experimental purposes have not been consistently successful, no doubt because of the lack of a single recipe that includes clearly defined plants and describes the amounts in which they are to be used and the ways in which the ointment is to be applied. Around the turn of the century, Dr. Karl Kiesewetter of Germany rubbed himself with a herbal ointment that caused him to dream about flying in spirals. He later killed himself with an experimental ointment. In the 1950s, German toxicologist Gustav Schenk experimented with inhaling a henbane smoke, which produced a headache, perspiration, malevolent hallucinations and the impression that the room danced. Then "the frightening certainty that my end was near through the dissolution of my body [a typical symptom of henbane poisoning] was counterbalanced by an animal joy in flight. I soared where my hallucinations—the clouds, the lowering sky, herds of beasts, falling leaves which were quite unlike any ordinary leaves, billowing streamers of steam and rivers of molten metal—were swelling along."

In 1958, George N. Conklin of Wesleyan University wrote about witch ointments in the *American Journal of Pharmacy*: "Indeed, the belief, followed by the effect of the drugs, easily, in my opinion, accounts for the oft-noted sincerity of the confessions; the belief a delusion, but the drugged experience real. . . . Any question of the toxicological effect of these ingredients used as a salve (as against the indubitable results if taken internally) must take into consideration that the ointment was mostly applied to the legs and the vaginal membranes, which could convey the toxins to the bloodstream. Further, it should be borne in mind that the louse-bitten skin of a witch was unlikely to be unbroken." It is noteworthy that all of today's common poisons, such as pesticides, have both oral and dermal toxicity ratings—the skin, even unbroken, is more like a sieve than a barrier.

In Carlos Castaneda's *The Teachings of Don Juan*, the power to fly came from a datura ointment smeared on the legs and genitals. Castaneda also drank an extract of datura root, which has been accorded a place in some flying-ointment recipes. He wrote: "I looked down and saw Don Juan below me, way below me. . . . I remember coming down once, and then I pushed up with both feet, sprang backward and glided on my back. I saw the dark sky above me and the clouds going by me. I jerked my body so I could look down. . . . My speed was extraordinary." He ended up physically removed by about half a mile from the place he started, which differs from most accounts of earlier flights. But Don Juan told Castaneda that he had flown not "like birds" but "as a man who has taken the weed," suggesting that he may have wandered or run to his destination. Unfortunately, the veracity of Castaneda's accounts is disputed.

In 1954, Germany's *Kosmos* magazine published an account of the preparation of a witches' ointment. The author, Siegbert Ferckel, who did not divulge the recipe he obtained "from a secondary source," reported having become frighteningly swollen and dizzy and feeling powerless and helpless. He then "floated upward with great velocity. Again, it became light, and through a pink veil, I vaguely noticed that I was floating over the city." He felt himself surrounded by a dancing circle of ill-tempered faces. "More and more of these figures joined in, surrounding me in a circle as they danced. Time passed with a snail's pace, and every minute seemed to last an eternity." He awoke the next morning "to a new life," his heart still beating rapidly.

Some of the herbs used in flying ointments have also produced, in some subjects, the sensation of turning into an animal, which might explain the witches' supposed ability to do so. The symptoms of poisoning by atropine, an alkaloid present in several of the witches' most favoured plants such as henbane and belladonna, include extreme thirst, impaired vision and a staggering gait and were reported by an early Greek, Paulus Aegineta, as signs of those suffering from lycanthropy. Giambattista Porta stated in the 17th century that "to make a man believe he was changed into a Bird or Beast," a potion containing henbane, mandrake, stramonium, or *Solanum manicum*, and belladonna was drunk, after which "the man would seem sometimes to be changed into a fish; and flinging out his arms, would swim on the Ground. . . . Another would believe himself turned into a Goose and would eat Grass and beat the Ground with his Teeth like a Goose, now and then sing and endeavour to clap his Wings." Similar experiences were also reported by Carlos Castaneda.

As with atropine, the active ingredients in these witches' plants are alkaloids, nitrogenous "-ine" substances that have powerful pharmacological effects on animals and humans, are present in the greatest concentration in seeds and roots and include such well-known plant products as nicotine, cocaine, strychnine and quinine. Atropine, hyoscya-

mine and scopolamine are potentially toxic hallucinogenic alkaloids found in four of the witches' choice plants – henbane, datura, mandrake and nightshade – all members of what Linnaeus called "a suspicious family," the Solanaceae. (More respectable members of the family, such as the tomato and potato, also contain these alkaloids, but they are concentrated in parts of the plant not eaten.) Atropine is, incidentally, used by ophthalmologists to dilate the pupils – useful for anyone who wishes better night vision – and scopolamine has been used as a truth serum.

On the next few pages are the chief plant ingredients in witches' ointments, listed in increasing order of their frequency of occurrence in the available recipes. Their proportions are not known, and I strongly urge the reader not to experiment with these dangerous plants. As Harold A. Hansen writes in *The Witch's Garden*, the wise women knew exactly what amounts and proportions were safe: "One might get the impression that the witches risked their lives every time they smeared themselves with the ointments, but there is no evidence that they ever ran into trouble. The reason for this is undoubtedly that the preparation of the ointment was entrusted only to those witches who knew their plants so well that any risk was ruled out in advance."

PARSLEY (*Petroselinum* spp) was the herb of the Greek hero Archemones, the forerunner of death, and was dedicated to Persephone, queen of the underworld. It became the sacred herb of burials and was frequently used at funerals, an oddly weighty role for a plant now considered little more than a garnish for salads and baked potatoes.

But although the "persil" included in some witches' recipes is sometimes thought to refer to hemlock, a parsley relative discussed later, even common parsley has powerful characteristics, especially the seeds and their oil. The oil contains high concentrations of

Because the mandrake root resembles a human body, the hallucinogenic plant was assumed to have human attributes.

apiol and myristicin, both of which are uterine stimulants; parsley oil was traditionally used to speed childbirth and to bring about abortions. Myristicin is the principal constituent of nutmeg oil, which is hallucinogenic. Apiol resembles myristicin chemically and has similar physical effects. According to Pliny the Elder, two authorities determined that there were male and female strains of parsley and that the female was known because, among other things, it "breeds grubs, and because of this, those who have eaten it, whether male or female, become barren, and sucking babies become epileptic if their nurses have eaten parsley." Parsley seed, Pliny main-

tained, "aids the menses and the after-birth."

MANDRAKE (*Mandragora officinarum*), a native of the Mediterranean region, has a broad disc of leaves, cup-shaped, purplish blossoms and round, plumlike, sweetish fruit —the "love apple," a name later bestowed upon the tomato, one of mandrake's New World relatives greeted with understandable suspicion by Europeans. The plant's Latin name may derive from the Sanskrit *mandros* (sleep) and *agora* (an object or substance), because the mandrake has long been respected as a powerful poison and tranquillizer. Henri Boguet wrote that the devil, via witches, induced in men a profound sleep "with mandragora or some other narcotic drought" so that a woman could go to Sabbat and be back without her husband waking.

Magical and maligned, the mandrake was the ideal plant to complement the witch's own mystery. In early Christian times, it was said to be God's first shaping of man, later rejected by the Creator when He shaped Adam from the red earth of paradise. And true enough, its fleshy root does bear some resemblance to the torso and legs of a man or woman (some specimens were called womandrake). The plant was so "human," it was supposed to shriek when pulled from the ground, a sound that would kill any harvester who heard it. Elaborate rituals once surrounded the harvest of mandrake, including tying the plant to a dog so that the dog, rather than a person, would be killed by the sound of the plant. In another tradition, three circles were drawn around mandrake with the tip of a sword, and the would-be harvester then danced around the plant, reciting words of love. Mandrake was also rumoured to glow in the dark.

But if mandrake was feared for its magic and its poisons, it was also considered therapeutic. From prehistoric times, people have believed mandrake capable of granting fertility (as one species apparently did for Rachel,

A page of a herbal devoted to witches' plants includes tomatoes, which were suspect because they are nightshades.

〜

an annual up to three feet tall with narrow leaves, white or pale blue flowers and prickly, walnut-sized capsules that give it one of its names, thorn apple. Another name, jimson-weed (or Jamestown weed), arose from an accidental poisoning of some soldiers who "turn'd Fools upon it for several Days" in Jamestown, Virginia, in 1676. "One would blow up a Feather in the Air; another would dart Straws at it with much Fury; and another stark naked was sitting in a Corner, like a Monkey, grinning and making Mows at them . . . ."

Carlos Castaneda, in *The Teachings of Don Juan*, noted that Don Juan called datura "the devil's weed," which "sneaks up on you like a woman" and often kills quickly. The root, stem, leaves, flowers and seeds all have different properties, said Don Juan, the roots being capable of enabling one to "soar through the air to see what is going on at any place he chooses." Exceedingly dangerous, thorn-apple preparations have nevertheless been prized as love potions. One indignant German writer said that the plant was used as "a tool of brothel-keepers, wicked seducers of girls, depraved courtesans and shameless lechers."

But John Gerard wrote in his 16th-century *Herbal* that "the juice of Thornapples boiled with hogs' grease to the form of an unguent or salve cures all inflammations whatsoever, all manner of burnings or scaldings, as well of fire, water, boiling lead, gunpouder, as that which comes by lightning, and that in very short time, as my selfe have found by my daily practise, to my great credit and profit." Datura has also been used to treat epilepsy, melancholia, convulsions, insanity and rheumatism, and as recently as the 19th century, Sarah Wallis Bowdich Lee called it a "celebrated remedy for asthma."

All parts of the plant, however, can cause hallucinations and rapid pulse, and an overdose results in convulsions, coma and death.

Jacob's aged wife) and of acting as an aphrodisiac. Too, Hippocrates maintained around 400 B.C. that "a small dose in wine, less than would occasion delirium, will relieve the deepest depression and anxiety." Chief among its active ingredients is scopolamine, a hallucinogen.

DATURA (*Datura* spp), with species native to both the eastern and western hemispheres, is another source of scopolamine. Datura species have been used in shamanism, voodoo and witchcraft in Europe, Asia, Africa and America.

Datura stramonium, one of the species most commonly mentioned in witches' recipes, is

HENBANE (*Hyoscyamus* spp) is a native Mediterranean solanaceous plant with sticky, hairy, grey-green leaves and flowers that Harold A. Hansen, author of *The Witch's Garden*, called "yellow, almost corpse-coloured, violet-veined, which remind one most of the 'evil eye.'" And they have an unpleasant smell, "a kind of Mr. Hyde to the potato's Dr. Jekyll." Earlier, I described the henbane-smoke hallucinations of German toxicologist Gustav Schenk. The same plant, which was noted in this century as having "the tendency to produce illusions of sight," has traditionally been burned throughout Europe on June 24, the birthday of St. John the Baptist (a holiday that replaces an earlier pagan celebration of the summer solstice), to fumigate stables to keep evil spirits from cattle and from children led through the stables.

As well as its reputation as a powerful smoke and a poison, henbane has a long history of use in herbal medicine as a love potion, sedative and painkiller.

POPPY (*Papaver rhoeas, P. somniferum*): Chief among sedatives and painkillers, the opium poppy, *P. somniferum*, a Middle Eastern and southeastern European native, is so well known for its high content of several alkaloids, especially morphine, that its value in witches' ointments needs little explanation. Seventeenth-century astrologist-physician Nicholas Culpeper considered the poppy's syrup "a gentle narcotic, easing pain and causing sleep. . . . An overdose causes immoderate mirth or stupidity, redness of the face, swelling of the lips, relaxation of the joints, giddiness of the head, deep sleep, accompanied with turbulent dreams and convulsive starting, cold sweats and frequently death." Both the opium poppy and the corn, or field, poppy (*P. rhoeas*) produce seed for baking and have cough-soothing and sedative properties.

HEMLOCK AND WATER HEMLOCK (*Conium maculatum* and *Cicuta virosa*) are small, extremely poisonous, herbaceous, native European plants whose close relationship to garden carrots and parsley has occasionally led to a tragic misidentification. However, the virulent poisons of hemlock and water hemlock, especially coniine, which is concentrated in the seeds and roots, will cause the sensation of flight if taken in a sufficiently small dose. Larger doses are often fatal—*Conium maculatum* was the Athenian state poison, used to execute such prisoners as Socrates.

The plants were also thought to have therapeutic uses, which may have been of interest to early herbalists. Dioscorides claimed that hemlock juice rubbed on a woman's breasts would stop the milk from flowing and could prevent them from growing too large, a belief recorded again 1,600 years later by Simon Paulli in *Flora Danica*, where he wrote, "Girls' breasts that are rubbed with the juice of this herb do not grow thereafter but remain properly small and do not change the size they are." Impotent men often claimed that witches had spread hemlock juice on their genitals as they slept. Pliny the Elder wrote, "What is certain is that an application of hemlock to the breasts of women in childbed dries up their milk, and to rub it on the testicles at the time of puberty acts as an antaphrodisiac." The unrelated hemlock tree is not poisonous.

WOLFSBANE, MONKSHOOD or ACONITE (*Aconitum napellus*), a European native, is a tall, attractive blue-flowered perennial member of the buttercup family that contains a very poisonous substance, aconitine, which may have been used on arrows in European prehistory. According to Greek mythology, the plant is the creation of Hecate, moon goddess and attendant of Persephone in the underworld. While centuries ago, Calpurnius Bestia apparently murdered one wife after another by smearing their genitals with aconitine as they slept (in early Rome, the plant's toxic properties were so well respected that growing it at all in that poison-happy society was a capital offence), modern flower gardeners grow wolfsbane in oblivious admiration of its beautiful blooms. Unfortunately, accidents do occur, including one, reported in an 1874 book, "from aconite roots being used instead of horseradish." Once used as a sedative and painkiller in small doses, aconite is now considered too toxic for anything but very limited external applications.

CREEPING CINQUEFOIL AND TORMENTIL (*Potentilla reptans* and *P. erecta*): More benign than most of the witch's favourites, these plants do, however, have a connection with her symbolism, being "fivefold" plants. Their leaves are arranged in groups of five, which alone is enough to grant them a magical reputation in the tradition of the witch's pentacle; the number five was especially important to witches (as it was to Christians, for similar reasons described in chapter five).

Tormentil, a Eurasian native, is a creeping plant that has been used as a red dye and as a treatment for various medical complaints, from diarrhea to fever to "the falling of the uvula," according to Nicholas Culpeper. It is still considered a useful simple for treating wounds; the powdered root is an especially effective styptic because of its high tannin content. Tormentil's main drawback is that excessive external application may cause scarring. Both plants were thought to enhance night vision – probably because of a high vitamin A content – which the witches may have found appealing.

NIGHTSHADE (*Atropa belladonna*), a solanaceous plant of dangerous reputation, is the most commonly listed ingredient in the witch-ointment recipes and is aptly named after Atropos, the eldest of the three Fates of Greek mythology, who severed the thread of life. Although the species name, *belladonna*, "beautiful woman," is usually assumed to have arisen from the plant's use as a dilator of the

Herbalist Susun Weed says humanity is still influenced by powerful plants.

pupils of fashionable Renaissance women, another theory has it that the name is derived from its use by good or beautiful women – that is, the early wise women, the witches.

All parts of what Elizabethan physician John Gerard called "sleepy nightshade" are extremely poisonous, mainly because of the presence of the alkaloid atropine. As few as three berries of this herbaceous, shrubby European native, especially if unripe, can kill a child. Poisoning has even been reported to result from using belladonna as a skin plaster, liniment or enema.

In translating Dioscorides' *De materia medica* in 1555, Andrés Fernandez de Laguna wrote of nightshade that "a dram of extract from the root when dissolved in wine produces fleeting images that please the senses, but if the dose be doubled, it drives a man mad for three days; if the dose be quadrupled, it can cause immediate death . . . ." The plant was said to be tended by the devil, who retired from caring for it only on Walpurgis Night, the eve of May Day, when he prepared for the witches' Sabbat instead. In the *American Journal of Pharmacy*, George N. Conklin associates the witches' tales of Sabbat dancing with the symptoms of belladonna poisoning and notes that "the delirifacient effects of *Atropa belladonna* alone could account for any bizarre confession on the part of the user."

In 1854, in *Trees, Plants and Flowers; Their Beauties, Uses and Influences*, however, Sarah Wallis Bowdich Lee wrote that *Atropa belladonna* "allays pain and irritation of the nerves, hence it is much employed in neuralgia." It is still available in several prescription pharmaceuticals, especially for digestive disorders and ulcers. "The action of belladonna in relaxing smooth muscles by depressing cholinergic stimulating effects is well recognized," says the 1976 *Physicians' Desk Reference* of one medicine, Chardonna. For Prydon Spansule tablets, which also contain atropine, the overdose symptoms are "dryness of the mouth and throat, hot, dry, flushed skin, dilated pupils, disorientation, delirium, rapid pulse and respiration," as well as photophobia, discomfort caused by light.

Other herbal ingredients in witches' ointments include celery, sweet flag, yellow flag, water lily, spurge, lettuce, purslane and poplar.

As any herbalist, alchemist or physician knew, such plants had to be not only properly prepared but also properly harvested. Every herb, mild or powerful, was best picked at a specific time and during a certain season. While early Romans may have been romanticizing when they wrote of naked or black-clad witches using bronze sickles to reap their plants during a full moon, witches probably did harvest most of their plants at night, in part because they did not wish to be seen but also because most of their favourites were traditionally at their best if gathered at night – some while the moon was full, others while it was waning or waxing and yet others during a lunar eclipse.

The recitation of charms during harvest is common among tribal peoples worldwide, and witches were no different, although the church forbade the use of such charms as early as the seventh century A.D. Nevertheless, the witches persisted. In one incantation quoted by Reginald Scot, a "charme that witches use at the gathering of their medicinable hearbs," it is possible that Christian terms were substituted for pre-Christian ones to appease the church, but it is also possible that the woman who recited this charm for Scot was as devoted a Christian as he:

Haile be thou holie hearbe
growing on the ground
and healest manie a wound
first wert thou found,
Thou art good for manie a sore,
and healest manie a wound,
In the name of sweete Jesus
I take thee from the ground.

Was Scot's witch really harvesting her plants for the glory of "sweete Jesus?" The accounts of the work of witches, shadowed by fear and muddied with time, leave little insight into the true motives of the wise women, "the deadliest enemies of heaven." Perhaps as our own knowledge of plants increases, so will our understanding of the women who attracted such fear and wonder during at least three centuries of Western civilization.

Answers may come, too, from modern women still following the herbal traditions of the witches. A self-styled "green witch" – "Somehow the modification 'green' makes the word 'witch' less threatening" – Susun Weed runs her own Wise Woman Center in Woodstock, New York, where she has published books on herbal medicine. When I asked her about flying ointments, Weed said that the substances came from what she called "power plants. So long as there have been sentient beings on this planet, there have been power plants and there has been interchange between those power plants and those beings. We tend to think of the power plants as being something very extraordinary, and yet they associate very, very closely with people. The most commonly used power plants at this time are coffee, tobacco, cocoa and marijuana. And the nature of the power plant is that because it has power, one needs, first of all, to have respect for oneself and, second of all, to have respect for the plant. And if both of those things are functioning, there is an equality between the being and the plant. If one doesn't have respect for oneself, if one doesn't have respect for the plant, then the plant in a very real sense overcomes the power of the person.

"As we reconnect with that respect for ourselves and respect for women's power to heal the planet, we understand that the planet gives away to us in the form of the plants. Nourish the soil, nourish the animals, nourish us and heal us; there's that continuing cycle between women and the planet and then back from the planet in the form of plants and into women's hands to pass into the cycle of people. I truly trust and believe right now that this planetary transformation is in the hands of woman, not just the woman that is in women but the woman that is also in men. It is that female spirit that is being called forth now for healing."

Weed, who led me and a group of others on a walk along a Canadian country road, where she pointed out the therapeutic uses and dangers of every plant we passed, follows what she calls "the invisible lineage, because as descendants of Europeans, women's lineage was severely disrupted. I made very consciously and very clearly an agreement to speak for the earth, to be a voice for the earth in this form because she does not speak in this form right now. There are many people doing this. I'm certainly not alone. I'm not the only one."

Gardensong

Comfrey, chamomile, thyme and golden cup
Mother sends me down to pick, down to
　　gather up
Lily of the valley, rue and daffodil,
Monkshood and foxglove, these can kill.
Mother knows the difference, mother grows
　　them all,
Plants in the spring, gathers in the fall.

Midsummer solstice, come build a fire
Older than the churchyard, taller than a pyre,
Old as the hills, old as the moon
Light it at midnight, let it burn till noon.
Preacher doesn't like it, wants to make it part
Of his Sunday service, take away our heart.

People called us witches, turned the word
　　about,
Feared our quiet power, tore our gardens out.
Pulled up the roots, threw away the seeds,
Burned the harmless flowers, let in the weeds.
Burned a thousand women, took away
　　the child
Thought we had forgotten, thought the
　　flowers wild.

We searched them out again, brought them
　　back at night
Seldom spoke the reason, knew that we
　　were right.
Whispered the wisdom, sought out the lore
Traded roots and seedlings, planted more
　　and more.
See our pretty gardens shining in the sun,
Bringing back the witches, one by one.

—Wilma Kenney

V

"In a Fair Communitie Togeather"

*The Virgin Mary's plants
and convent gardens*

*The Virgin was a Garden round beset
With Rose, and Lillie, and sweet Violet.
Where fragrant sents without distaste of Sinne,
Invited God the Sonne to enter in.
But it was closed: Alma's shut up: we know,
What Gard'ner then might enter in to sow?
Or plant within this Eden? Or, what birth
Might be expected from a virgin-earth?
The Holie-Spirit, like a subtile wind,
Peercing through al, only a way could find.
As th'Earth brought forth at first, how 'tis not nowne:
So did this Garden, which was never sowne.*

〜

This bit of mediaeval poetry describes a mysterious garden, entirely walled and full of flowers that were "never sowne." It is a place of beauty and sweet scents, an Eden, paradise and refuge.

The poem is also a metaphor for woman, tempting but untouchable. It—she—is the Virgin Mary, the perfect woman, who was not only the garden itself but also the roses, lilies and violets within it—symbols within a symbol,

The plant associates of the new goddess, Mary, the
mother of Jesus, are not roots but flowers—delicate,
perfumed receptacles for reproduction.

all approachable by only one gardener, the "Holie-Spirit." It is a strange and unnatural image but a powerful one.

The Christian church influenced all areas of mediaeval and Renaissance life in Europe, including the way women were defined, how they lived and their association with plants. Nowhere was this clearer than in the perception of the Virgin Mary, whose role among saints had been burgeoning since the millennium. A mere patron saint in the early centuries of the church, Mary assumed an increasingly important role in the Middle Ages, until she attained a sort of cult status (now known as Mariolatry) by the 12th century. Considered the most accessible facet of God, the most responsive to human supplication, she dominated prayers and rituals. And her likeness in paintings and statues in churches, shrines, gardens and festivals was often associated with flowers.

The mother of Jesus went some way toward filling a generations-old gap in Western religion: the powerful, compassionate mother goddess associated with fertility and, by extension, plants. One of Mary's chief virtues, humility, has the same origin as the Latin *humus*, earth. But Mary was an unusual earth goddess. Conceiving while still a virgin and giving birth to both man and god in one baby were not unusual feats for an earth goddess, but Mary's childbearing was her entire *raison d'être*. Mary, least earthy of Earth Mothers, did not have the fecund, sometimes dangerous, power of seeds and roots of many earlier goddesses. Her plant associates were flowers: delicate, passive, perfumed receptacles for reproduction. Like the petals of a flower, Mary was "vessel and implement, herself a mandala," writes Eithne Wilkins in *The Rose-Garden Game*.

Despite the fact that little was known of the real woman, Mary's growing preeminence in the Middle Ages led to a concept of her that, while not quite one-dimensional, was certainly lacking in depth. (Torquato Tasso wrote in the 16th century: "The vertues proper to a man are Wisedome, Fortitude and Liberalitie. To woman, Modestie and Chastitie.") In paintings and prayers, Mary was depicted as devoted, quiet and compassionate but not quite human; she was never shown eating or angry or laughing or talking to her friends. The lady, that unearthly creature who would reach her zenith in the Victorian age, by which time she would actually be christened with the names of flowers like Rose, Lily and Violet, was being fashioned from the stuff of legend, longing and ignorance.

Emily James Putnam says in her 1970 book *The Lady*: "The lady's history has in all times been reflected and symbolized by that of her garden. . . . In both the lady and the garden, something primarily useful is maintained unproductively for its aesthetic value alone." The image of the lady as a flower – a cut flower without roots in the earth, as it were – was first fully realized in the Middle Ages in an ethereal portrayal of Mary that would prove to be a lasting ideal. As we shall see, however, the synthesis of this image with an earthier one occurred in the era of Mariolatry in convents where the "flowers of the church" had a freedom available to few women until this century.

Although Mary was most closely identified with flowers, she had links, fleeting or lasting, with scores of plants – virtually anything beautiful or sweetly scented, including various herbs and trees. What was important for a society not particularly attuned to ornamental gardening but very much in touch with herbal medicine was that the chief Marian plants were also healing plants. For the common person familiar with simples, the message was clear: Mary is good medicine.

The Song of Solomon, a long, sensual biblical love poem that is decidedly secular to most ears but was interpreted by early Christians as referring to God's immaculate relationship with Mary, mentions a list of plants which were consequently associated with the Holy Mother, including grapevines, apples, figs, pomegranates, wheat and plants prized for the preparation of perfumes, medicines or spices. They included spikenard (*Nardostachys jatamansi*) from northern India, highly regarded as a perfume; camphire, or camphor, derived from an Oriental evergreen, *Cinnamomum camphora*; saffron, from the saffron crocus (*Crocus sativus*); calamus (*Cybopogon martinii*), the aromatic palmeron oil grass of Egypt; cinnamon from the cinnamon tree (*Cinnamomum zeylanicum*); frankincense, a fragrant gum exuded from trees of the genus *Boswellia*; and myrrh, from the Arabian myrtle (*Balsamodendron myrrha*).

The mandrake (*Mandragora officinarum*), however, a powerful plant and one of the witches' favourites, was mentioned in the *Song* only as the source of "a smell." Like other poisonous plants, it was decidedly not Marian. Women could be divided metaphorically into two groups, then, according to their herbal affiliations: those who sided with Mary could be considered much like flowers or benign medicinal plants, while those who followed the ancient codes of the witches were considered to be as poisonous as the plants they grew.

Roses and lilies, the only two flowers listed in *The Song of Solomon* — "I am the rose of Sharon and the lily of the valleys" — became the most important of the Marian flowers. Indeed, the rose had been associated with beauty, wisdom, love and mystery since time immemorial and was the favourite flower of the Greek and Roman deities who governed love, while the lily had long been a symbol of purity and womanhood. In taking up the sign of the rose, Mary simply picked up the stem dropped by goddesses who had gone before.

According to one mediaeval legend, roses first appeared at Bethlehem, where, wrote Sir John Mandeville, a "fayre Mayden" was falsely accused (presumably of witchcraft) and sentenced to burn: "And as the woode began to brenne about her, she made her prayer to our lorde as she was not gylty of a thynge that he would helpe her that it might be knowen to all men. And whan she had thus sayd, she entered the fyre and anone the fyre went out, and those branches that were brennynge became reed roses, and those branches that were not kyndled became full of whyte roses, and those were the first roses and rosers that any man saw, and thus was the mayden saved through the grace of God."

Mary was called the Mystic Rose, Rose of Sharon, Peerless Rose. "And as in the morning the rose opens, receiving the first dew from heaven and the sun, so Mary's soul did open and receive Christ the heavenly dew," says a 15th-century sermon. Sometimes she appeared to believers in the form of the rose, as she did to the Mexican peasant Juan Diego, whose 16th-century vision of her, replete with red roses, led to the establishment of the shrine of Our Lady of Guadeloupe in Mexico City. At Fatima and Lourdes, she was also said to have appeared from a circle of roses. According to legend, St. Josbert daily repeated five psalms that began with the letters of the name Maria. When he died, five roses were found in his mouth, eyes and ears.

A circle of roses, too, is the rosary, the string of beads now closely identified with the Roman Catholic Church and with the Ave Maria, or Hail Mary, the short prayer based on Luke 1, verse 28. One early legend has it that upon saying his Ave Marias, a monk saw each prayer turn into a rose before his eyes. He created 50 such roses, enough to make a perfect chaplet, or rosary. The rosary is normally strung with multiples of 10 similar beads, with differently coloured or shaped beads separating each "decade," or set of 10. The usual rosary has 5 decades, while a

The rose is associated with Mary and with the church in general and thus appears in many ecclesiastical decorations, such as a tile from an English abbey.

～～

full rosary consists of 15. In a prayer cycle that first appeared in the 11th century, Ave Marias are traditionally recited as the devotee touches each of the smaller beads. The larger beads are reserved for the Paternoster (Our Father) and the Gloria. The custom of reciting prayers on beads had been practised by Buddhists and Hindus before it was adopted by Christians and Moslems, but the name "rosary," from the Latin *rosarium*, rose garden, is peculiar to Christian beads.

In the early Middle Ages, collections of poems or prayers or other bits of information were often given the name *hortulus*, flower garden, or *hortus*, garden. The *Hortus deliciarum*, or *Garden of Delights*, compiled by Herrad, a 12th-century abbess, is an illustrated encyclopaedia of biblical and mediaeval social information. (The only complete copy of it was, unfortunately, destroyed when the Germans bombarded Strasbourg in 1870.) Despite its title, it contains little horticultural

information, although there are the usual Christian symbolic references to certain flowers—crocuses shine with wisdom, and lilies have virgin purity. The word *rosarium* also denoted literary collections of various sorts, although it finally came to suggest only Marian devotions. By the 13th century, the rosarium, the series of Marian prayers said on the prayer beads, had lent its name to the beads themselves.

The number 5 and its multiple 50 are natural extensions of the symbolism of the rose. The sum of the first even digit (two) and the first odd compound of one (three), the number five has probably been considered special ever since human beings first counted their fingers, and so it seemed significant that there were five petals in the most sweetly scented, beautiful and medicinal of plants, the ordinary single rose. By connecting the centre of each rose sepal with the next, one obtains a pentagram, or pentacle, a star with five points, which became a symbol of magic and mystery. The pentacle was used as a talisman against witches and demons.

The protective power of the rose extended into conversations held *sub rosa*: secret, not for the public. In antiquity, such dealings were literally conducted under the sign of a rose. In the 16th century, the rose symbol was placed over confessionals. The Christian connections with the number five were equally powerful, especially the five joyful, five sorrowful and five glorious mysteries of Mary.

The apple, a close relative of the rose, which reveals the mystical five-pointed star when cut in half horizontally, has connections with Mary as well. St. Ambrose declared in the fourth century that "Eve caused us to be damned with an apple; Mary redeemed us with the gift from a tree": Jesus, the fruit of Mary's womb, who is sometimes represented as an apple in her hand. In fact, the apple has a split personality—the Latin word *malum* means both "apple" and "evil."

～～

Symbolic fruit of the downfall of humanity, the apple has long been associated with evil deeds done by women and was sometimes used as evidence of wickedness in the trials of witches.

Roses and apples also played an important role in the life and death of Dorothea, the only woman among three patron saints of gardening, the other two being Phocas and Fiacre (who is also the patron saint of cab-drivers). Dorothea, believed to have been martyred around 303 A.D., is most commonly portrayed with a sword (the vehicle of her martyrdom), a wreath of roses on her head, a spray of roses or a basket of roses and apples in her hand. The story has it that she was taken in front of a judge, accused of witchcraft and tortured because of various miracles she had performed. Then, according to an anonymous 15th-century account, the judge said to Dorothea, "Howe longe wilte thou drawe us along with thy wychcrafte? Eyther doo sacryfyse and lyve or ellis receyve the sentens of thy hede smytyng of." Dorothea replied that the judge might proceed at his pleasure, because "I am redy to suffer for my lorde Jhu Criste, my spouse, in whose gardeyn full delycious I have gaderd rosis and apples."

The next day, she was sentenced to be beheaded. When Theophilus, a notary of Rome, saw her, he scornfully requested that she send him some roses and apples from the garden of her spouse, even though it was the middle of winter. Despite the season, a child appeared with a basket containing three roses and three apples. Dorothea told the child to take the basket to Theophilus. And so, concludes the story, Theophilus and the city of Caesarea in Cappadocia (now Iraq) were converted to Christianity.

Sharing equal standing with the rose among Marian flowers was the white lily, later called the Madonna lily (*Lilium candidum*), a native of the Middle East. Fragrant and beautiful, the lily had been dedicated by the Romans to Juno, queen of heaven, special protector of marriage and women. According to one legend, it grew from the tears of Eve after her expulsion from Eden. The lily appears frequently in mediaeval paintings of Mary, especially in depictions of the Annunciation, when Mary was told by the angel Gabriel that she would give birth to the Messiah.

The violet, third in importance of the Marian flowers, was a symbol of humility or modesty. "O Mary," prayed Saint Bernard in the 11th century, "thou art the violet of humility, the lily of purity, the rose of love."

But if Mary was violet, lily and rose, she was also the entire garden, as mentioned in *The Song of Solomon* — "A garden inclosed is my sister, my spouse; a spring shut up, a fountain sealed" — and as described in Henry Hawkins' 1633 *Parthenia sacra*, where the Virgin appears "not in the habit of fashion of a Gardener, which office she rather yealds (as proper) to her Sonne, but of a Garden," the closed garden, or *hortus conclusus*. Part of the poem introduces this chapter. Hawkins recalled the Garden of Eden when he wrote that "no Serpent . . . could have acces." In fact, the garden is "shut-up from al invasions of Enemies," an image that is simultaneously sexual and suggestive of the earlier reign of the earth goddess, friend of the serpent. Even though the garden is secured against those old symbols of fertility and power, Mary still has an outward resemblance to the goddesses of old, looking, said Hawkins, "as if she were clothed with the Sunne, crowned with the Starres, and trampling the Moone. . . . Nor would I wish you perfunctoriously to view her only, and passe her over with a slender glance of the eye, but to enter into her Garden, which she is herself, and survey it well."

And what is this garden like? "It is a Monopolie of al the pleasures and delights that are on the earth amassed togeather . . .

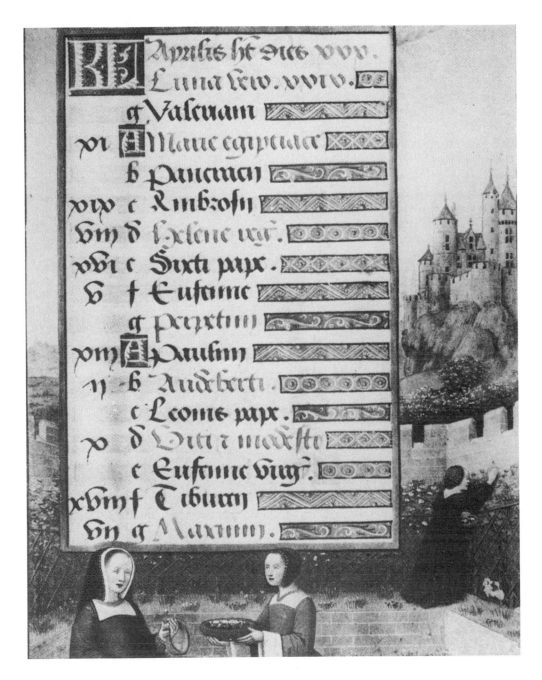

The walled garden, or hortus conclusus, *was the symbol of the Virgin Mary and the reality of women who chose the cloister.*

where are Arbours to shadow her from the heats of concupiscence; flowrie Beds to repose in with heavenlie Contemplations; Mounts to ascent to with the studie of Perfections: where are hearbs and Simples, soveraigne medicines of all spiritual maladies, where (I say) are the Flowers of al Vertues: The Lillie of spotles and immaculate Chastitie, the Rose of Shamsastnes and bashful Modestie, the Violet of Humilitie, the Gilloflower of Patience, the Marygold of Charitie, the Hiacinth of Hope, the Sun-flower of Contemplation, the Tulip of Beautie and gracefulnes." It was "a most delicious Paradise and Garden."

The trees also had qualities that reflected Mary's. "The Cedar of high Contemplation, the Cypress of odoriferous fame and sanctity of life, the Laurel of Constancie, the Palme of glorious Victorie, the Mulberrie of Patience" and many more. Hawkins gave Marian qualities to other aspects of the garden: the dove that inhabited it, the sea that surrounded it, the house that was within it and the "deaw" that fell upon it. The "moone" that illuminated it at night was "the Dowager and Queen-Regent of the Firmament," the ancient goddess now subdued as Mary.

An earlier book, *The Myroure of Oure Ladye*, written for the Sisters of Sion, who lived in England from 1415 until the dissolution of the monasteries under Henry VIII, also compared Mary with a host of plants, many of them mentioned in *The Song of Solomon*, including cedar, cypress, palm, rose, olive, plane tree, cinnamon, balm tree and myrrh tree. Again, certain qualities of each were equated with Mary's. For instance: "The palm tree ys smale byneth and large above and yt is evergrene. So oure most excellente lady was smale byneth from the love of all earthly thynges and large upwarde by love and desyre of hevenly thynges." Mary is here described as turning away from the earth, for which she had only "smale" love, and toward more ethereal pleasures.

Many healing plants were associated with Mary, including the pot marigold, emblem of the feast of the Annunciation.

In honour of this new earth goddess, some monasteries of the Middle Ages sprouted Mary gardens filled with Marian plants. In form, most of these gardens were symmetrical, designed according to the earliest Eastern notion of paradise, where two rivers (or pathways) bisected one another, dividing the garden into quarters, in the centre of which was a fountain or pool. Many plants in the Mary garden had the epithet "Our Lady's," an extension, in some cases, of the pre-Christian epithet "Lady's," that either stood for all women or honoured a woman long forgotten.

A 16th-century Mary garden at a Cistercian seminary in Scotland included Our Lady's smock (*Cardamine pratensis*), also called the cuckooflower or bitter cress, which is thought to resemble linen laid to bleach on the grass; Our Lady's garters, or ribbon grass (*Phalarus arundinace*); Our Lady's, St. Mary's, holy, milk or blessed thistle (*Silybum marianum*), whose white-spotted leaves had supposedly been coloured with drops of Mary's milk; Our Lady's fingers, woundwort or kidney vetch (*Anthyllis vulneraria*), which bore yellow or deep red flowers; Our Lady's bunch of keys, or St. Peter's keys, the primrose (*Primula veris* or *P. officinalis*), a medicinal simple whose fragrant yellow flowers bloom profusely in spring; Our Lady's thimble, the harebell (*Campanula rotundifolia*), a tall flower with bright blue thimblelike blooms; Our Lady's tears, or lily of the valley (*Convallaria majalis*), with its small, beautifully fragrant white blooms. Our Lady's, or blessed, thistle (*Cnicus benedictus*) was described by Culpeper as "good for all sorts of malignant and pestilential fevers and for agues of all kinds. It destroys worms in the stomach and is good against all sorts of poisons." Also in Mary gardens were Lady's bedstraw, Lady's cushion, Lady's delight, Lady's teardrops, Lady's hair, Lady's tresses and Lady's seal, as well as hollyhocks, marigolds, daisies for innocence and flowers of the family Cruciferae (now changed to Brassicaceae), whose blooms were thought to resemble the cross, hence the name. Lavender, too, was grown in the Mary garden because, according to legend, the plant became sweetly scented after Mary hung Jesus' washing upon it to dry, while rosemary, similarly, was said to have begun to produce blue flowers only after Mary threw her cloak over a bush.

Lady's mantle (*Alchemilla vulgaris*) was a prized Marian plant. Although the shape and texture of the leaves were compared with a cloak or mantle worn by Mary, more importantly, the plant extrudes drops of excess water from its leaf edges, a liquid alchemists imagined was water from heaven that could restore fading beauty and might even be a panacea for all ills, a truly heavenly benefit. Alchemilla can also set seed without fertilization, because the male parts wither before the female parts mature, a seemingly miraculous virgin birth, though not a rare occurrence in the plant world. The plant's genus name indicates its importance to alchemists, who believed the plant to be so magical it could be distilled into gold, an idea that must have meant years of frustration to the most determined of them.

The pot marigold (*Calendula officinalis*) was, like many plants, associated with Mary because it was a medicinal simple that was also beautiful. St. Mary's gold, later Marygold or marigold, was the floral emblem of Lady Day, March 25, the date of the feast of the Annunciation of the Virgin (and until 1752, the official beginning of the year), a day when statues of Mary were hung with garlands and coronets of marigolds, just as the statues of Greek and Roman gods had been decked with flowers in earlier times. The name *Calendula* was given to the marigold because of its habit of blooming at the beginning of the year or because it could bloom for several months.

The Assumption of the Virgin, a late-summer celebration of Mary's entrance into heaven, was also associated in some places with healing herbs. In this case, too, the celebration of Mary took its cues from ancient rites held on the same date. In 1896, Lina Eckenstein wrote in *Woman Under Monasticism* that at the time, "a number of days, frauentage, come in July and August and are now connected with the Virgin, on which herbs are collected and offered as sacred bunches either on the altar of Our Lady in church and chapel or on hilltops, which throughout Germany are the sites of ancient woman worship. This collecting and offering of herbs points to a stage even more primitive than that represented by offerings of grain at the harvest festival."

Convent gardens are worth examining within the context of the relationship between women and plants and of that between Mary and plants, not because cloistered women were unusual in having gardens – monasteries, too, had gardens, some of which are well documented – but because, in an era when women had little personal freedom, many nuns flourished in comparison with those who had not taken the veil.

Perhaps this was because the cloistered situation mirrored most closely the *hortus conclusus*: in becoming part of the metaphor of the walled garden, the nun was relatively free to transcend it, to reach over the wall, as it were. Less encumbered by educational disadvantage and childbearing, women in convents could pursue a religious vocation, follow a pious road to intellectual growth or simply seek refuge. Nuns could educate one another and the laity, exchange letters with eminent scholars and theologians, minister to the sick and live surrounded by gardens designed for contemplation as well as for the production of medicine and food. Henry Hawkins' description of Mary as the *hortus conclusus* may well apply to the best of the convents: "It is, in a word, a world of sweets that live in a fair Communitie togeather, where is no envie of another's hapines or contempt of others' povertie; while everie flower is contented with its own estate; nor would the Dazie wish to be a Rose nor yet the Rose contemnes the meanest flower."

Convent gardens, mostly tended by the nuns themselves, were important to their self-sufficiency. But they also became places where the nuns could express their collective delight in plants. When, in the sixth century, the Roman bishop, poet Venantius Fortuna-

Depicted here in a garden, Christine de Pizan was one of the most popular female intellectuals of the late 14th and early 15th centuries. She wrote several books in defence of women.

tus, was invited to dinner at the convent of St. Croix, whose gardens had already inspired him, he said that the table was covered with so many roses it was scarcely visible and that foliage and flowers were strewn about the room. Established in Poitiers, France, by Radegund, the fifth of the seven recognized wives of the king of the Franks, this convent had a garden on the surrounding slopes. To express his passion for Radegund, Fortunatus sent her violets and other Marian blooms, writing, "O mighty queen, to whom gold and purple are of little worth, with a few flowers your lover reveres you. And though colour has no substance, yet it is present through these growing things – purple in violets, and the crocus with its golden form. Rich in the love of God, you have shunned the world's rewards; despising that wealth, you will keep this. Take up the gift of varied flowers I send you, flowers to which your blessed life summons you yet more strongly."

The garden of the famous Dominican abbey of Poissy, about 20 miles west of Paris, was an attempt to create an earthly paradise: "*Ce semble estre un très doulz paradis,*" according to Christine de Pizan, one of the most popular female intellectuals and writers of the late 14th and early 15th centuries. De Pizan, who visited the convent after her daughter joined it, lyrically described her stay in *Le Livre du dit de Poissy.* At Poissy, she found a garden where

. . . were paired
Fruit-bearing trees, and wild beasts lair'd,
And in high enclosures, well ensnared;
Nothing proper to an Eden compared
Was not there found.
A fine and private place, wherein much
*   was bound,*
And of the things it held, I found
Were antler'd hinds that ran across
*   the ground*
Most fleetingly;
Hares and rabbits were there abundantly,
And two fish ponds, gushing naturally,
Well fashioned, albeit artlessly,
And of fish full;
Wild deer were there, and plentiful,
What else? In neither summer, winter, spring
*   nor fall*
Was everything not beautiful,
So God me save . . .

Christine de Pizan recorded her visit to the convent where her daughter was staying, a place that, she said, resembled an earthly paradise.

Delight in gardens was not restricted to the French. Visiting an English convent, Bishop Atwater recorded his 16th-century complaint that on feast days, the nuns "did not stay in church and occupy themselves in devotion between the hours of Our Lady and the High Mass but came out and wandered about the garden and cloisters." At the Cistercian priory of Nuncotham, England, some of the sisters had private rooms and gardens, and occasionally in the evening, according to Atwater, one or other would be absent from the last service of the day "because she was so busy looking after her flowers."

The convent garden might help both actively and passively in the curing of the sick. Actively, it supplied simples, the curative herbs, and so was a more institutional version of the herb gardens described in previous chapters. Passively, the cloistered garden provided solace to the sick.

Euphemia, abbess of Wherwell Benedictine nunnery in England between 1226 and 1257, "built there a place set apart for the refreshment of the soul, namely a chapel of the Blessed Virgin, which was erected outside the cloister behind the infirmary. With the chapel, she enclosed a large space which was adorned on the north side with pleasant vines and trees. . . . She surrounded the court with a wall and the necessary buildings, and round it she made gardens and vineyards and shrubberies in places that were formerly useless and barren and which now became both serviceable and pleasant."

The garden of Grace Dieu priory of Loughborough, England, was designed to resemble Gethsemane. The history of this small priory of White Nuns, established in the 13th century not many years after the Magna Carta was signed, is similar to that of many convents. Its founder was a countrywoman, Roesia de Verdun. On the death of her father, Roesia, sole heir to her father's estate and probably a widow, paid the king a fee for "her relief and livery of the lands of her inheritance, as also that she might not be compelled to marry" and, with her inheritance, established a convent, a not uncommon action for a relatively wealthy older woman. The convent was granted additional parcels of property by various neighbouring landowners such as John Comyn, Count of Boghan, who, in the late 13th century, did "give and assign one hundred acres of waste land in Whitewyke and Shepshed to the Prioress of Grace Dieu . . . to enclose with a ditch and a wall and to make a park there." Another landowner leased to Grace Dieu all his land for 80 years—for the price of one red rose a year.

The nuns kept a "brew-house"—beer was a universal beverage that often included herbs such as tansy and sweet gale instead of hops—and a "yele-house," ale house. Beer and ale must have contributed to the happiness of the nuns. The cellarer of Grace Dieu, Margaret Bellers, was once accused of going out "to work in autumn alone with Sir Henry, he reaping the harvest and she binding the sheeves, and at evening she comes riding with him on the same horse."

A report on the convent in 1534 and 1535 by two employees of Henry VIII, who began the dissolution of the monasteries the following year, stated that the nuns venerated part of the tunic of St. Francis, which was supposed to help women in childbirth, perhaps, intimated the report, because the nuns themselves were giving birth. (It was more likely because the nuns were acting as midwives.) Also, Henry's men noted, "This house standeth low in a valley upon a little brook, in a solitary place, compassed round with an high and strong stone wall within which the nuns had made a garden, in resemblance of that upon Mount Olivet Gethsame . . . ."

By 1804, long after Henry VIII had had his way and the convent had been closed and sold, an observer wrote that "the whole of Gracedieu was a park and is still so denominated. The outer wall of the garden still remains in many parts of it perfect. It originally included a space of about two acres, and a piece of ground within the inclosure is to this day called Paradise."

While the convents were not necessarily gardens of delight that could measure up to Henry Hawkins' description of the *hortus conclusus*, they did allow women to grow and blossom intellectually and spiritually. It is no wonder that the outstanding 19th-century English garden designer, Gertrude Jekyll, said of her home, "One of the wishes I expressed to the architect was that I should like a little feeling of a convent." An ongoing challenge to women lies in discovering how to find the best of the convent in lives beyond the walls of the closed garden.

VI

"The Only Thing Like Civilized Life"

*Transplanted women and their
New World gardens*

When I started to make a herb garden in
Ontario, I tackled a little plot that someone had
evidently gardened long before—barely
visible traces of a wheel of stones outlined
raised beds. But since those beds
had been made, the soil level had risen almost a
foot, thanks to the accumulation of
needles and leaves from overhanging pines
and soft maples, and the entire area
had become a tangle of weeds or, rather, plants
I considered to be weeds: nettles
and motherwort. Not until I began to unearth
the beds did it occur to me that I was
rooting out one generation's medicinal herbs in
order to plant the culinary herbs of
another. The nettles and motherwort had
probably not been deliberately planted in this
garden—they are such successful plants
that they grow almost everywhere the soil
is arable—but they were certainly the
offspring, however many generations removed,
of plants used medicinally by women

who had come here from distant lands. Motherwort (*Leonurus cardiaca*) and nettles (*Urtica dioica*) are legacies of pioneer women. The plants are not native to North America but are two species among hundreds brought to a new continent because they were too valuable to leave behind. The story of the pioneer gardeners is an interesting facet of the relationship between women and plants, for it illustrates the way in which plants, always women's helpmates, eased the transition to a new life on a different continent. In the gardens of the settlers, plants were not only food and medicine but also beauty, entertainment, education and solace.

This was particularly true for women, who tended the home gardens in the New World as they had done in the old. In the early 19th century, Anne Grant wrote of New York's Hudson River Valley: "Not only the training of children but of plants such as needed peculiar care or skill to rear them was the female province. . . . A woman in very easy circumstances and abundantly gentle in form and manners would sow and plant and rake incessantly." Such women had brought to the New World both aesthetic and practical ideas about how a household should be run, along with mortars, pestles, cooking pots and seeds bred an ocean away. For the most part, the immigrants were prepared to carry on as they had formerly, drying, brewing and distilling familiar plants to make familiar foods, ornaments, cosmetics and medicines.

Plants native to the new lands satisfied different needs. Women in remote places were particularly likely to see wild plants as "dear friends, soothing and cheering by their unconscious influence hours of loneliness and hours of sorrow and suffering," as Catharine Parr Traill wrote from the Canadian backwoods in the 19th century. Generous, uncultivated and sometimes anonymous, wildflowers offered, especially in places where there were few books and little social life, the intellectual excitement of botanical exploration as well as practical and medicinal benefits of their own.

The wildlings, like imported flowers, also contributed beauty, no small virtue in a life in which one might work like a pack animal from dawn till dusk. Mary Jane Megquier, who settled in San Francisco in the mid-19th century, declared, "If I had not the constitution of six horses, I should [have] been dead long ago." A bouquet of unknown wildflowers she had gathered was "the only thing like civilized life in the room."

Catharine Parr Traill advised settlers in Upper Canada: "Do not allow the lusty teams and the broad acres, the grass, the grain and the trees to occupy all your time, but give a thought and an eye occasionally to the beautiful. . . . Here are the mixed balsams and carnations, the mignonette, mourning bride and columbine; there, love-lies-bleeding and, in the corner, love-in-a-mist, the candytuft and Canterbury bell." In 1754, Esther Edwards Burr wrote from Newark, New Jersey: "A few days ago, I had six sorts of flours in the garden and court-yard [so] that it looked like summer. And in two days more, I should have pinks blown the second time." And Anne Grant wrote of the women in the Hudson River Valley: "These fair gardeners too were great florists. Their emulation and solicitude in this pleasing employment did indeed produce 'flowers worthy of Paradise.' "

Cotton Mather had urged American women to grow medicinal plants in their gardens and to keep their closets stocked with "several harmless and useful (and especially external) remedies for the help of their poor neighbors." Beds of flowers, salad plants and herbs were planted near the house, and seeds of the most successful species escaped to become familiar weeds of today—motherwort, nettles, mullein (*Verbascum thapsus*) and horsetail (*Equisetum arvense*), all imported as medicinal herbs. Dandelions (*Taraxacum*

Catharine Parr Traill urged pioneer women to devote time to flowers.

～

officinale) were valued from flower to root, not at all the objects of disdain they are today. Their high-vitamin leaves became spring salad greens, beers and tonics, their roots ersatz coffee, their petals golden wine. The plant is also an effective diuretic and liver medicine—*officinalis* means therapeutic, "of the apothecaries." Purslane (*Portulaca oleracea*), lamb's-quarters (*Chenopodium album*) and chicory (*Cichorium intybus*) were, like dandelions, very nutritious salad greens that, if now overlooked in the kitchen, have nevertheless maintained their visibility in gardens and fields.

Some of the introduced plants were less able to adapt to their new climate. Mary Thomas, a reluctant Australian pioneer, wrote in 1836 that she had planted in her garden "the fruits and vegetables of the known world," but "the vegetables have not the sweetness of those in England and generally run to seed before they have attained half their size. This may, perhaps, be remedied by proper management, the plants being, like ourselves, not yet acclimatized." Elizabeth Macarthur, an earlier Australian immigrant, wrote, "Our garden produces nothing, all is burnt up; indeed the soil must be allowed to be most wretched and totally unfit for growing European productions."

But pioneer women persisted in cultivating familiar plants, in part because they were remedies against that most disheartening of ills of the New World, homesickness. Since return trips home across vast oceans were largely out of the question and even letters took months to change hands, the "strangers in a strange land" valued any connection with the happier aspects of the world they had known. Martha Logan of Charles Town, South Carolina, expressed in 1761 her desire for tulips, ranunculas, anemones, narcissus and hyacinths, all remembered from England. Even Catharine Parr Traill, usually optimistic and resourceful, wrote in *The Canadian Settler's Guide*: "Woman, whose nature is to love home and to cling to all home ties and associations, cannot be torn from that spot that is the little centre of joy and peace and comfort to her, without many painful regrets. . . . As the seasons return, she thinks of the flowers that she loved in childhood, the pale primrose, the cowslip and the bluebell, with the humble daisy and heathflowers— and what would she not give for one, just one, of those old familiar flowers!"

But simply getting the old familiar plants and seeds to their new homes presented settlers with many logistical difficulties. Seeds— and, even more so, cuttings or rooted plants —are, after all, living things with a limited shelf life, especially when storage conditions are less than ideal. Dampness and warmth make seeds sprout and rot; drought and too much heat or cold kill cuttings and entire

～

plants. Such pioneer precautions as keeping seeds in metal canisters and inserting shrub roots in potatoes could be expected to work for only a certain amount of time. And until this century, it was at best a month's sea voyage to the New World from Europe, while people who travelled farther inland might not settle down for months longer.

Once they arrived at their destination, the newcomers often had to wait at least a season before they could begin gardening. In the roughest and most distant places, the first priorities were clearing land and building shelter. And when it was time to establish a garden, they could not simply send home for seeds, at least not with much hope of receiving them quickly and in good condition. Shipping seeds from the old country was just as time-consuming as the settlers' journeys.

In October 1851, on Canada's West Coast, James Douglas ordered "garden seeds" from England and asked that they be sent "by the way of York Factory . . . as the sea voyage to this country by Cape Horn generally proves destructive to seeds." If the seeds were sent overland immediately upon receipt of his letter, they would "reach this place in April 1853, early enough for sowing"—a year and a half after Douglas had placed his order.

Even at the beginning of the 20th century, Edith Cuthell, who gardened in India, wrote, "Most of the seeds sent out to me weeks ago in tins arrived mildewy and spoilt." Were such seeds lost or found to be not viable upon arrival, the pioneer's only hope was to buy replacements in local towns or, better, to borrow or buy them from neighbours who had been more fortunate.

"If you have more than a sufficiency for yourself, do not begrudge a friend a share of your superfluous garden seeds," was Catharine Parr Traill's advice in 1855.

Seeds, then, were high-priority items, gathered, saved and carried whenever and wherever possible. Traill advised "female emigrants" to bring to Canada "seeds of Balm, Thyme and Sweet Basil, for these are rarely met with here—Sage, Savoury, Mint and Peppermint are easily got. Sweet marjoram is not commonly met with. I would also bring out some nice flower-seeds, and also vegetable seeds of good kinds, especially fine sorts of cabbage."

M.L. Borowsky writes of Ukrainian immigrants to Canada: "They would always take with them as a memento a lump of their native soil. . . . The farmers took with them various useful seeds and domestic implements, while their wives and daughters, immigrating at the same time or a while later, brought along the seeds and the roots of favourite flowers and aromatic herbs. These plants often served medicinal purposes . . . ." Among the seeds the Ukrainian women brought were those of hollyhocks, wormwood, mint, fennel-flower and marijuana. In the carefree manner with which seeds disregard boundaries and legislation, the offspring of that medicinal marijuana still sprout in gardens and manure piles abandoned by the pioneers.

"We brought an assortment of seed from Cincinnati with us over the mountains," wrote missionary Narcissa Prentiss Whitman in Vancouver, Washington, in 1836. "Husband has sent for the seeds of the large locust, Chestnut & Walnut trees. I should like to have the butternut included for experiment. . . . When Brother Weld comes, please remember to fill his pockets with peaches, plums and pear seeds, some of the best kind, and some good apple seed; what they have here is not of the best kind nor a great variety. Another very important article for us housewives, some broom-corn seed." (Broom corn is a maize relative that grows, instead of ears, a tuft of strawlike stems which can be tied together to produce a very serviceable broom.) Later, Whitman wrote, "The grapes are just ripe & I am feasting on them finely. . . . I save all the seeds of those I eat for planting and of apples also. This is a rule of Vancouver."

A combination of ingenuity, native plants and painstakingly imported plants made for the most successful gardens. Missionaries like Whitman were often the first to settle permanently in new areas and were consequently often the first to plant the alien corn. "New" is, of course, relative: the Atlantic coast of North America had a thoroughly European culture by the end of the 18th century, while settlement farther north and west came as much as a century later. In 1893, after a visit to the Holy Angels convent in Lake Athabasca, Alberta, a mother superior wrote, "There is no ground that can be tilled. The patch on which our Sisters try to grow potatoes and barley was a morass . . . ." Nevertheless, the dedication of the sisters to their task of growing non-native plants paid off. By 1902, a convent chronicle recorded: "Our garden has grown 75 heads of cabbage (rather small), a sack of beets, 30 ears of wheat, 32 tomatoes, 5 bunches of celery, some cucumbers, a melon, half a bushel of onions, some turnips, lettuce and radishes, as well as some flowers for the decoration of the altar. . . . Last year, Sister Brunelle said she had not tasted a cucumber before for 34 years, Sister Superior for 18, Sister St. Peter for 17 and so for the rest."

That the sisters were not moved to glean their vitamins as the natives had for thousands of years by dining on various barks, herbs, grasses, mosses and lichens is understandable, if impractical. (Modern-day North Americans, too, include remarkably few indigenous plants in their diets.) This insistence upon growing what was well known had its costs. As the "European productions" had been "burnt up" in Elizabeth Macarthur's Australian garden, so locusts and frosts tried the spirits of even the Holy Angels nuns, and in one incident, Sister Brunelle, "after lavish-

ing on them what may be called a mother's care, had the consolation of bringing home one carrot."

But while such imported, well-loved species were apt to be fickle, the indigenous plants were not, and they sustained and cured immigrants who could take advantage of native knowledge. Lichen offered by an Indian woman saved the starving crew of Alexander Henry in the 18th century. Henry wrote, "The woman was well acquainted with the mode of preparing the lichen for the stomach, which is done by boiling it down into a mucilage as thick as the white of an egg. In a short time, we obtained a hearty meal; for though our food was of a bitter and disagreeable taste, we felt too much joy in finding it and too much relief in eating it not to partake of it with appetite and pleasure."

Native herbal medicines also saved lives. In 1624, Nicolaes van Wassenaer wrote of the Indians: "There is not an ailment they have not a remedy for . . ." which was true only until the Europeans arrived, bringing their diseases with them. As Father Louis Hennepin noted in 1698, the natives had "none for smallpox." But he also wrote, "They are versed in roots and herbs, with which they cure all sorts of illness." In the early 18th century, James Isham wrote to England that Indian tea (or Labrador tea, an infusion of *Ledum palustre*) "intirely cur'd me, being Very much Efflicted with a Nervous disorder." In dozens of recorded cases, native remedies cured settlers of ailments ranging from stomach aches to scurvy.

In fact, the Europeans, with their plagues and pockmarks and bad teeth, had arrived in the new lands to discover races of people who, without the questionable benefits of civilized medicine and sophisticated cuisine (including refined sugar and alcohol) and without many of the diseases of the Old World to contend with, presented a picture of enviable good health. The Dutch recorded in New Amsterdam in 1624 that "it is somewhat strange that among these most barbarous people, there are few or none cross-eyed, blind, crippled, lame, hunchbacked or limping men; all are well-fashioned people, strong and sound of body, well fed, without blemish."

This was due, in part, to the native pharmacopoeia, some of which had been introduced to Europe by explorers as far back as the 15th century. Those plants were familiar to the immigrants, while others quickly gained popularity. Catharine Parr Traill wrote that "settlers are often well skilled in the use of the native plants – they may possibly have learned the value of them from the Indians or from long experience taught by necessity . . . ." In *Women and Men on the Overland Trail*, John Mack Faragher writes that "women seemed to know substantially more than men the value of wild plants and Indian concoctions." Goldenseal (*Hydrastis canadensis*) and North American ginseng (*Panax quinquefolium*), which was remarkably similar to the Oriental species, were almost exterminated by early drug collectors.

Sassafras was another native remedy loved by the immigrants, thanks, in part, to the pleasant flavour and aroma of the tea made from the bark of the tree *Sassafras albidum*. Reputed to cure syphilis, rheumatism and dropsy, sassafras was the object of a flurry of excitement after its introduction to Spain in the 16th century, when there were fortunes to be made in supposed cures for syphilis. But syphilis remained rampant, and by the time Pehr Kalm wrote about North America in 1748, he reported of sassafras merely that "the people here gather its flowers and use them instead of tea" and that "the bark of this tree is used by the women here in dyeing worsted a fine lasting orange color, which does not fade in the sun." The natives, said Kalm, used the plant for eye diseases.

Among the pioneers, sassafras was more likely to be drunk in a spring tonic, a herbal restorative with which women "purified the blood" of their families as soon as they could obtain the ingredients from the cold spring soil. The benefits of such tonics probably came chiefly from vitamins that had been in short supply all winter. Along with sassafras, the tonic might include wintergreen (*Gaultheria procumbens*), an American native that contains vitamins and painkilling salicylates; tips of white pine (*Pinus strobus*), a native expectorant; and pennyroyal (the introduced *Mentha pulegium*). Also useful in spring tonics was a member of the lily family, sarsaparilla (*Smilax* spp), another plant first touted as a syphilis cure. Much later, sarsaparilla had a better-deserved reputation as a flavouring for soft drinks. According to one spring-tonic recipe, it was mixed with the bark of wild cherry and black birch, the roots of sassafras, false sarsaparilla (*Smilacina racemosa*) and sweet flag, as well as burdock, dandelion leaves, boneset, motherwort and the blossoms of white daisies. The resulting brew would have contained bracing quantities of vitamins A and C, both deficient in the winter diet of the pioneers.

For "dysentery in children," Catharine Parr Traill recommended the related spikenard (*Aralia racemosa*), also known as Indian root or spicebush. "I lost two infants who were under the care of the most careful medical men but saved another by the use of a wild herb that was given me by a Yankee settler's wife. A plant called spikenard (or spignet, as she called it) that grows in the forest with a long spindle root, scraped, and a small quantity boiled in milk thickens it as if flour had been put in it; it has a sweet, astringent taste, slightly bitter."

For a family as isolated as Traill's – herself, a husband and nine children in a place where "the only habitations beyond our log cabin were one shanty and the log house of a dear brother" – some knowledge of medicinal plants was a necessity. In fact, Traill became an eminent recorder of Canadian natural life. Born in England in 1802 – her life would span almost the entire century, until 1899 – she had declared "a passion for flowers" even before she emigrated with her husband in 1832. The wildlife that surrounded her in Canada West "became a great resource, and every flower and shrub and forest tree awakened an interest in my mind so that I began to thirst for more intimate knowledge of them." To satisfy her thirst, she borrowed Frederick Pursh's *A Systematic Arrangement and Description of the Plants of North America*, which, "unfortunately for me, was chiefly written in Latin." Traill managed to learn enough Latin for her needs and, in the meantime, depended upon "the eye and the ear. . . . My next teachers were old settlers' wives and choppers and Indians." While recording her observations in a series of books, she noted that some plants had no name at all that she could discover, and so "I consider myself free to become their floral grandmother and give them names of my own choosing," an ephemeral luxury, to be sure, but one hardly available at all back home in England.

Her 1868 *Canadian Wild Flowers* was followed in 1885 by *Studies of Plant Life in Canada*, the first popular work on Canadian botany. Both were illustrated with colour lithographs by her niece Agnes FitzGibbon. The books were meticulous records of Traill's own observations. Of squirrel corn (*Dicentra canadensis*), for instance, she wrote, "In studying the habits of this and the next species of the genus *Dicentra*, I have noticed some peculiarities of growth in these interesting plants which appear to have escaped the attention of the more learned botanical writers. One thing may here be mentioned, which is the total and very rapid disappearance of the whole plant directly the flower has perfected and ripened the seed, which is about a month after the plant has bloomed."

Knowledge about plants of their adopted lands came to settlers from the natives.

In 1855, in *The Female Emigrant's Guide* (reprinted as *The Canadian Settler's Guide*), Traill told women what to expect and how to survive on North American land: how to decorate a house, cure a few ailments, cook, make yeast, wine and other necessities; and how to garden, especially how to raise vegetables. "With a little attention and labour, the vegetable garden may be carried to great perfection by the women and children with a little assistance from the men at the outset in digging the ground and securing the fences or any work that may require strength to effect." (This gender-based division of labour is much like that of the tribal farmers described in chapter two.)

Women could even attend to fruit trees, a notion Traill admitted was unusual – "My female readers will say . . . 'We women have nothing to do with nurseries, except in the

The garden could be planted only after the land was cleared and the shelter built.

house.' " But if they did not, the trees might be neglected, because the men were busy with other chores: "The tending of a nursery of young trees from the first sowing of the seeds in the ground is rather a pleasure than a labour and one which I have taken a delight in from my earliest years." (In fact, New World women, by sheer necessity, had long been stretching the boundaries that kept them out of Old World orchards and other male preserves. Almost three centuries earlier, in Jamestown, Virginia, Mistress Pearce, the first non-native American woman known to have kept a garden, had been able to grow "neere one hundred bushels of excellent figges . . . .")

Catharine Parr Traill's application of the discipline of botany to the wilds of North America was not unique. "I consider this country opens wide a fruitful field to the inquiries of the botanist," wrote Traill after she and her husband settled in the virgin forests of what is now Ontario. Botany was "the fertile source of mental enjoyment, especially to those who, living in the bush, must necessarily be shut out from the pleasures of the large circle of friends and the varieties that a town or village might offer."

Botany as a woman's science will be further discussed in a later chapter, but it is worth noting here that it could be both entertaining and intellectually stimulating for lonely pioneer women. Fanny and Adelia Penniman, for instance, created a herbarium of the plants they found growing around their northern-Vermont home in the early 19th century. But the first American woman to gain recognition in any field of science — appropriately enough, botany — was Jane Colden. She was the daughter of Cadwallader Colden, himself an eminent botanist, a physician, a historian and an anthropologist and the lieutenant-governor of New York from 1761 until his death in 1776.

Jane, the fifth of 10 children, was born in 1724. When she was 4, the family travelled north from New York City to a place they dubbed Coldenham, near Newburgh, on

3,000 acres of wild Catskill country that Colden described as "the habitation only of wolves and bears and other wild animals." While Jane was growing up, tutored in botany and natural history by her father, visitors included such notable botanists as John and William Bartram of Philadelphia, Dr. Alexander Garden of Charleston, South Carolina, and Pehr Kalm of Sweden, all of whom trekked into the wilderness to visit the amazing Coldens.

Jane's accomplishments in this outpost, if outstanding, nevertheless had a familiar pioneer ring to them: she was described by observers as being an excellent florist and physician and producer of the best cheese in America. She was also beloved by her father, who once wrote to a friend, "Our second daughter, Jane, is too good to part with; neither can she bear the thought of leaving us, so that I am in hopes we shall have her company and affection as long as we live." In 1759, however, Jane married a doctor, and her botanical writings apparently ceased. She died in 1766, as did her only child.

Jane had taken her knowledge of botany into the wild countryside around Coldenham, making notes about the plant life and, as Catharine Parr Traill would later do, asking the inhabitants for local names and medicinal uses. "The Pedicularis is called by the country people Betony: they make Thee of the Leaves, and use it for the Fever and Ague." Butterfly milkweed (*Asclepias tuberosa*) she described as "an excellent cure for the Colick. This was Learn'd from a Canadian Indian, and it is called in New England Canada Root. The Excellency of this Root for the Colick is confirm'd by Dr. Pater of New England, and Dr. Brooks of Maryland likewise confirmed this." And there was "Aralia Shrub, *Aralia spinosa*, Called here Prickly Ash. The Indians make a Decoction of the Bark of this Shrub & use it for long continued Coughs, & likewise for the Dropsy."

Her father was delighted and wrote to one of his botanical correspondents, J.F. Gronovius, in 1755: "I have a daughter who has an inclination to reading and a curiosity for natural philosophy or natural history and a sufficient capacity for obtaining a competent knowledge. . . . She has already a pretty large volume in writing of the descriptions of plants. She was shown a method of taking an impression of the leaves on paper with printer's ink, by a simple kind of rolling press, which is of use in distinguishing the species. No description in words alone can give so clear an idea as when assisted with a picture. She has the impression of three hundred plants in the manner you'll see by the samples." The illustrated notebook to which her father referred now rests in the British Museum and was recently reprinted by the Garden Club of Orange and Duchess counties in New York.

Jane and Dr. Garden independently discovered in New York State a North American species of St.-John's-wort (*Hypericum virginicum*), and she wanted the species name to be *gardenia* in his honour. As it turned out, Garden's name had already been used for cape jasmine (*Gardenia jasminoides*), so the gift was not given, but Jane did have the satisfaction of having her dissertation on hypericum published in Scotland.

A few other pioneer women penetrated the inner circle of 18th-century corresponding botanists, albeit briefly. One was "Mrs. Lamboll of Charles Town," South Carolina, who had "a garden which was richly stored with flowers and other curiosities of nature in addition to all the common vegetables for family use" and who sent "a little parcel of very curious fresh Florida seeds" to John Bartram in Pennsylvania. Martha Daniell Logan, also of Charles Town, received an income from selling "seeds, flower roots and fruit stones" from her garden, according to an advertisement in 1753. At 40, Logan managed a plantation of native trees, roses, a lily pond and experimental gardens. Describing her, Bartram wrote a colleague of "the favor of a elderly widow Lady who spares no pains or cost to oblige me; her garden is her delight and she has a fine one: I was with her about 4 minutes in her company, yet we contracted such a mutual correspondence that one silk bag of seed hath repast several times."

As an elderly woman, Logan published what was possibly the first horticultural treatise in the United States, a "Gardener's Kalender" (signed simply "A Lady," in the modest fashion of the times), which appeared in the 1764 *South Carolina and Georgia Almanack*. Although Logan was an expert flower gardener, the Kalender describes only vegetables, herbs and fruits. For November, for instance, the full entry reads: "Earth up Celery and tie up Endive for blanching. Continue to sow Seeds, as Parsley, Spinage, Radish and Lettice of all kinds. The latter end of this Month, begin to prune Fruit-Trees, especially Vines, which may now be done safely."

Logan also grew native plants, such as "Our Wilde Lilly, which is Called the golden," that she sent to Bartram. The adoption of native plants in the gardens of immigrant women signified, as much as anything else, their recognition that the new land was home. Settlers like Mary Jane Megquier, with her wild bouquet that was "the only thing like civilized life in the room," easily appreciated the flowers so freely given from surrounding fields and woods. Lady Jean Skipwith, an Englishwoman who moved to Virginia in the late 18th century, listed, along with an impressive collection of domesticated plants in her garden, several natives such as dog's-tooth violets, bloodroot, wild orchids, Solomon's-seal, columbines and blue-eyed grass (*Sisyrinchium*), "the blue flower with grasslooking stalks and leaves, plenty in the orchard."

Catharine Parr Traill encircled her Canadian garden with a hedge of honeysuckle, spirea, wild roses, raspberries, gooseberries and red and black currants, "with here and there a standard hawthorne." Later, she wrote, "The Wild Cucumber, Orange Gourd, Wild Clematis and a number of other shrubby climbing-plants will thrive and cover the rocky pile with luxuriant foliage. Thus by the exertion of a little ingenuity, the garden of the settler may be rendered not only highly useful but very ornamental."

As John Ruskin wrote of such women who arrived to find wilderness and left gardens as their legacies, "The path of a good woman is indeed strewn with flowers, but they rise behind her steps, not before them."

As late as 1913, Elinore Pruitt Stewart still cited "loves growing things" as a necessity for any pioneer woman; in this case, in Wyoming, part of the western frontier once described as "great country for men and horses, but hell on women and cattle."

Whenever and wherever it existed, the frontier was likely to be difficult for women. Plants provided comfort, food, medicine and beauty, but the pioneer life was nevertheless a difficult one. In the 1850s, a farm woman in the American West could expect to raise five or six children, at least one of whom would die before its fifth birthday. Furthermore, a wife was "legally little better than a slave," writes Stevenson Whitcomb Fletcher of early life in Pennsylvania: "Pioneer farm women paid a fearful price for early marriage and constant childbearing. Frontier graveyards were populated with worn-out mothers who were quickly succeeded by youthful stepmothers. Many pioneer farmers were laid to rest beside two or three wives." And over those graves, a spread of native grasses, with perhaps a few of those omnipresent herbal weeds—the nettles and motherwort and dandelions that now spring up in my own garden—marked the passing of the women who were themselves exotic flowers in a new land.

VII

"Your Sweetest Empire
Is to Please"

*Floral femininity in the 18th
and 19th centuries*

The image of woman as flower — as shrinking
violet or wild Irish rose or any of a
gamut of other petalled things — became
brightest in the 18th and 19th centuries, when
almost everything done by the *Homo sapiens*
cultivar known as "the lady" had some
connection with flowers. Roots, herbs and
medicines were relegated to the poor and the
past. Ladies were beyond such mundane
concerns. Counselled by Sarah Josepha Hale,
the editor of an early magazine for
women, to "cultivate those virtues which
can only be represented in the finest flowers,"
they were pretty, passive and perfumed. They
dressed in flowers, talked about flowers
and fashioned flowers from all kinds of
materials. They were even named for flowers:
Daphnes, Hazels, Camellias, Irises, Heathers,
Myrtles, Rosemarys and Violets occupied
Victorian cradles. Older names such as Rose
and Flora experienced revivals, while the
ancient and venerable Margaret became Daisy.

Victorian ladies practised many floral arts, such as the creation of phantom leaves.

～

Emily James Putnam, in *The Lady* (1970), compares ladies with black tulips and blue roses, the elusive goals of plant hybridizers. (A black tulip was, in fact, created in the Netherlands in 1986 and a blue rose soon after in the United States, but ladies were by then a far rarer breed.) Like the black tulip and the blue rose, the lady, argues Putnam, was an artificial creation, something neither natural nor useful except as a decoration and a cultural achievement.

But unlike blue roses, an epithet that, incidentally, later described Laura, the fragile heroine of Tennessee Williams' *The Glass Menagerie*, ladies came about quite naturally as products of a society rich enough to allow a select group to live pampered lives as far as possible from realities that were often very harsh. Childbirth was dangerous for both mother and child; child mortality rates were high; diseases such as tuberculosis, typhoid and cholera were mysterious and deadly; and air and water pollution in some areas were appalling, thanks to home coal fires, inadequate sewage and the furnaces and gutters of the Industrial Revolution. The poor took comfort in their gin and their babies, while ladies sheltered themselves within the home and the flower garden.

The extent to which the upper classes took seriously the woman/flower metaphor now seems almost incredible. The following poem by Mrs. Barbauld, an 18th-century Englishwoman, sets it out in rhyme. Here, women are flowers, men the trees that shelter them:

Flowers, the sole luxury which Nature knew,
In Eden's pure and guiltless garden grew.
To loftier forms and rougher tasks assign'd;
The sheltering oak resists the stormy wind,
The tougher yew repels invading foes,
And the tall pine for future navies grows;
But this soft family, to cares unknown,
Were born for pleasure and delight alone.
Gay without toil, and lovely without art,
They spring to cheer the sense and glad
  the heart.
Nor blush, my fair, to own you copy these;
Your best, your sweetest empire is—to please.

Women "born for pleasure and delight alone"? In a time when the socially advantaged had servants to do most of the dirty work, even to raise the children, well-born women needed do little else than amuse themselves and others. The day's routine might consist of tending to the servants and—in small doses—the children, visiting friends, playing cards and practising certain arts and crafts that were fashionable: a little painting, a little music and dancing and almost certainly something to do with flowers. Never had floral crafts been so popular, nor had so many people had enough time to pursue activities of such questionable value.

Some of these activities and their attendant handbooks are worth a look. There was, for instance, the creation of artificial flowers, manufactured, according to a 19th-century author who signed herself simply "A Lady," of "ribbon, velvet, feathers, wax, paper, the pith of plants, dyed grasses, satin, mother-o'-pearl, wings of beetles and other insects, glass, hair, muslin, beads, porcelain, shells and thin sheets of whalebone & c." The wax variety was described in *The Wax Bouquet*, also by "A Lady" of London. (Modesty and social pressure encouraged this habit of authorial anonymity. One such "Lady" wrote in her 1721 book, "I presume not so far upon the Merits of what I have written, as to make my Name publick with it . . . the Consideration of the Tenderness of Reputation in our Sex [which as our delicatest Fruits and finest Flowers are most obnoxious to the Injuries of Weather, is submitted to every infectious Blast of malicious Breath] made me very cautious, how I expos'd mine to such poisonous Vapours.") *The Wax Bouquet* was one among hundreds of how-to books that helped fill the long hours of upper-class women and simultaneously opened the door of authorship to many of them. These books, true pocketbooks, are usually tiny — no more than three by five inches — painstakingly illustrated volumes no doubt thought suitable for a woman's small hand and dainty intellect.

A diminutive 1855 example, subtitled *The Art of Raising All Flowers at All Seasons: A Manual of Clear Instructions for Ladies Making their Own Wax Flowers*, described how to make petals, sepals and leaves from thin sheets of coloured wax, which, said the author, one could purchase for eight pence a dozen at the Whitaker Wax Counter in Soho. The sheets were cut with warmed scissors according to the shapes of actual flower parts or purchased paper patterns for lilies, violets, crocuses, camellias and other popular blooms: "Always, when practical, copy from a natural flower, as the aim of the art is to copy, not invent." A "curling pin" gave petals lifelike curves, and stems of wire were added. An advertisement in the back of a book published 20 years later in Boston declared that "a lady in this city has, during the past year, realized $1,600 from the sale of wax flowers. This fascinating art is becoming nearly as popular here as in Europe, where ladies of all classes practise it in common with painting, drawing, embroidery & c." Some of these ladies did not reach the standards of the Boston craftswoman, however. A contemporary female observer wrote that "nothing is meaner than some of the productions called wax flowers."

"A Lady" who wrote another tiny volume, *The Floral Knitting Book*, hoped that "with a few skeins of wool and a little wire," one could "form accurate representations of natural flowers, which will be found an elegant and interesting amusement." The resulting fuzzy lilies, fuchsias, geraniums, narcissus and such could be made somewhat realistic, promised the author, if the reader took living flowers to the wool shop to find good colour matches. Unlike wax flowers, these decorations had their practical side. "As these flowers will bear washing when soiled, they not only form pretty ornaments for the room in vases but, from their durability, might be used for trimming ball dresses; the smaller kinds also, if knitted in silk, look well in bonnets or caps." Meanwhile, Miss Grounds' *Crochet Chenille Flowers from Nature* advised readers, who paid a shilling for her pamphlet, that "these flowers possess all the richness and beauty of velvet, with the advantage of shades, and are admirably adapted for trimming Ball Dresses, Wreaths for the Hair, & c. & c."

Stranger than the craft of artificial-flower making was the creation of skeletonized, or phantom, plants, a curious pursuit that originated in the Orient and was popularized in Britain "to embellish the home of taste," according to Edward Parrish, author of a manual on the subject, *The Phantom Bouquet*, for which his wife provided him with expert information.

To create skeletonized plants, real leaves, flowers, seedpods and such were treated to a process that removed all of the softer tissues, revealing "the delicate veinings of these plant-structures deprived of their grosser particles and of such brilliant whiteness as to suggest the idea of perfectly bleached artificial lace-work or exquisite carvings in ivory." Leaves, especially those of deciduous trees, were covered with boiling water and kept submerged with weights for four or five weeks. Next, the leaves were removed and swept lightly on both sides with a soft toothbrush or shaving brush until they were clean. After an optional further softening, they were soaked in a solution of one to four ounces of calcium chloride to a pint of water and removed in a few hours, or as soon as they were white. The now-bleached remains of the leaves and seed-pods were dried and arranged on a background, which, "to our taste, may best be of green velvet, recalling the image of verdure in contrast with frost," wrote Parrish. Covered with a glass bell or convex glazing in an oval frame, the result was called a Phantom Case—"Hundreds of pier-tables and étagères in city and country are garnished with its airy forms, and its photographic miniature, under the well-chosen motto, 'Beautiful in Death,' is displayed in almost every stereoscope . . . ."

Producing phantom leaves was, according to the anonymous female American author of a book by that name, an art which "seems designed for female hands exclusively. If some of its attendant operations are unpleasant

The well-decorated home included various horticultural items, such as an ivy screen for the fireplace, "leaf prints from nature" and elaborate table centrepieces.

[she had already explained that after weeks of soaking, the decaying leaves might seem to the practitioner 'decidedly unpleasant to her olfactory organs'], all are yet delicate and gentle. . . . Everywhere the effect will be to elevate and refine."

As was the case with the florification of the Virgin Mary, so these floral arts were supposed to "elevate and refine" women, to "deprive them of their grosser particles," like the skeletonized leaves. Woman's character "should be rather divine than sensual," wrote the author of a handbook on table manners in his instruction that women should not be given too large a slice of meat nor should their plates be filled too full. And indeed, some of these women did seem like fragile phantom flowers protected under a dome of glass. In the mid-19th century, an American, Harriet Garnett, wrote in letters of her "strange, introverted sister Fanny," who "on good days, bathed, pressed flowers or collected shells." Fanny "nurses pots of cuttings and young seedlings with maternal love and really understands the culture of flowers extremely well," wrote Harriet. Later, Fanny took up another popular hobby of the time: collecting seaweeds, "her present delight." Harriet noted that Fanny was "much amused with sea weed, which she dries extremely well, and has really a pretty collection of them." This sort of pastime, amassing collections of dried flowers, seaweeds, shells and many other things, appealed both to shy, fey creatures like Fanny and to relatively worldly women such as Mary Delany, whose outstanding paper flowers are described in chapter nine.

The well-decorated Victorian home included many other horticultural items besides dried-flower collections and phantom bouquets. Annie Hassard's *Floral Decorations for the Dwelling House*, published in London and New York in the 1870s, told "Ladies and Amateurs" about the very modern skill of "leaf printing from nature," in which smooth leaves produced a photographic image on paper treated with silver nitrate. The book also described how to make an ivy screen for a fireplace and how to arrange a bowl of fruit for dessert—"Peaches and Apricots look handsomest . . . resting on a mat of bright green Moss and decorated only with a spray of Creeping Fern twined through them, so as just to tone down their bright colours but nothing more, their individual beauty being too great to be hid." Hassard also divulged the secrets of lighting the dining room to best illuminate a vase on the table—an illustration shows three tall arrangements, the middle one with three tiers, that must have made conversation and eye contact across the table almost impossible. This, despite the insistence of an earlier (male) author, Shirley Hibberd, that "a dinner table is intended for the enjoyment of those who sit at it and should never be made an occasion for ostentatious display of plants or cumbrous ornaments."

Hibberd's 1856 *Rustic Adornments for Homes of Taste*, however, described fantastic tiered arrangements that can only be considered ostentatious. Hibberd described one that won first prize in the 1870 Birmingham Horticultural Society show as having, on the "lowest tazza . . . circles of scarlet geranium, white eucharis and crimson roses relieved with sprays of astilbe, stipe, milium and maidenhair. The middle tazza was dressed with pink heaths and white and crimson roses, with grasses and ferns to soften the outlines. The trumpet top was filled with astilbe and scarlet geraniums, with grasses to give a feathery finish." Such arrangements were not generally displayed alone but flanked by "modified repetitions of the centre."

Houseplants were also used in decorating. In the 19th century, enormous glazed conservatories, often filled with exotic plants, became extensions of almost every wealthy home. More universally, women were encouraged to tend a small relative of the conservatory, an indoor, glass-covered planting box called a wardian, or Ward's, case. This was an early sort of terrarium, the legacy of Nathaniel Bagshaw Ward, a physician interested in horticulture who stumbled upon a technique that gave plants a fighting chance to survive transoceanic voyages. A container of soil covered with a tightly fitting glass lid became a closed environment which would protect a plant from damage by wind, drought or cold so that rare specimens could travel long distances. Not only did wardian cases carry 20,000 tea plants from Shanghai to the Himalayas, but filled with ferns and mosses, they soon travelled from table to table in the parlours of the upper class, where the same self-sustaining qualities made them encouragingly easy garden projects. "The case need only be opened for the removal of dead leaves or for a little trimming when required," instructed one guidebook.

The care of wardian cases was described in almost every gardening manual for women, including Cornelia J. Randolph's 1884 *The Parlor Garden*. Randolph promised her readers, whom she addressed throughout as "ladies" or "dear madam," that if they were to follow her instructions, "the refined and refining pleasures which the practice of gardening affords will have been enjoyed by you, in all their variety, without your leaving the house." One chapter told these housebound horticulturists about a new variation of the wardian case, the parlour aquarium, "a conservatory of a square or oval form, with a ridged roof, the interior of which encloses a basin in which ornamental aquatic plants are cultivated." This water garden, which in its transformation into the modern aquarium became less focused on plants and more on fish, was cultivated in part for beauty and in part for educational purposes, demonstrating "the mutual dependence of animal and vegetable life," as one author put it, to women increasingly interested in science.

Another parlour accomplishment was the window garden, described in manuals like Shirley Hibberd's. The window garden was a small greenhouse, a variation of the wardian case, that projected outward from the window on iron brackets. It was poetically described in the unsigned (but said to have been written by Elizabeth Talbot) *Flora Domestica or The Portable Flower-Garden* of 1823, which alphabetically listed plants suitable for indoor culture, their Latin names and uses and care, along with the mediocre poems that so often fattened such books:

So did the maidens with their various flowers
Deck up their windows and make neat their
* bowers:*
Using such cunning as they did dispose
The ruddy peony with the lighter rose,
The monkshood with the bugloss, and
* entwine*
The white, the blue, the flesh-like columbine
With pinks, sweet-williams; that far off
* the eye*
Could not the manner of their mixtures spy.

Rows of these gardens in the windows of crowded streets must have been as attractive as the window boxes that still decorate European cities. Such gardens, wrote Hibberd, were "peculiarly adapted for the window that commands an unpleasant look-out, or where inquisitive eyes impose a limit on privacy, or perhaps tongues that defy propriety make unseemly noises without."

The lady was unlikely to find labouring on her knees in the garden attractive, however—such work was seen as an unpleasant necessity for the lower classes. Any kind of serious work outdoors could damage her hands, break her nails, freckle her skin and, worst of all, make her smelly and dirty. Jane Croly, an American who wrote essays under the pen name Jenny Juneiana, let it be known in 1864 that "Delicate personal cleanliness, even if it verges upon an extreme, is a very attractive thing in a woman, much more so than, as a sex, they at all understand. Men are naturally dirty—they can go to sleep at night with bodies reeking with the exhalations which they have accumulated during an active day."

Another American, Sophie Johnson, wrote about 20 years later that this sort of attitude was dishonest if it kept women from gardening: "Mrs. Japonica and Miss McFlimsey hold up their hands in holy horror at the very idea of any of their kindred soiling their hands with the work . . . yet how much harder do they work at the crowded party or ball! To dance the 'German' requires quite as much physical strength as to plant a flower-garden and rake off the weeds; but that is the fashion, and beef tea and stimulants must be resorted to, to sustain the feeble knees, uplift the nervous fingers." Mavericks like Johnson might attempt to lure the lady to more intimate contact with plants, but it was the burgeoning science of botany, described in the next chapter, not enthusiasm for gardening, that would expand female horizons a lit-

The window garden, festooned with ferns and other
popular plants of the day, allowed the lady to
garden without resting on her knees or freckling her
skin. She was as sheltered as the plants she tended,
kept safe from the world outside.

~~

99

~~

tle beyond paper chrysanthemums and embroidered camellias.

Of course, once girls were old enough to dress according to fashion, even those few who might have wanted to do some physical work outdoors would have been shackled by their clothing. For at least a century, ladies' dresses had "rendered out-of-door exercise entirely out of the question," as one woman wrote. "A white muslin gown, damped to cling more closely to the figure, and satin slippers are not an equipment even for a walk on the London pavements; they would make a country ramble still more completely out of the question."

Mary F. Thomas wrote in a letter to the journal *The Lily* in 1852: "A short time ago, a lady, evidently suffering severely the penalty of the slave of fashion, said, on my remonstrating on her course, that she could not change, for she had worn stiff whalebones so long that she could not support her body in an upright position without them." Ladies of the 18th and 19th centuries were decorations, not workers. In the garden, they might languish on a bench under a parasol or pick the odd rose. Captain James Mangles proposed creating a " 'lady's flower-garden,' where immediately after rain she may step out, dry shod, and enjoy the fragrance of her flowers, while their beauty and progressive development will be ever present from the window of her apartment." Women's ancient love affair with plants was, for the moment, confined to touching them from the neck up.

Love affair is an apt description indeed for one lady's clandestine forays into her garden. In an unsigned book of 1898, *Elizabeth and Her German Garden*, "Elizabeth" — actually Mary Russell, the Countess von Arnim — wrote, "I did one warm Sunday in last year's April, during the servants' dinner hour, doubly secure from the gardener by the day and the dinner, slink out with a spade and a rake and feverishly dig a little piece of ground and break it up and sow surreptitious ipomaea, and run back very hot and guilty into the house and get into a chair and behind a book and look languid just in time to save my reputation."

"Your sweetest empire is to please" was something of a curse. Marie Bashkirtseff, a young woman who kept a journal in the 19th century, spoke for a generation like herself when she wrote: "I stopped in the garden and looked at a stone vase in which a lovely canna rose was just unfolding. I thought how pretty my white dress and leafy crown must look in that entrancing garden. Is that all I am ever to do in life — dress myself carefully, put leaves in my hair and think about the effect?" With leaves in her hair, Marie's effect was, of course, that of a flower.

As women became flowers, so the flowers became linked with certain human qualities. Since antiquity, rosemary had stood for remembrance, pansies for thought, narcissus for vanity, and so on. But now, every flower had its own definition. This was the language of flowers, a fad given the Oriental seal of romanticism by its relationship with a Turkish code introduced to Europe by several travellers, including Lady Mary Wortley Montagu, English poet, monitor of social manners and bluestocking. In the 18th century, she brought home from Constantinople a sampler of what she called the Selam floral code, which gave meaning to objects such as pearls, cloves and flowers. (Montagu, no shy flower herself, was a brilliant, smallpox-scarred woman who would also acquaint English high society with such Eastern exotica as bloomers and the fez.)

Of this simple code, apparently devised by illiterate women in Eastern harems, Montagu wrote, "There is no colour, no flower, no weed, no fruit, herb, pebble or feather that has not a verse belonging to it; and you may quarrel, reproach or send Letters of passion, friendship, or Civillity, or even of news, without ever inking your fingers." The pearl, she said, meant "fairest of the young"; paper, "I faint every hour"; a pear, "give me some hope"; a piece of gold wire, "I die—come quickly." Within a century, cloves, paper, straw, gold wire and all of the other nonfloral trinkets were abandoned, but the Turks' language of flowers had become a great hit among European ladies. A romantic bouquet of ferns, daisies, lilacs, columbines and lily of the valley might signify sincere (fern), innocent (daisy), first love (lilac), tinged with folly (columbine), bringing a return of happiness (lily of the valley) to the lover who sent it. The recipient, properly versed, might realize that she had been given more than a simple bunch of flowers. The subject proved another fruitful ground for female authors.

Manuals such as *Garland of Flora* and *Tell the Wish of Thy Heart in Flowers* and Sarah Josepha Hale's 1838 *Flora's Interpreter* helped spread the message, which was declared on valentines, in address books and in verse.

In Eastern lands they talk in flowers,
And they tell in a garland their loves
*   and cares;*
Each blossom that blooms in their garden
*   bowers,*
On its leaves a mystic language bears;
Then gather a wreath from the garden
*   bowers,*
And tell the wish of thy heart in flowers.

Promising further examples of "the best specimens of American poetry" and "choice extracts from the British poets," Hale's book was republished in 1850 as *Flora's Interpreter and Fortuna Flora,* which included a system for divining one's fortune by combining birth date and floral meanings. In keeping with the growing scientific knowledge among women, this edition also offered an explanation of botanical terminology and, for each plant, its Latin name and habitat.

In Grandville's book, the tulip becomes half flower and half woman.

But it was not science that made the language of flowers appealing. In a time of good manners and sexual repression, at least for women (during Victoria's reign, a woman known as Aunt Etty dug up phallic stinkhorn mushrooms "to protect the morals of our maidens"), this was a language of emotion with origins in the passionate East. "We are told that in Persia, the tulip, whose blossom in its native country is scarlet while the centre of its glowing cup is black, is used to express warm affection; and, when sent by a lover, will convey to the object of his attachment the idea that, like this flower, his face is warm and his heart consumed as a coal," wrote a female author. Perhaps this language was so attractive simply because it gave flowers—and hence women—a voice with which they could express the sensual, the provocative, even the rude. Was there, in that era, ever a lady who served her husband endive for dinner, taking quiet satisfaction in knowing that she was calling him frugal?

Albert Grandville took the woman/flower metaphor still further—perhaps as far as it could go—in *Les Fleurs Animées*, a wonderfully illustrated volume in which each flower, depicted as a woman dressed in petals and leaves, is involved in an activity corresponding to the language of flowers. The wallflower is carried over a wall by a lusty man; the sweet pea idly drinks cider; the water lily is a nun.

A short essay accompanies the illustration of each flower. The marsh mallow, a medicinal plant described as "beneficence" in the language of flowers, is represented as a nurse caring for beetles and frogs. "In her devotion to these cares, she manifested a sort of monomania," observed Grandville wryly. The regal lily became the Queen of France, but not until she had fallen in love, a loss of innocence that occurred because, as she later regretfully admitted, "I was no longer a flower, I was a woman. My weakness was that of my sex." Tulipa—half tulip, half woman—was, according to Grandville's mythology, loved for a short time by the Sultan Shahabaan, who, when he tired of her simple charms, dropped her into the Bosporus. The beautiful but unperfumed camellia was transformed into Imperia, a stunning but cold woman. After her husband killed himself because of her lack of warmth (scent), Imperia declared that while a woman could not live without love, a flower could exist without scent.

No flower, in fact, captured the Victorian imagination like the camellia. In the mid-19th century, Alexandre Dumas' *La Dame aux Camélias* was produced in Paris. In English, it became the play *Camille*, the basis of Verdi's *La Traviata*. The delicate heroine of Dumas' play, to this day a model of floral femininity taken to its extreme, Marguerite Gautier could not bear scented flowers because they made her cough and so preferred camellias: "Those are the only flowers I like; it is quite useless to send me any others. . . . Perfumes make me ill." Almost overnight, camellias became the rage, and members of the upper class sought to outdo each other in collecting and growing this touchy greenhouse ornamental that suffers in full sunlight and in temperatures too high or too low. One author claimed that camellias were popular only because they were difficult to grow.

If a woman were not frail enough to be a hothouse camellia, what flower could she be? "The rose spoke of burning loves, the lily of her chaste delight," wrote George Sand in *Consuelo*, in a mid-19th-century passage that gave flowers female voices. "The superb magnolia told of pure enjoyment and lofty pride, and the lovely little hepatica related the pleasure of a single and retired existence. Some flowers spoke with strong and powerful voices which proclaimed in accents trumpet-tongued, 'I am beautiful, and I rule'; others murmured, in tones scarcely audible but exquisitely soft and sweet, 'I am little, and I am beloved.' " George Sand was, of course, Aurore Dupin, discreetly veiled by a male pseudonym.

Like the phantom leaves and crocheted flowers in their glass cases, Dupin, as a woman unabashedly writing fine literature, needed to protect her identity from the damage that her era would surely inflict. And if upper-class women had privileged lives as cosseted flowers, the fact that they had little choice in the matter made them prisoners much like the glass-covered artificial flowers they created. Marie Bashkirtseff wondered, "Is that all I am ever to do in life?" And "Elizabeth," the German Countess von Arnim, wrote longingly, "I wish with all my heart I were a man, for of course the first thing I should do would be to buy a spade and go and garden, and then I should have the delight of doing everything for my flowers with my own hands."

VIII

"That Pleasing Study"

Botany, a science for ladies

Not all Victorian ladies were content
with artificial flowers. One of the curiosities of a
curious age was the sight of a woman out
in a field, parasol in one hand, a flower in the
other, proclaiming the plant to be monogynia
or digynia with the same authority
she might have said it represented "lost love" in
the language of flowers. In a time when
interest in all the natural sciences burgeoned,
botany became such an accepted study for
women that an American observed in 1822,
"I believe more than half the botanists in New
England and New York are ladies."
By the end of the century, thousands of women
had taken to the fields, guidebooks in
hand, and a male botanist had responded to
the insecurities of his readers by
publishing an answer to the pressing question:
"Is Botany a Suitable Study for Young Men?"

The development was an interesting one,
because the sciences, as intellectual pursuits,

were traditionally deemed masculine. But something intrinsically female seemed to be present in plants, and thus their study, unlike that of, say, rocks or stars, was socially acceptable, even encouraged, for women. Now, the relationship between women and plants, at one time entirely practical, became almost entirely intellectual. There was nothing really useful about knowing that a plant belonged to the order monogynia. One wanted to know not so much what a plant could do as what it should be called; what its relationship was to other plants rather than to people. Botany was, in large part, a memory game, although it could, of course, also be linked to such activities as making floral crafts or gardening.

"The study of botany seems particularly suited to females," wrote Almira Lincoln in her *Familiar Lectures on Botany* in 1831. "The objects of its investigation are beautiful and delicate." To the anonymous female author of the 1864 American book *Phantom Leaves*, botany represented "a world of novelties to which [a woman] had heretofore been a stranger." By learning such a craft as phantom-leaf making, described in the previous chapter, the lady would "insensibly become a botanist. . . . From a desire to extend her knowledge of the subject, she will consult the numerous botanical authorities which crowd the shelves of the nearest library, and thus her interest in a study so elevating and refining will be increased."

Thus elevated and refined, a woman could, without losing her grasp of the Victorian notion of fragile femininity, take a greater part in the world in an age that became defined by its knowledge of the natural world—"the era," said Victorian Robert Kerr, "of Omnium Gatherum." Biological specimens gathered all over the world by explorers and collectors had been arriving in Europe by boatloads for more than two centuries. John Loudon, one of the 19th century's leading botanists, esti-

mated that there were about 1,000 non-native plant species available in England in 1700 and about 6,000 by 1800—magnolias, rhododendrons, forsythias, mock oranges and scores more of the plants which would eventually inhabit almost every Western garden. During her remarkable horseback journey through England in the 18th century, Celia Fiennes described several of the new arrivals at the "Physick Garden" at Oxford, including "ye Sensible plant, take but a Leafe between finger and thumb and squeeze it, and it immediately Curles up together as if pained, and after some tyme opens abroad again, it looks in Coullour like a filbert Leafe but much narrower and long."

In 1753, in the midst of all this adventure and wonder, Swedish scholar and physician Carl Linnaeus published his *Species plantarum*, which described 6,000 species of plants and used a scheme that would unravel the previously bewildering tangle of plant taxonomy. This was the Linnaean system of binomial nomenclature, which is still in use. Binomial nomenclature works much like the Chinese system of naming people—surname first. The genus name, showing the relationship to other close family members, is followed by the species name. A plant can be positively identified by a binomial such as *Lactuca sativa*, lettuce, whose genus name, *Lactuca*, suggests the milklike sap of the plant and whose species name, *sativa*, means cultivated. Sometimes a subspecies or a variety (or, in this century, a cultivated variety, or cultivar) name adds further clarity to the binomial label. The genus belongs to a plant family, which in turn belongs to a larger order, and that, in turn, to a class, phylum and kingdom.

Maria Jackson wrote in her 1816 volume *The Florist's Manual or Hints for the Construction of a Gay Flower Garden*, "The Florist will increase her amusement ten-fold by making herself familiar with the ingenious system of the great parent of botany, Linnaeus, and some knowledge of which seems unavoidable in those ladies who, in cultivating their favourite flowers, exercise the mental along with the corporeal faculty."

Despite its advantages, the Linnaean system did have its critics when it first appeared, some of whom objected to its "lewd" and "licentious" descriptions. It worked strictly according to the number of stamens (male organs) and pistils (female organs) in a flower. In establishing classes, a prefix for the appropriate number of stamens was attached to the Greek-derived male suffix -andria. A flower with one stamen, then, was in the class monandria. To place it in a smaller group—its order—the plant was further defined by its population of pistils, which received the female suffix -gynia. A plant with one pistil belonged to the order monogynia; if it had two pistils, it was digynia, and so forth. The poet Wilfred Blunt said that botany had now been brought within the range of "any young lady who could count up to twelve."

But flowers might have many stamens and just one pistil, or more than one of each, a situation unsuited to 18th-century ideas of propriety, particularly with a straight-laced god at the helm of nature. Linnaeus described monandria as "one husband in a marriage," but diandria was "two husbands in the same marriage" and polyandria "twenty males or more in the same bed with the female." One Russian scholar said that "such loathsome harlotry as several males to one female would never have been permitted in the vegetable kingdom by the Creator." In his *Botanical Tables*, Lord Bute assured readers that his book was suitable for the use of ladies, as "no improper terms will be found in it."

Plants—and their official Linnaean names, for how else could one positively identify all of these newcomers?—were now on everybody's mind, even those of cosseted women. A genteel tea party might well include mention of the health of a lady's *Dahlia rosea* or *Chrysanthemum frutescens*. As Maria Edgeworth wrote in her 1810 *Letters for Literary Ladies*, "Botany has become fashionable; in time, it may become useful, if it be not so already."

At Longwoods, a famous garden in Delaware, is a 19th-century house, once owned by a Quaker family, that contains a journal kept by Rachel Peirce Lamborn around 1830 or 1840. In it, the Linnaean system is carefully written out by hand, accompanied by a sketch of a group of ladies going on a botanical walk, all in dresses and Quaker bonnets and all holding bouquets of flowers. Such "amateur botanizing expeditions" were a popular exercise.

As usual, royalty provided a lofty example of what was acceptable for all ladies. The Queen of Sweden was instructed in the new taxonomic system by Linnaeus himself, and Queen Charlotte, wife of George III of England, was a student of botany in the 1780s. One text on "exotick plants" of the era noted "the rapid progress her Majesty and the Princesses her daughters have made in the most difficult parts of that pleasing study." The sanction of the clergy came in 1795, when the Reverend John Bennett wrote in *Letters to a Young Lady*: "Attention to a garden is a truly feminine Amusement. If you mix it with a Taste for Botany and a knowledge of Plants, you will never be in want of an excellent Restorative."

Restorative indeed: science as therapy. The recommendation that ladies learn a little botany to improve their health was, at first, the entire reason for them to engage in a science whose serious study was still seen to be the province of men. At the time, fresh air alone was considered good medicine. On the other hand, sitting in a stuffy classroom poring over one's books was likely to overtax and damage the delicate female constitution. The Scottish geologist Hugh Miller wrote to his

As interest in all sciences burgeoned in the 19th century, only one, botany, was dominated by women. This illustration by Thorza Lee appears in Familiar Lectures on Botany *by Almira Lincoln.*

~~

fiancée, "Take little thought and much exercise. Read for amusement only. Set yourself to make a collection of shells or butterflies or plants. Do anything that will have interest enough to amuse you without requiring so much attention as to fatigue." (A collection of plants, dried and properly labelled – the herbarium – was, in fact, a respected tool of botany, but Miller undoubtedly had something less serious in mind.)

The idea of female intellectual weakness was criticized by Antoinette Brown Blackwell, who wrote in the late 19th century that "Nature" would take care of women, whom Blackwell compared not with the usual flowers but with the much more stalwart trees: "Deciduous trees perform a large amount of work even in winter. They look desolate, lifeless; yet in the midst of their covering of ice and snow, their slow activity is steadily nurturing every bud and fibre of the whole plant. February finds all growth much

farther advanced than December. When the sap begins to circulate freely in the vegetable veins, the tree is ready to burst into sudden greenness and blossoms. If Nature can accomplish this much out in the cold, she ought to be able steadily to mature her young women in harmonious strength and vigor amid the warmth and comfort of well-regulated homes and school rooms."

The belief that women could not physically tolerate intense mental concentration crippled their desire to pursue serious studies, but there was consensus that "an agreeable and rational exercise for the body" was quite a different thing, as Charles Mackintosh wrote in Louisa Johnson's 1845 *Every Lady Her Own Flower Garden.* To achieve it, a woman need only observe plants outdoors. Even if she did not move at all, she would be breathing fresh air while performing mildly invigorating mental calisthenics: "The mind will be agreeably exercised in contemplating the beauty of the flowers, but much more so still if the study of their respective parts, natures and structures, in a botanical or physiological point of view, be at the same time attended to." Lady Charlotte Murray agreed, according to her 1799 book, *The British Garden*: "The Garden and the Field offer a constant source of unwearying amusement, easily obtained, and conducing to health, by affording a continual and engaging motive for air and exercise."

Closely tied to botany's promise of healthful exercise was its supposed ability to enhance spiritual health, to lead the minds of its students to the contemplation of God, the creator of all natural philosophy, as 16th- and 17th-century science was called. Astronomer Johannes Kepler called himself "the priest of God in the temple of nature," while 17th-century chemist Robert Boyle wrote in one treatise that the most virtuous religious activity one could perform was to learn about the world and therefore about God.

Botany, too, was expected to lead one's thoughts to the sublime. As William Cowper put it in a poem quoted on the first page of *The British Garden*, "Nature is but a name for an effect whose cause is God." It was a matter of convention to include a dedication to God in the preface of a botanical text: to record the author's "object throughout the work, to direct the attention to the wisdom and goodness of God, as exhibited in the structure and arrangement of the vegetable kingdom," as Anne Pratt wrote in 1838 in *The Field, the Garden and the Woodland*.

Priscilla Wakefield wrote in the preface of *An Introduction to Botany* in 1796, "The design of the following Introduction to Botany is to cultivate a taste in young persons for the study of nature, which is the most familiar means of introducing suitable ideas of the attributes of the Divine Being, by exemplifying them in the order and harmony of the visible creation." In 1829, Almira Lincoln wrote in her *Familiar Lectures on Botany*, "These lec-

tures, although written with a view to teach science, have yet a higher aim, that of leading the youthful mind to view the wisdom, power and goodness of the Almighty, as manifested in his creation—and no commendation which this work has received has been so gratifying to its author as that which has ascribed to it a religious tendency."

If a woman failed to make the proper mention of God in her preface, she was taken to task, as was Elizabeth, Countess of Kent, for omitting any such reference in her 1823 book, *Flora domestica*. In her subsequent publication, the unsigned *Sylvan Sketches* of 1825, Elizabeth said that her previous book had been judged "wanting a spirit of religion and that frequency of grateful reference to the Creator." As a result of her apparent oversight, "some conjectures, likely to be injurious to [me], have been formed with regard to the cause of this omission." What the conjectures were, one can only wonder—that she was heathen? A witch?

She settled the account in an intriguingly oblique fashion in *Sylvan Sketches*: "If a man stand upon a rising ground and look abroad upon a fertile country, must he be told the source of all that beauty? Must he be reminded what he ought to feel before his heart will swell with a fulness of gratitude and love? Oh, surely not . . . ." Still, Elizabeth managed to avoid mentioning God. But the book was conventional in other respects. Along with a few mediocre botanical poems, like those which often appeared in otherwise serious books for women, she described various trees, giving their histories, uses and Latin names, the names Linnaeus had organized.

Dr. Cadwallader Colden, an influential 18th-century scientist, philosopher and writer living in New York, thought that women's lack of schooling in Latin would hamper their interest in botany. He wrote to the botanist J.F. Gronovius in 1755, "I often thought that Botany is an amusement which may be made greater to the Ladies who are often at a loss to fill up their time. . . . The natural curiosity & the pleasure they take in beauty and variety of dress seems to fit them for it far more than men. The chief reason that few or none of them have hitherto applied themselves to this study, I believe, is because all the books of any value are wrote in Latin & so filled with technical words that obtaining the necessary previous knowledge is so tiresome and disagreeable that they are discouraged at the first set out & give it over before they can receive any pleasure in the pursuit."

Colden "took the pains to explain Linnaeus's System" to his daughter Jane "and to put it in an English form for her use by freeing it from the technical terms, which was easily done by using two or three words in place of one. . . . Though perhaps she could not be persuaded to learn the terms at once, she now understands in some degree Linnaeus's characters, notwithstanding that she does not understand Latin." (After Jane's death, an admirer wrote in the preface of her botanical notebook, "She possessed such a love of botany that she learned Latin.") Indeed, in her own botanical notebook, Jane listed the Latin terms she would use: "Radix, the root; Caules, the stalk; Folia, the leaves; Calix, the general cup; Corola, the compound flower . . ."

Of course, one could memorize the Latin name of a plant and not understand its meaning at all. "Cold-heartedness" in the language of flowers could represent lettuce just as easily as *Lactuca sativa* in the language of botany. But one could progress beyond mere parroting to an understanding of rudimentary Latin, which could be learned gradually. *Officinalis*, for instance, is a common plant species name meaning medicinal or "of the apothecaries." Also, the species name had to agree in gender with the genus: masculine *albus*, feminine *alba*, neuter *album*. Compre-hending the basics of the terminology meant that by simply seeing a plant name, one would have some understanding of the plant's relationship to others and probably something of its appearance or use. After all, as Agnes Catlow pointed out in her 1855 *Popular Garden Botany*, a lady would certainly want to know the background of a visitor to her home before inviting the stranger inside; the same ought to be true of the plants in her garden.

In books written initially by men for women, later by women themselves, the authors taught science as painlessly as possible by using literary styles and conventions that the women already knew from romantic novels and poetry. Sumptuous description, for instance, was a teaching tool used by the respected botanist Sarah Wallace Bowdich Lee, who said that her 1854 *Trees, Plants and Flowers: Their Beauties, Uses and Influences* was an attempt to make a botanical work accessible to readers who lacked knowledge of plant taxonomy or Latin. An enthusiastic plant explorer and likely the first person to collect systematically in West Africa, Bowdich Lee described a hurricane in her textbook: "A distant murmuring is first heard, then come sighs and wailings, almost amounting to shrieks and loud moans. The leaves are agitated and produce a violent rustling. Then the branches crack, and twigs fall, and presently the whole forest gives a mighty roar. The commotion becomes universal, one bough presses against another till the weakest gives way with a loud crash, the noble trees bow their heads, and the tops fall to pieces, every branch is snapped off, and then the uprooted giant comes to the ground, bringing its lesser brethren with it in the fall, while huge fragments are borne onwards and around, like feathers."

And many otherwise serious texts of the day were sprinkled with the saccharine poetry that must have been thought to help the factual medicine go down. Some of these poems, like "The Chaplet" by a poet simply designated "Richardson," reminded the reader of her obligation to appear decorative, however scientifically competent she might be:

To thee, sweet Maid, I bring,
The beauteous progeny of Spring:
In every breathing bloom I find
Some pleasing emblem of thy mind.
The blushes of that op'ning rose,
Thy tender modesty disclose;
These sno-white lilies of the vale,
Diffusing fragrance to the gale,
No ostentatious tints assume,
Vain of their exquisite perfume;
Careless, and sweet, and mild, we see
In these a lovely type of thee . . .

In another concession to the styles of the day, textbooks might be written in the form of letters between friends or between teacher and pupil. Reading someone else's letters, even if they are all about botany, is more interesting than reading a lecture. In 1796, Priscilla Wakefield published An Introduction to Botany, which became so popular that, within half a century, it had been republished 11 times and translated into French. (Pressed between the pages of the copy I saw at Ontario's University of Guelph was a figure eight of very fine blond hair, wound and tied in a fashion so precise and complex that it seemed a suitable memorial to the era.)

An Introduction to Botany took the form of a series of letters. Instead of chapter one, Wakefield wrote Letter I from Felicia at the "Shrubbery, February 1" to her "dear Sister" Constance. The first letter gives some indication of the role of botany in the life of the Englishwoman of the late 18th and early 19th centuries.

Felicia explains at the outset that she greatly misses her sister Constance: "Even the approach of spring, which is marked by the appearance of snowdrops and crocuses, affords me but little pleasure; my kind mother, ever attentive to my happiness, concurs with my governess in checking this depression of spirits and insists upon my having recourse to some interesting employment that shall amuse me and pass away the time while you are absent; my fondness for flowers has induced my mother to propose Botany, as she thinks it will be beneficial to my health, as well as agreeable, by exciting me to use more air and exercise than I should do without such a motive. . . . How should I enjoy this pursuit in your company, my dear sister! But as that is impossible at present, I will adopt the nearest substitute I can obtain, by communicating to you the result of every lesson."

Felicia's teacher, who is also, appropriately enough, female, is as careful as the book's author to point out the link between God and nature. Mrs. Snelgrove "leads me by her amiable reflections to consider these pleasing objects not only in a botanical view but by pointing out the peculiar uses of the different parts of their structure, to perceive and admire the proofs of Divine Wisdom exhibited in every leaf and in every flower . . . ."

The following year, 1797, "A Lady," Maria E. Jackson, published Botanical Dialogues Between Hortensia and Her Four Children, which was, the author declared, "designed for the use of schools." The four children, Charles, Harriet, Juliette and Henry, display a peculiarly Georgian sobriety, young Charles saying to his mother at the outset, "Indeed, ma'am, you made me ashamed, when we parted, of my idling character; and Harriet and I resolved that we would no more give you reason to say that you could not attempt to instruct us in botany, because we did not seriously apply to our more necessary studies." Meanwhile, Hortensia (whose name means "of the garden") has "prepared this little room, which opens into my flower garden, for our study. Hither you may at any time come; and you will find books and glasses, and every thing that you may want." In this garden classroom, she would teach the children the system of Linnaeus. Harriet points out that "Charles will have the advantage of us, as he understands Latin," but Hortensia answers that that is not necessarily the case, as botany has "a language peculiar to itself."

Written in the form of fiction was a botanical text by "A Lady," published in 1824. *The Juvenile Gardener*, "written by a lady for the Use of her Own Children with a view to giving them an early taste for the Pleasures of a Garden and the Study of Botany," had two children as main characters, Agnes and Frank Vernon. "Frank's mamma had desired him to cultivate a few wild flowers first; for then he would be more able to attend to richer flowers when he had gained a little knowledge by beginning with such as were hardy. Besides, she said it would teach him to value the most simple works of nature as well as the more splendid tribes of Flora; and all are alike the work of the Giver of all good things." (When Frank asked his mother if he could have a botany book, she told him she would find Priscilla Wakefield's *An Introduction to Botany*, "which is a very good one.")

Besides the books written in the form of letters and stories, some were dialogues, much like plays, featuring two or three characters having odd, stilted conversations: "I am, for my part, quite contented to gather a sweet-smelling nosegay of beautiful garden monsters, as botanists denominate them, without troubling myself about their scientific names," says "Caroline" in the unsigned 19th-century *Conversations on Vegetable Physiology*. The more knowledgeable protagonist, "Mrs. B.," replies that she felt much the same until she heard the lectures of the distinguished Swiss botanist, Augustin Pyramus de Candolle, inventor of the so-called natural system of plant classification, which she then proceeds to explain. The characters in the 1817 *Conversations on Botany*, unsigned but attributed to Sarah Mary Fitton, a notable botanist and one of the few women to have a plant genus named for her, were "Edward" and his teacher, "Mother," who tells Edward all about a subject "your aunt and I were talking of yesterday in the garden": Linnaeus.

Although these introductory texts had more to do with taxonomy—with simply learning a new language—than with exploratory science, some authors, such as Fitton, were thoroughly knowledgeable about their field and could not only explain taxonomy but also venture some educated speculations about plants. The path taken to attain that level of expertise by another notable author, Jane Webb Loudon, was interesting and unusual.

"It is scarcely possible to imagine any person more completely ignorant than I was of every thing relating to plants and gardening," wrote Jane of herself in 1830, when, at 23, she married 47-year-old John Claudius Loudon, a distinguished botanist and the most influential garden writer of the time. Having made a mark upon the world of science fiction with the publication of *The Mummy* in 1827, Jane could not have foreseen that her future lay in true science. "When I was a child," she wrote, "I never could learn Botany. There was something in the Linnaean system (the only one then taught) excessively repugnant to me; I never could remember the different classes and orders, and after several attempts, the study was given up as one too difficult for me to master. When I married, however, I soon found the necessity of knowing something of Botany, as well as of gardening." Eventually, tending their eclectic quarter-acre garden with her husband and helping him write his books, Jane gained "with unparalleled ardour, an extensive knowledge of botany," according to John.

Soon, she began to write her own series of

Botany was considered good for women because it did not require great intellectual exertion and encouraged mild, healthful exercise.

horticultural and botanical books, many of which were for women. In the manner of late beginners who can still remember how ignorance feels, she had a facility for making her work appealing to novices. For instance, of *Fritillaria imperialis*, Jane wrote in an otherwise scholarly description, "It flowers in May, and it is said to have an unpleasant smell, like that of a fox, but I cannot say that I ever perceived it, though I remember when a child being particularly fond of peeping into the flowers to see drops of water within them and wondering why they did not fall like rain."

By the time she wrote *The Ladies' Flower Garden of Ornamental Bulbous Plants* in 1841, Jane had the conviction that came from a thorough knowledge of her subject: "The genus *Gladiolus* ought to be divided into at least two sections or sub-genera. I consider a sub-

genus to be such a portion of any genus as will not intermingle with the rest and has some distinctive appearance, but insufficient to induce a belief of their original diversity."

Like Jane Loudon, most female botanists concentrated on studying local plants. Few women had the financial means or the social support to travel to other countries and gather specimens on their own as did the distinguished male botanists. Rare were women like Lady Sarah Amherst, an amateur English botanist who was able to collect plants in distant lands because her husband travelled to China and later became governor general of India. But as middle-class women travelled with their families to new colonies, they took seeds and plants with them, sent seeds and plants home and asked for seeds and plants to be sent to them, thus dispersing familiar plants around the world and increasing the introduction of foreign species in Europe. The dahlia, for instance, a native of Mexico, was introduced to Britain from Spain in 1789 by Lady Jane Bute; it was subsequently lost and then reintroduced in 1804 by Lady Holland. On June 12, 1786, Mary Dickinson of Wilmington, Delaware, wrote in a letter that "a relation of mine in England, who is wife to David Barclay, has requested me to send her some seeds of the most curious natural productions of America." Priscilla Bury noted of her 1838 painting of the great bombax, or silk-cotton, that it was drawn "from a description and dried specimens brought by a lady of Caraccus."

In June 1840, a Mrs. Molloy, then living in Western Australia, wrote to her friend Captain Robert Mangles, a botanist, "I gathered all the seeds but those of the isopogon up to the very hour before I sent off my last box. . . . I should very much like to have some common red flower pots. . . . As soon as I know the method of managing my seedlings, I will collect a nursery of plants for you and range them under my verandah, which I make into a sort of conservatory. I will promise seedlings of nuytsia, isopogon, petrophila, the blue geranium, only found here, anigozanthes, verticordia and, in short, everything I should like myself. Pots will be useful for these, but for raising my own seeds, I use perforated raising boxes." From Mangles, Molloy said she had received lily of the valley, apricots and hyacinths, while verbenas, myrtles and camellias "were all dead" after their long trip from Britain.

Several Western Australian plants were named after Mangles, including *Helipterum manglesii* and *Anigozanthos manglesii*, but no such record remains of Molloy. The Latinization of someone's name into a plant name, as in *manglesii*, was the ultimate tribute one botanist could pay another or, indeed, could pay a friend, a regent, an amateur plant collector, a priest, a physician, a pharmacist, a gardener or an astronomer—all of whom have been remembered this way. To a plant that had not yet been scientifically named—and these were quite common in the era of Omnium Gatherum—a botanist could give someone's surname with an appropriate Latin suffix and have the name approved: Fuchs became fuchsia, Nicot nicotiana, Forsyth forsythia, and so on. Many plants, of course, especially those already familiar in Europe and western Asia, had already been named before Linnaeus drew up his system and bore such names from Greek mythology as *Achillea, Centaurea* and *Narcissus*.

Although women interested in botany were legion, their near absence in plant names is noteworthy. Linnaeus sent his pupils, whom he called his apostles, plant collecting around the globe and so had the opportunity to grant many of the names in his own herbal lexicography. This was a matter of consternation to England's Earl of Bute, who said of Linnaeus: "I cannot forgive him the number of barbarous Swedish names, for the sake of which he flings away all those fabricated in this country. . . . I own I am surprised to see all Europe suffer these impertinences. In a few years more, the Linnaean Botany will be a good Dictionary of Swedish proper names."

The Earl need not have worried. The overall effect of a list of Latin plant names is not particularly Swedish. But if the English were well enough represented, other groups of humanity were not. What a list of plant names reveals is the history of botanical power and influence in Europe in the 16th, 17th, 18th and 19th centuries; with few exceptions, the names based on surnames are based on those of influential European men, their friends and regents.

Most of the name granting was accomplished by a core of botanists—all male in the inner circle, although an occasional woman

Both genus and species names of Victoria regia *honoured Queen Victoria.*

～

did contribute marginally—who wrote and visited one another, travelled to new lands and exchanged seeds, cuttings, information and support. As one historian noted, "The 18th-century world seems strangely small. Almost all the important men knew each other." For example, Frederik Allamand of Switzerland (genus: *Allamanda*), Carl Linnaeus of Sweden (genus: *Linnaea*), John Clayton of England and Virginia (genus: *Claytonia*), Johann Frederik Gronovius of the Netherlands (species: *gronovii*), Pehr Kalm, a Swede who researched the natural resources of eastern North America (genus: *Kalmia*), Thomas Jefferson of the United States (genus: *Jeffersonia*) and Peter Collinson of England (genus: *Collinsonia*) all corresponded with one another about botanical matters. Many more examples exist, including namesakes of amateur male botanists and gardeners who were

acknowledged by their more expert friends.

Women who gathered and studied plants at home, however, were generally unrecognized by the central committee of botanists. This is in part because any woman serious about plant studies was entirely barred from the larger male scientific community—from membership in such influential organizations as the Royal Society, founded in 1642, the Linnaean Society, founded in 1788, and the Royal Horticultural Society, founded in 1804. Women were encouraged to dabble in botany, certainly, but not to excel in it. As late as 1899, Sarah Farquharson, F.R.M.S. (a Fellow of Britain's Royal Microscopical Society) reported to the International Congress of Women, "There are at least three Societies, namely, The Royal, The Linnaean, and The Royal Microscopical, which will not permit entrance to full fellowship of any female. I say full fellowship because the latter Society (The Royal Microscopical) permits women to compete for election on exactly the same terms as a man, but if duly elected, women may not have the benefit of attending the meetings on account of their sex. The Royal and Linnaean Societies have not gone so far even as this and admit no women to membership or fellowship.

"No one who has taken up seriously any biological subject with the view of becoming as perfect in it as possible will, I am sure, question what the drawback is to be thus debarred from the interchange of thought and ideas which this want of realisation means.

"To give a single instance that has come specially under my notice, of the way in which women are prevented from reaching the summit of achievement in science, I may mention that during the time I was bringing out a work on British ferns, it was of the utmost importance to me to have access to the Herbarium of Linnaeus as well as to hear Cryptogamic discussions at the meetings of this great centre of Biological Science. I applied to the Linnaean Society, but alas, although I was told my election would have been easily carried, it could not be, on account of my sex."

There are, then, only a few plant names that remember women. Some of them honour the wives of botanists – the species name *moraea* for Sara Moraeus, the wife of Linnaeus; *lucilae* for Lucile Boissier, who died while accompanying her husband, Swiss botanist Edmond Boissier, on an expedition in Spain. Many more names honour queens, who often patronized botanical gardens or the voyages of discovery that brought new plants home.

The most memorable of the names in honour of a queen was *Victoria regia* for the giant South American water lily dedicated, both genus and species, to Queen Victoria, who was also given, in person, the first flower the plant produced in England. This behemoth among plants, with leaves five to six feet wide, was something of a midway attraction in Kew gardens in the mid-19th century, when it was sketched growing in its own special pond, a child or two perched on its leaves. *Victoria regia* seemed a suitable tribute to a monarch who not only ruled her own country but influenced many tropical ones as well. The plant did, however, later regain its previous species name, *amazonica*; even as a tribute to a monarch, a gift of both the genus and species names was excessive, especially when a more appropriate species name had already been chosen.

There is just a handful of names that commemorate female botanists, including *Hutchinsia*, a genus of low herbs named for Ellen Hutchins of Ireland (1785-1815), who excelled in the botany of flowerless plants; *Fittonia* for Elizabeth and Sarah Mary Fitton, well-respected botanists; and *Portlandia* for the Duchess of Portland, Margaret Cavendish Bentinck (1715-1785), a keen botanist who had her own botanic garden in Buckinghamshire. The species name *robbiae* honours Mary Ann Robb of Hampshire, England, who introduced *Euphorbia robbiae* to the West by bringing back rooted plants from Turkey in her hatbox in the 1890s, a feat that won the plant the epithet "Mrs. Robb's bonnet."

That there are few women's names in the plant lexicon is not surprising, given the restrictions placed upon the sex in an era when plants were being introduced into Europe at a great rate and named just as quickly. Less comprehensible is the dearth of names that have anything at all to do with the environment, language or country of the plant's origin, even though the "discovered" plants usually already had names in the native tongues. A few original names remain, among them *Pothos*, from a Sinhalese name; *Akebia*, Latinized Japanese; *Argania*, Latinized Moroccan; *Luffa*, Arabic; *Datura*, East Indian.

The 18th and 19th centuries were good times to be white, European, privileged and male. Nevertheless, while women who wanted to further their botanical studies were certainly hobbled, the study itself likely did not disappoint them. No doubt many agreed with the sentiments of Dr. J.F.A. Adams, who wrote in his 1887 article for *Science* magazine, "Is Botany a Suitable Subject for Young Men?" that botany was, indeed, suitable not only "for young ladies and effeminate youths" but also for "able-bodied and vigorous-brained young men who wish to make the best use of their powers." Adams had several reasons for his opinion: botany was "an admirable mental discipline," it would "promote physical development," it was "of great practical utility," and most important, it was "a source of lifelong happiness." Adams explained, "If one's surroundings are uncongenial and life proves full of cares and disappointments, it is great solace to be able to say with Aurora Leigh, 'I was not therefore sad. My soul was singing at a work apart.'"

IX

"New Wonders to Paint"

Plants, flowers and women's arts

"Flowers are a woman's most perfect adornment," write the authors of *Domestic Needlework*, "but as flowers soon fade, it is no wonder that women should try to produce in needlework a lasting imitation, which they might have always at hand."

~~

Art, like science, is a field in which plants have provided a means of expression and fulfillment for women, whose artistic heritage is humble and often anonymous, much of it bound up with needle and thread, loom and yarn. Botanical arts allow the artist to bring the outdoors in, turning winter homes into summer gardens and introducing the colours of nature to dark, musty corners. All of life can become a garden, unrestricted by time or place.

~~

During the Renaissance, when little other inexpensive art was available, pillows, curtains, upholstery, fire screens and pictures on the walls were decorated alike with leaves, vines and flowers. Women also carried a movable garden with them – as they continue to do – on their clothing and in perfume sachets. Sometimes fashion called for flowers scattered here and there, sometimes for intertwined, continuous patterns that suggested stems and vines. Still other designs reproduced entire gardens, real or imaginary. An 18th-century dress worn by the Duchess of Queensbury was described by artist Mary Delany as "white satin embroidered, the bottom of the petticoat brown hills covered with all sorts of weeds, and every breadth had an old stump of a tree that run up almost to the top of the petticoat, broken and ragged and worked with brown chenille, round which twined nastersians, evy, honeysuckles, periwinkles, convolvuluses and all sorts of twining flowers which spread and covered the petticoat, vines with the leaves variegated as you have seen them by the sun, all rather smaller than nature . . . the robings and facings were little green banks with all sorts of weeds, and the sleeves and the rest of the gown loose twining branches of the same sort as those on the petticoat . . . ."

Textile arts have found eager practitioners among women for several reasons. For one thing, articles made of cloth are utilitarian and, at that, almost always used for household goods and clothing, women's traditional responsibilities. Needlework is neat, clean and portable enough to suit a mother of young children or a woman visiting friends, the little equipment required is inexpensive, and the small investment is recouped in something practical.

Plants suit textile arts; women suit plants; textile arts suit women. It is an ancient *ménage à trois*, probably as old as the first spun yarn. In various types of needlework such as embroidery, lace, petit point, cross-stitch and crewel (whose name refers to the special two-ply worsted yarn it requires), flowers are favoured subjects because they are colourful and relatively easy to portray with a needle and thread – not quite the right tools for rendering the detail and perspective needed for portraits and landscapes. However, even in embroidery, the most flexible of the techniques, flowers must be designed appropriately to suit the limitations of the medium. William Morris wrote, "Though the pattern be a veritable flower garden, the embroideress will not forget she is gardening with silks and gold threads, i.e. the needlewoman must work according to the needle and do what the needle commands best and be content with that." The textile arts provided challenges that took generations of designers to solve.

Until this century, virtually all women practised needlework, the sort of universal skill that today can best be compared with literacy: one was simply expected to master it. Little European girls learned from their mothers and their governesses, first creating samplers of various stitches. The title page of *The Needles Excellency*, a 1636 instruction book, shows three women: "Wisdom" holding a book in her hands (perhaps *The Needles Excellency*), "Follie" chattering and gesturing and "Industrie" busily embroidering. The devil, one knew, might well find work for idle hands.

In the previous century, the European interest in embroidery had reached a peak. The technique was known on the continent as English work, *opus anglicanum*, and virtually anything made from cloth was a candidate for some sort of floral decoration. The production of steel needles helped speed the creation of so much inexpensive embroidery that, for a time, its display in public was restricted by law to the upper classes. Queen Elizabeth I herself was an embroiderer and sent a scarf to Henry IV of France with the request that he "hide its defects under the wings of his good charity."

*An outward sign of a subtle relationship is seen in
the floral decoration of women's clothing.*

～～

In her portraits, Elizabeth sometimes appears dressed in blackwork, in which repeated, botanically inspired patterns are embroidered entirely in black silk on a white linen background. A style especially appreciated in Spain and possibly introduced in England by Eleanor of Aquitaine, its geometric intricacy suited the Elizabethan love of puzzles of all types, including garden mazes. Meanwhile, Mary, Queen of Scots, a skilled needlewoman, established a school for embroidery at Chateaudun while she was in France.

This era marked the beginning of the most delicate of textile arts, the most feminine, if you will. Lace, a European art form most highly developed in France, Italy, Belgium and Spain, was an offshoot of openwork, in which threads were pulled from fabric to create an airy design popular on underclothing.

As needlework imitated gardens, so did gardens imitate needlework.

~~~

Poor women earned a meagre living by working 18 hours a day making lace, which generally consisted of stylized patterns of flowers, vines and leaves fashioned, in truth, from air; only the outlines were actually created. The finest lace was as light as a spiderweb and was highly valued for the collars and cuffs of the upper classes. In his 1520 *Elegy upon a Collar* (*Elegia sopra un collaretto*), Agnolo Firenzuola wrote:

This collar was sculptured by my lady
In bas reliefs such as Arachne
And she who conquered her could ne'er excel,
Look on that lovely foliage, like an Acanthus,
Which o'er a wall its graceful branches trails.
Look on those lovely flowers of purest white,
Which, near the pods that open, hang
    in harmony.

As plants arrived in Europe from around the world in the age of Omnium Gatherum, everyone—including women with their needles—began to look more closely at plants, to try to copy them as accurately as possible. Botanical gardens were established. Five existed at the end of the 16th century; two centuries

later, there were about 1,600. Here, where plants were collected by the hundreds and displayed according to their botanical relationships, embroiderers and artists found patient subjects. Plants exotic and familiar were crowded together where they could be conveniently studied and sketched. In fact, it was partly for the use of artists and embroiderers that the Jardin des Plantes was established in Paris in the early 17th century. There, Pierre Vallet, official *brodeur* to the king, designed embroidery patterns to be worked by Marie de Medici and the ladies of her court. (A passionate embroiderer, de Medici was the subject of the dedication of Vallet's 1608 *Le Jardin du très chrestien Henry IV*, a "florilegium," a book of flower portraits that could be used as embroidery patterns.)

One notable woman artist—not a needleworker but an illustrator—who took her inspiration from a botanical garden was Elizabeth Blackwell. She moved to Swan Walk, near the Apothecaries Garden in London (now Chelsea Physic Garden), so that she could draw its collection of medicinal plants. She did so after showing some of her drawings to the founder of the garden, Sir Hans Sloane, and other physicians, one of whom, she wrote, displayed "some of the first Drawings at a publick Herbarizing of the Worshipfull Company of Apothecaries and recommended me to the Friendship of Mr. Isaac Rand," curator of the garden. Rand, in turn, encouraged her to produce a series of botanical illustrations. At Chelsea, Blackwell made about 500 "drawings taken from the life." She prepared copper engravings from the drawings, watercoloured the engravings by hand and made enough money from the resulting two volumes of *A Curious Herbal* to secure her husband's release from debtor's prison. Published in 1737 and 1739, the herbal was reissued with reengraved plates in 1757. When Elizabeth died the following year, she was buried in Chelsea churchyard,

~~~

THE NEEDLES EXCELLENCY
A New Booke wherin are diuers Admirable
Workes wrought with the Needle. Newly inuented and
cut in Copper for the pleasure and profit of the Industrious.

WISDOME · INDVSTRIE · FOLLIE

On the title page of "The Needles Excellency,"
three women in a garden act out a morality lesson.

near the garden that had provided her with so much toil and pleasure.

Most women, of course, were not able to visit a botanical garden, nor would most have been confident that, even if they were, they could have copied the plants accurately. Nevertheless, there were plenty of patterns that could be traced and painted or embroidered. Herbals such as Blackwell's—or, even better, earlier books with simple woodcuts rather than the more detailed engravings—had been popular for needlework almost as long as they had been available. The woman placed the illustration over a sheet of paper and poked a needle all around the edge of the

illustration, piercing the paper below. When she removed the illustration, she pressed powdered charcoal through the holes in the paper to mark a piece of cloth held beneath it. She could then redraw the follow-the-dots design on the cloth and shake off the charcoal dust.

Defacing herbals became unnecessary as embroidery became more popular and book publishing more economical. Special pattern books appeared, such as Jacques Lemoine's 1586 *La Clef des champs*, which consisted of 98 hand-coloured woodcuts, mostly of flowers, plants and fruits. The book is a virtual dictionary of the flowers embroidered by

*A group of women works to bring the garden
indoors on various textiles.*

Elizabethans, including irises, peonies, daisies, borage, several types of roses, small-bloomed pansies and the usual gillyflowers, or carnations. Its dedication to Lady Mary Sidney explains that the book was published to serve embroiderers and tapestry makers, among others.

In the next century, *A Schole-House for the Needle* offered "patternes of Cut-workes" that would "fitly serve to be wrought, some with Gould, some with Silke, and some with Crewell, in coullers: or otherwise at your pleasure." The book became so popular that it had reached its 12th edition within two decades. *The Flower-Garden Display'd*, an anonymous work of 1734, advertised that it contained "above 400 curious representations of the most Beautiful Flowers . . . very useful Not only for the Curious in Gardening, but the Prints likewise for Painters, Carvers,

Japaners, & c. also for the Ladies, as Patterns for Working, and Painting in Water-Colours, or Furniture for the Closet."

In such books, the Garden of Eden was an enduring theme, a morality lesson that, while claiming idle hands from the devil, also gave the needleworker a chance to practise rendering an interesting selection of plants, birds and animals. *A Schole-House for the Needle* included four panels based on the story. In the first, Adam and Eve are happy in Eden; in the second, Eve is tempted by the fruit; in the third, she eats it; and in the fourth, she and Adam flee the garden. Woman's temptation and fall were painstakingly rendered over and over in tiny stitches by female fingers. In the late 17th and early 18th centuries, trade with the Orient brought an Eastern influence to Eden: pavilions, bridges, blossoming trees and exotic birds.

Not only the Orient, but politics, too, influenced needlework subjects. Few women had any influence on changes of government, yet repercussions of the most exalted events appeared even on handkerchiefs and pillowcases. One could make a quiet political statement by choosing one's botanical themes carefully. The fleur-de-lis represented the French royal family and, by extension, many things French, and the Tudor rose was the banner of English monarchs from Henry VII to Elizabeth I. Mary, Queen of Scots, created a work that included the French fleur-de-lis, the Scottish thistle and the English rose—symbols, as it turned out, of her childhood, adulthood and death. During the Restoration, the motifs of Charles I, the acorn and oak, appeared triumphantly in the work of English monarchists.

If women's art reflected the changing political scene, it actually affected, however subtly, the largely male skill of landscape gardening. As embroiderers copied plants growing in gardens, so the gardens themselves echoed the curving designs and repeat patterns so suitable for embroidery. This influence was enhanced by the Elizabethans' fading interest in religious images and increasing enthusiasm for nature-oriented decorations and for plants and gardens as objects of beauty rather than just utility. Knot gardens—intricate interweavings of various low-growing, closely cropped plants best appreciated when viewed from overhead—were very popular, if impractical, and can still be seen in the grounds of palaces whose gardens were designed in a century that had gone mad for embroidery. Embellishments of just about everything, clothing and gardens included, were in vogue for an increasingly affluent populace with more time to spend dallying on details.

In the early 17th century, certain flowerbeds were known in France as *parterres de broderie*. A century later, George London described garden "Imbroidery" in his book

This "French knot" is meant to instruct gardeners, not embroiderers.

The Retir'd Gardener as "those Draughts which represent in Effect those we have on our Cloaths." By the 1780s, William Beckford, travelling in Holland, described gardens "with stiff parterres scrawled and flourished like the embroidery of an old maid's work bag." And a century later yet, Shirley Hibberd described "leaf embroidery," a garden bed devoted to plants with interesting foliage, which "may be likened in a general way to a hearthrug or Turkey carpet pattern." The style bore "such general resemblance to embroidery as to justify the name by which this system is to be henceforth known."

Similarly, Jane Loudon wrote in *The Villa Companion* in 1850, "There are very few ladies indeed who are competent to lay out a flower garden; though the skill required to do so is within the capacity of every woman who can work or embroider patterns for the different parts of a female dress."

The most remarkable example of an embroiderer who had the capacity to lay out a flower garden was Gertrude Jekyll. Born in

Hand watercolour etchings illustrate botanist Jane Loudon's "The Ladies' Flower Garden of Ornamental Bulbous Plants."

England in 1843, she was an accomplished woodcarver, photographer, painter and needleworker—two of her designs, one based on periwinkles, one on irises, appeared in the 1880 *Handbook of Embroidery*—before failing eyesight necessitated that she turn to creating what she described as "pictures of living beauty." Jekyll became one of the world's foremost garden designers because of her intimate knowledge of plants coupled with her artistic sense of colour and design. In one of her many books about gardening, she wrote, "What I have endeavoured to describe about arrangements of colour and the making of pictures with living plants was helped by some early training; for when I was young, I was hoping to be a painter, but, to my lifelong regret, I was obliged to abandon all hope of this, after a certain amount of art school work, on account of extreme and always progressive myopia. But my interest in and devotion to the fine arts has always been one of my keenest joys and, with it, a love of Nature, with all its beauties and wonders."

Jekyll's botany lessons began when she was 9, in an era when the inclination of many women to use plants as artistic subjects took a scientific turn. Botanical illustration would, in fact, give the more talented of them a comfortable living, as it had done for early practitioners like Elizabeth Blackwell and Maria Sybille Merian, an entomologist and skilled needleworker who published three volumes portraying various insects on their host plants. An additional book by Merian, the 1680 *Neues Blumen Buch*, a compendium of hand-painted engravings of garden flowers, was intended to be a source of embroidery designs. She also invented a process of painting on silk or linen that would make the fabric both reversible and washable.

Another notable needlewoman whose artistic reputation would be gained beyond the embroidery hoop was Mary Delany, whose life spanned most of the 18th century. De-scribed by Dr. Samuel Johnson as "the highest bred woman in the world and the woman of fashion of all ages," Delany befriended an assortment of famous contemporaries, including Jonathan Swift, George Frederick Handel, Lady Mary Wortley Montagu, Philip Miller (author of the famous *Gardener's Dictionary*), botanist Joseph Banks and the founder of the Methodist church, John Wesley. Described by her friends as virtuous and charming, "Dearest Mrs. Delany," as King George called her, left six volumes of diaries and letters that reveal her to have possessed both insight and humour.

After her first husband died, Delany, an expert needlewoman who was always on the lookout for new plants to portray, took up drawing and then, at 40, oil painting, working most days from 6 in the morning until late in the afternoon. It was not until she was in her 70s, however, that she invented "paper mosaics," studies of flowers created from bits of coloured paper glued to a black background. She wrote in her autobiography that the inspiration for her first flower came from a piece of Chinese paper that exactly matched the colour of a scarlet geranium. To amuse herself, she cut out the shapes of the petals, laid them on a background and then cut other plant parts from green paper, pasting them down as well. When Delany's close friend the Duchess of Portland, a noted gardener, entered the room, the Duchess mistook the paper flower for a real one and asked Delany what she was doing with the geranium.

From the age of 72 until she was 85, Delany worked at an amazing pace to create a 10-volume herbal, or as she called it, a hortus-siccus, or paper garden, *A Catalogue of Plants Copied from Nature in Paper Mosaick*, "finished in the year 1778 and disposed in alphabetical Order according to the Generic and Specific names of Linnaeus." Because her work, dubbed the Flora Delanica by one viewer, demanded many colours and tints of

*Mary Delany's paper mosaics were
botanically accurate.*

~~~

paper, Delany asked her friends to be on the lookout for raw materials, which were shipped to her from as far away as China. She obtained her models from botanical gardens such as Kew and the Chelsea Physick Garden; took care, as a student of the Linnaean system, to portray the correct number of stamens and styles; and painstakingly layered various tints to create exactly the colours she wished, with results that Sir Joseph Banks praised for their botanical accuracy. A collection of Delany's mosaics now resides at the British Museum, where they are still considered fine examples of botanical art.

The demands on later female artists, the "paintresses" of the Georgian and Victorian eras, were not for scientific accuracy, though, but for sentimental illustrations that could decorate poems, maxims, greeting cards and children's books. Although Beatrix Potter, for instance, was a talented botanical illustrator, she earned her reputation with a series of books for children. Kate Greenaway, whose work has not been widely considered either botanically accurate or aesthetically pleasing, managed to achieve a personal style despite the rigid and unimaginative art instruction of her time.

Although a Female School of Art and Design was established in 1852 in London, the students were generally not women who loved art but ladies seeking new hobbies or poorer women wishing to become art teachers. The techniques taught were mostly imitative and inflexible. Much to Greenaway's economic benefit in a romantic era yet to her disadvantage in the long run, she revelled in Victorian themes, portraying round-cheeked cherubs flying in baskets and pale-skinned ladies trailing garlands of flowers. Her work also suffered from the gaudy medium of chromolithography.

Greenaway, however, was satisfied with her subjects and her work, which she aimed to make botanically accurate. She wrote to John Ruskin, "I've got a liking to put Flower branches along the top of things and dont seem to mind if You dont see where they come from, and yet want it quite correct in its way of growing and the shape of its flowers and leaves."

Illustrating botanical books provided a living for other talented women. In the introduction to Alice Lounsberry's 1899 *A Guide to the Wild Flowers*, Dr. Nathaniel Lord Britton thanks the illustrator, Mrs. Rowan, whose "figures have been drawn from plants growing in their natural surroundings, and they are accurate and elegant." Many more women illustrated the increasing number of botanical textbooks and magazines. A list, published in 1987, of 103 artists, engravers and lithographers employed by *Curtis' Botanical Magazine* over the past 200 years indicates that almost half of them were women. By

*Margaret Brownlow illustrated her book
with her own paintings.*

～～

1977, the year of the Fourth International Exhibition of Botanical Art and Illustration at the Hunt Institute in Pittsburgh, art curator John V. Brindle reported "a high percentage of women in the list — 55 percent of the names in all four catalogues and nearly 59 percent in the current exhibition." This was "not unexpected," added Brindle, as "it merely reflects a long-standing trend."

Some botanical artists fell into the work by default: they were interested primarily in the plants, needed illustrations and, lacking assistance, did the work themselves. Under other circumstances, they would likely not have been artistically involved at all.

Agnes Chase, for instance, an authority on North American grasses at the turn of the 20th century, portrayed her subjects simply to record them, usually in pen and ink, but always "with technical exactness," as one critic pointed out. One of a surprisingly large group of botanically oriented women pressed into work because of the debts left after the deaths of their husbands, Chase said that her interest in grasses began when her grandmother told her that grass did not have flowers — and she insisted that it did. She published a text in 1922, the *First Book of Grasses*. Active in various reform movements, she worked for the U.S. Department of Agriculture for more than 60 years. When interviewed at the age of 87, she said that she would rather talk about grass than herself: "Grass is much more interesting. If it were not for grass, the world never would have been civilized." Barbara McClintock, winner of the 1983 Nobel prize for her work in corn genetics, at age 81 expressed a similar sentiment, passing congratulations on to the corn plant.

Other women combined two equal pleasures. Horticulturist Margaret Brownlow illustrated *Herbs and the Fragrant Garden* with her own crayon and watercolour paintings.

For many women, the life of a botanical artist was a pleasant one, as its outdoor themes encouraged travel, a luxury that was becoming increasingly possible, especially for women unencumbered by young families. Marian Ellis Rowan (1848-1922), widowed at an early age, travelled to Australia to record its plant life. Mrs. Charles Hentley journeyed through New Zealand for four years to portray plants in their native habitats. Kate Furbish, of the United States, who learned botany from her father when she was 12, aimed as an adult to draw all the native flowers and shrubs of Maine, and for 35 years, she wandered the rugged countryside, collected and classified the plants and created

～～

Marianne North progressed from copying the
flowers in Kew gardens to searching for elusive
plants around the world.

⌇⌇

⌇⌇

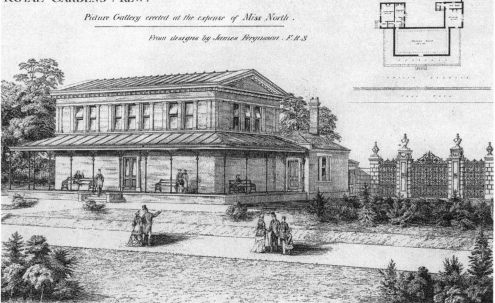

A new version of the hortus conclusus *is the gallery North had built at Kew gardens, England.*

fine, botanically accurate watercolours. Margaret Mee, who died in 1989, penetrated the rainforests of South America to do her work *in situ.* An Englishwoman, Mee moved to Brazil in 1952, where she taught art and collected and painted tropical flora in the endangered Amazonian jungle on trips that often lasted for weeks. She endured malaria, hepatitis and near drowning and subsisted "for days on packets of dehydrated soups boiled in swamp water."

Similar in her enthusiasm for her subjects was Marianne North, an extraordinary woman whose name is hardly recognized today but was well known in turn-of-the-century Britain. Her art gallery at the Royal Botanical Gardens at Kew, England, represents, I think, a new version of the *hortus conclusus*, the closed garden that at one time symbolized not only the Virgin Mary but all floral

femininity. Stepping through the doors of the Marianne North Gallery, one enters an entirely different kind of closed garden: a small, brilliantly coloured paradise created by North alone. She commissioned the construction of a gallery to enclose a world of her own work, arranged country by country according to its plant life.

Born in 1830, North, in the manner typical of Victorian ladies, took lessons "in flower-painting from a Dutch lady" in London when she was 20 and then practised copying flowers at Kew. Flower painting was so condoned as a female accomplishment at the time that John Loudon wrote in his *Gardener's Magazine* that "to be able to draw flowers botanically and fruit horticulturally . . . is one of the most useful accomplishments of your ladies of leisure living in the country."

North had the opportunity to paint outside England quite early by accompanying her father—"from first to last the one idol and friend of my life"—on his travels throughout Europe and the Middle East. After his death in 1869, she travelled alone and continued to do so for the next 15 years, searching for places of particular botanical interest at a time when not only was a woman travelling alone a rare creature but hotels were scarce and medical facilities often nonexistent. There were compensations, however: the English were treated deferentially almost everywhere she went, and there were few enough of them abroad that they formed a sort of elite hospitality network. North was entertained by a magistrate, a princess, an archdeacon and a rajah and was introduced to U.S. President Grant. Encouraged in her work by Charles Darwin, she even received a thank-you letter from Victoria regia herself, Queen Victoria.

Her gallery is overwhelming. High on the walls, the names of the countries and continents she visited are printed in large capitals —Ceylon, India, Singapore, Jamaica, America, and so on—and under each name hang paintings from that country or continent, more than 800 in all. Enormous blooms entirely fill some canvases, while others show landscapes, caterpillars or fruits whole or cut open; the leaves and fruit of the banyan, the sacred lotus and, in a privileged position directly above the front door, Queen Victoria's namesake, the water lily *Victoria regia* (as it was then called), floating upon a Brazilian pool. Even the door frames and lintels are decorated with flowers. Like countless other women who created their own versions of Eden—some as small as a handkerchief— Marianne North seems to have felt that the old *hortus conclusus* needed to be reworked from scratch and on her own terms.

North embraced an acceptably female art form—the portrayal of flowers and plants— and took it as far as she could in her day. And in doing so, she stretched the definition of "femininity" to allow herself a life of freedom, adventure and worldwide friendship. She rode a stagecoach from Salt Lake to the Pacific Coast, "got wet through in the mist" under Niagara Falls and galloped on horseback through an Australian brush fire. In the latter half of the 19th century, she visited every continent except Antarctica, usually alone, and wrote that she "scarcely went out without finding some new wonders to paint, lived a life of the most perfect peace and happiness and got strength every day with my kind friends."

Those words come from the journals edited by her sister, *Recollections of a Happy Life* and *Some Further Recollections of a Happy Life*, which reveal North to be fascinated by life in general and by the natural world in particular. In Jamaica, she wrote that she stayed in a room overlooking "bananas, rose-apples (with their white tassel flowers and pretty pink young shoots and leaves), the gigantic bread-fruit, trumpet-trees (with great white-lined leaves), star-apples (with brown and gold plush lining to their shiny leaves), the mahogany-trees (with their pretty terminal cones), mangoes, custard apples and endless others, besides a few dates and cocoanuts." She was, she said, so overwhelmed by the luxuriant Jamaican plant life that she "was in a state of ecstasy and hardly knew what to paint first."

Just before her gallery opened in 1882, someone wandered in while she was arranging her paintings and asked if they had all been done by one person. "I said simply that I had done them all," wrote North, "on which he seized me by both hands and said, 'You! Then it is lucky for you that you did not live two hundred years ago, or you would have been burnt for a witch.'"

If one generation's witch is another's artist, then we are indeed fortunate that North's *hortus* was created in a relatively tolerant age.

X

"These Are My Conquests"

Privileged women in the flower garden

"Incarceration in the flower garden" is
how Eleanor Perényi, author of *Green Thoughts*,
a wonderful collection of essays related
to horticulture, interprets the modern
relationship between women and plants. In the
chapter "Woman's Place," Perényi points
out that women are most benign, in any
horticultural sense, when they are relegated,
indeed confined, to the task of tending
flowers, "of all plants the least menacing and
the most useless." Other writers, such as
Emily James Putnam, who saw the lady, like the
flower garden, as "protoplasm . . . moulded and
coloured by art like so much wax or plaster,"
agree. Nevertheless, while the trend toward
women spending increasing amounts of energy
in the flower garden is easy to trace, it
is not so clear whether incarceration or free
choice is involved—or a combination of both.

~~

If women have been imprisoned in the flower
garden, it has happened only within the past

few centuries, as documented by many written references to woman's rightful place among the blooms. In 1860, in *The New American Gardener*, Thomas Fessenden wrote, "The cultivation of flowers is an appropriate amusement for young ladies. It teaches neatness, cultivates a correct taste and furnishes the mind with many pleasing ideas." In fact, Fessenden continued, it was because ladies were so like flowers that the association would probably be a beneficial one: "The splendid lustre and variegated hues (which bid defiance to the pencil) of the rose, the lily, the tulip and a thousand others harmonize with the fair, fostering hand that tends them—with the heart susceptible to the noblest impressions—and with spotless innocence."

It has, like so many floral images of women that preceded it, overtones of the Virgin Mary. As such, it presents a distorted and unattainable ideal of earthly womanhood. But the question remains: Have men like Fessenden been responsible for the incarceration of women in the flower garden, as Perényi suggests, or have women themselves freely chosen to work with flowers instead of with other plants or, indeed, rather than not garden at all?

Certainly, some women have urged their fellows in the direction of the blooms. Louisa Johnson wrote in her 1840 *Every Lady Her Own Flower Garden*, "Floriculture ranges itself under the head of female accomplishments in these our days; and we turn with pity from the spirit which will not find in her 'garden of roses' the simplest and purest of pleasures." The Countess von Arnim wished that "I may grow in grace and patience and cheerfulness, just like the happy flowers I so much love." And in her 1810 article, "Horticulture as a Profession for Women," Laura Blanchard Dawson referred to "the peculiar sympathy which exists between womankind and flowers." Obviously, some women prefer flowers to other plants (as do some men), a matter of individual taste. But by Fessenden's day, virtually anyone who called herself a lady was involved, in some way, with flowers; the flower garden was a place where "a lady may display her taste," as Johnson wrote. Was coercion to blame?

For the answer, it may be helpful to look at the wealthy and privileged, those who are "not like you and I," as Ernest Hemingway expressed it. While the poor cannot follow fashion because they have neither the money nor the time to spend on inessentials and those in the middle class feel they need to follow fashion to keep their jobs and their social standing, the rich can, presumably, do pretty much what they like. And wealthy women have, by choice, frequently been outstanding flower gardeners. After World War II, one of England's best known of that elite breed, Vita Sackville-West, "concentrated on flowering plants," writes Victoria Glendenning in *Vita: The Life of V. Sackville-West*. "Growing vegetables was part of the discarded wartime mentality . . . ."

Many of these unordinary women were unordinary flower gardeners, not the kind who buy a few zinnia seeds from the local grocer and prune a tea rose or two every spring. They were, and often are, superb horticulturists, followers of the female botanical tradition that began in the age of Linnaeus. "Nearly every great lady in England takes a personal interest in her gardens and conservatories and knows all about the plants and flowers," wrote Helena Rutherford Ely early in this century, when she also noted that "flower gardening is preeminently a woman's occupation and diversion." Almost 80 years later, in *The Englishwoman's Garden*, in which 36 outstanding English flower gardens are described by their owners, almost half of the gardeners are titled—duchesses, marchionesses, and the like. No mere slaves to fashion—or coercion—are these people. They

Vita Sackville-West's innovativeness
as a flower gardener was foreshadowed by a
childhood photograph.

〜〜

〜〜

demonstrate that, given a choice, women will often choose to garden and, more specifically, to work with ornamental plants. If the beautiful, fleeting, vulnerable aspects of flowers seem less attractive to some readers than the strong, powerful aspects of herbs, the former qualities are historically just as much part of being women as the latter — and who should understand that better than women themselves?

In *The Englishwoman's Garden*, the idea of the flower garden as a place of peace, tranquillity, refuge and inspiration is expressed time and again. From Philippe Rakusen: "I confess I enjoy giving pleasure to others and am delighted when people find the garden restful." From Esther Merton: "I am a very lucky woman who lives for her garden, adores it, warts and all, and enjoys every moment of every hard-working day. What more can you ask of life?" From Sarah, Countess of Haddington: "For me, this garden, a corner of Tyninghame, is a miniature paradise. It is by no means perfect, but it has come to be an oasis of rest and quiet, where visitors can wander at ease and where each winding path can bring a fresh surprise. This is surely something of value in our turbulent world."

Flowers have in them something of luxury and grace, something allied not just to being female but to being privileged. J.B. Whiting wrote in the 1849 *Manual of Flower Gardening for Ladies* that "to watch and tend the delicate seedling through all the stages of its gradual development until it becomes a perfect plant, to mark the unfolding of the tender young leaves and to observe the progressive expansion of the flower-buds into full-blown flowers seems a peculiarly fitting employment for a refined and gentle female." Princess Grace of Monaco wrote of her own interest in flower arranging: "Through working with flowers, we began to discover things about ourselves that had been dormant. We found agility not only with our fingers but with our inner eyes in searching for line, scale and harmony. In bringing out these talents within ourselves, we gained a dimension that enabled us not only to search for harmony in an arrangement but also to discover the importance of carrying it into our lives and our homes."

Such florally involved, upper-class women have been around for at least four centuries — members, in a sense, of a mini-race that survives all other social changes. John Evelyn's 17th-century diaries leave traces of several, such as "my Lady Brook's garden, which was one of the neatest and most celebrated in England"; the estate of Lady Clarendon, where "my lady being so extraordinarily skill'd in ye Flower part and my lord in diligence of planting" that the garden "perfumes the aire"; and the Countess of Bristol's "rare collection of orange-trees, of which she was pleas'd to bestow some upon me." Orange trees were, incidentally, grown as much for their sweetly scented flowers and their ornamental evergreen leaves as for their decorative fruit. In social terms, one might say that the oranges grown in European gardens were more like gardenias than apples.

The Duchess of Beaufort was a renowned gardener of the early 18th century. Of her estate at Badminton in Gloucestershire, Charles Evelyn wrote that "by her Knowledge and Management, she has given the greatest Example of female Horticulture, perhaps, that any Nation can produce. Her Greenhouses and Parterres were fill'd with the utmost Variety, not only of all Sorts of beautiful Flowers and the finest and most valuable Greens and Plants that this Climate affords but also that are to be met with in any other Country whatsoever. And at length she arriv'd to so great a Perfection that she could challenge any foreign Gardens to produce greater Curiosities than her own."

The second Duchess of Portland, Mary Bentinck (close friend of Mary Delany), was similarly disposed. Owner of an envied collection of plants exotic enough to be considered "Curiosities," she supported botanical expeditions, as did other wealthy, horticulturally inclined women, many of whom were royalty. Among the skills the Duchess perfected was the propagation of newly introduced North American magnolias, although she was remembered most for her roses. H.C. Andrews wrote in the *Monograph of the Genus Rosa* in 1805 that the title of the Portland rose was "received in compliment to the late Duchess of Portland, a great admirer of this charming tribe of plants and in whose collection at Bulstrode they were cultivated in great luxuriance."

Although these women were described by observers, they seldom left their own gardening records. Thus, the journals of Lady Mary Coke from the late 18th century offer a valuable insight into the passionate interest one titled woman took in her flowers. Mary frequently recorded the number of hours she spent in her garden, obviously an important place in her life: "At half an hour after [9 a.m.] went out into the garden; came in to write my journal. 'Tis now one O'clock & I am going out again. I worked in the garden from one O'clock til half an hour after three; had but just time to dress before dinner." At various times, she also "set several flowers"; had "twelve dozen of honeysuckles, which, added to those of the last year, will make a very great quantity"; and "planted a hundred perannual flowers that I had this morning from Mr. Lee . . . ." Lady Blandford, she said, "out does us all in flowers; [her garden] looked as gay & smelt as sweet as if it was the middle of summer."

These women do seem to have enjoyed their incarceration. Of course, unless they were exceptionally talented in the arts, they had few ways, other than begetting children, of making a mark upon the world. "These are my conquests," Josephine, wife of Napoleon Bonaparte, is reported to have said of the roses and lilies in her renowned garden showcase at Malmaison near Paris. (In a book Josephine commissioned, however, the author noted in his dedication to her that the plants of Malmaison "gently commemorate the conquests of your illustrious husband.") Napoleon's conquests may have been far more substantial, but Josephine had enough money, time and influence to have her own sort of power—in the garden. Josephine, as Napoleon dubbed Marie-Joseph-Rose de Tascher de la Pagerie, was perhaps the most memorable of all women flower gardeners—although the term "flower collector" may be more appropriate.

Like many tropical expatriates, she had a lifelong yearning for greenery, sweet fragrances and floral colour, qualities often taken for granted in warm countries but missed by those who move to temperate places. She was born of an upper-class Creole mother and a poor father in Martinique and, until she was 14, received the standard modest education of the day, learning how to read, write, dance and embroider (flowers, no doubt). A fortune-teller predicted that little Marie would be unhappily married, widowed and crowned as "more than a queen." After separating from her first husband, she moved to Paris, where she married Napoleon in 1796.

Josephine began to collect flowers as soon as she acquired, in 1799, the 300-acre farm west of Paris that would become her own centre of power, Malmaison. Many of the plants at Malmaison reflected Josephine's longing for the tropics she had left behind: hibiscus, camellia, magnolia, mimosa, geranium and sweet potatoes, some of which survived the winters in a greenhouse. She is reported to have once plucked a branch of jasmine that had been brought from her native Martinique and said, "The seeds were sown and tended by my own hands—they re-

Empress Josephine collected plants as her husband
Napoleon Bonaparte conquered countries.

mind me of my country, my childhood and the ornaments of my adolescence."

But it was her floral eclecticism, almost as strong a passion as her husband's desire to collect countries, that made Malmaison famous. In 1801, Josephine told the agent of the French government in London of her interest in acquiring English trees and shrubs and suggested that the gardener at the *"beau jardin de Kew"* might provide her with some unusual seeds. She also requested seeds of her mother in Martinique. The French botanist Aimé Bonpland, who also exchanged plants with the Kew's Sir Joseph Banks, brought her mimosa, heliotropes, cassias and lobelias from his travels in America. Ambassadors and travellers in Europe, Morocco, Guyana, Mexico, Australia and the Cape of Africa sent her specimens of gladiolus, pelargonium, eucalyptus, hibiscus, the monkey puzzle tree and many more. Like a true *botaniste*, she, in return, sent occasional specimens to her donors.

Napoleon sent her hundreds of different

plants and seeds from Schönbrunn during his campaign of 1809, and he forwarded others later, including seeds of mignonette from his Egyptian campaign. These Josephine placed in pots in her drawing room, helping to establish the flowers—literally "little darlings"—as the sweetly scented favourites of the French elite. She also introduced to France eucalyptus, hibiscus, phlox, cactuses, rhododendrons, double jacinths and rare tulips.

English diarist Bertie Greatheed, a self-styled "Englishman in Paris" of the early 19th century, wrote in his memoirs, "Bonaparte always sleeps with his wife: in her dressing room, there were four or five books on botany: the only ones I saw in the house." Soon, however, there were botany books but no husband; Napoleon annulled his marriage to Josephine in 1809 because of her supposed sterility, not her reputed indiscretions, and married the Archduchess Marie Louise of Austria. Later, Josephine's obituary notice in the *Moniteur* noted: "Extremely unhappy during her husband's reign, she sought refuge from his roughness in the study of Botany." It is said that Josephine conquered Napoleon with a bouquet of violets she gave him after they first met. When Napoleon died, he was wearing a golden locket containing dried violets gathered from her grave.

Almost 200 new species of plants flowered at Malmaison from 1804 until her death in 1814. "You have gathered around you the rarest plants growing on French soil," wrote the botanist Etienne Pierre Ventenat to her Majesty, in the dedication to *Jardin de la Malmaison*, a two-folio work containing scientific descriptions of more than 200 plants. "Some, indeed, which never before had left the deserts of Arabia or the burning sands of Egypt, have been domesticated through your care."

Josephine's horticultural ambitions were unrestrained. She amassed one of the finest collections of dahlias of her time—some were sent to her by the German naturalist Alexander von Humboldt—and attempted to keep a few specimens solely for her enjoyment; but when some tubers were stolen, she banished the flower from the royal gardens. She would spend as much as 3,000 francs on a single rare bulb and constantly expanded the area devoted to cultivation, hiring a succession of expert gardeners.

Josephine is most closely associated, however, with roses, especially the white 'Souvenir de Malmaison,' even though it was developed in 1840, after her death. Before her time, roses had not been particularly popular as decorative flowers in France, less so than tulips, hyacinths and carnations. They were considered more useful than ornamental and were valued mostly for their scent, which gave fragrance to rose water, a great deal of which was manufactured in the French town of Provins. (Napoleon was one of a long list of important people, including Joan of Arc and Louis XIV, who received gifts of rose water in Provins.) The flower used there was the apothecary rose, or *rose de Provins*, *Rosa gallica officinalis*. But Josephine would gather many more roses. The tea-scented, ever-blooming China roses had begun to arrive in Europe in 1810 and were quickly brought to Malmaison. Her rose garden eventually displayed about 250 different kinds.

Her roses are most beautifully remembered in *Les Roses*, a collection of paintings by Pierre-Joseph Redouté, the "Raphael of Flowers," who also helped with the interior decoration of Malmaison, decorated the principal greenhouse and illustrated eight volumes of *Liliaceae*. Josephine, who encouraged and patronized Redouté, spent almost 25,000 francs to buy many of his original drawings. She died before he completed his most famous work, *Les Roses*, published between 1817 and 1824 in 30 parts, each consisting of six plates. Josephine also contributed almost 20,000 francs to the 1813 *Description des plantes rares cultiveés à Malmaison* by Aimé Bonpland, which included 64 colour plates by Redouté. As a patron of the arts, Josephine, like many other wealthy women, supported gardening in the background by financing the work of botanists, botanical authors and artists.

If Josephine was the first of the famous women flower gardeners, two others are Ellen Willmott and Vita Sackville-West, both English. Willmott belonged to the late 19th century and Sackville-West to the early 20th.

Ellen Willmott was a proud, ostentatious person of independent means and no formal scientific training, who was described by Gertrude Jekyll, a great gardener herself, as "the greatest of living women-gardeners." Willmott's life was one of constant, extravagant attention to the plants she loved, especially roses. Besides her most famous garden at Warley Place in Essex, she had gardens in France and Italy, and she spent her entire fortune on the three. In the heyday of Warley Place, an army of more than 100 gardeners clad in navy aprons, knitted green silk ties and straw boaters cared for 100,000 different kinds of plants. A mere 13 or so gardeners worked at Treserve in France, yet one plant order for Treserve fills four pages.

"She must at one time or another have grown virtually every species of flowering plant that can be grown in the temperate zone," writes Perényi in *Green Thoughts*. "But her passion was roses, and in these, she outdid even the Empress Josephine, with whom it is more than probable she identified herself." And as Josephine was associated with *Les Roses* by Redouté, so Willmott is best known for *The Genus Rosa*, a two-volume opus published between 1910 and 1914, with illustrations of the roses in her own garden.

Like Josephine, Willmott was a flower aficionado who mixed with the cream of society—Princess Victoria often visited Warley Place, and Edward, Prince of Wales, broke one of the instruments in her music room. She was also a plant collector; many of her specimens were being cultivated for the first time. She was known as an extremely careful and able gardener who could save prized exotic species that might otherwise falter.

Willmott owned a microscope and a telescope, joined the Royal Horticultural Society (RHS) in 1894 and was one of the first woman Fellows of the Linnaean Society. More scientifically inclined than Josephine, she was able to combine her financial resources with her botanical skills in a manner that made her famous in a more scholarly way. "I have a man collecting Pelargoniums for me out on the Cape," she wrote in a 1908 letter; and in 1909, "I have had a very beautiful series of *Primula viscosa* hybrids. I have been working at them 10 years crossing and re-crossing them with every Primrose I could get in flower at the same time. I gave sets of some 60 different ones to Kew, Edinburgh and Dublin . . . ." The Arnold Arboretum of Harvard University sent her many plants, and she helped fund the collecting expeditions of the Arnold's E.H. "Chinese" Wilson.

She was most passionately involved in working with irises, roses and daffodils. Every year from 1904 until 1907, she won the Gold Medal of the RHS for various groups of fine and rare daffodils, and from 1900 until 1906, she took many RHS Awards of Merit for her own breeds of daffodils, including 'Eleanor Berkeley' (1900), 'Dorothy Wemyss' (1901), 'Incognita' (1902) and 'Moonstone' (1903). She won the RHS Victoria Medal of Honour in 1897, as did Gertrude Jekyll.

A woman described by her biographer, Audrey le Lievre, as "absolutely infuriating and quite impossible to deal with," Willmott is nevertheless remembered in the names of many gentle, unopinionated plants: *Iris willmottiana alba*, *Tulipa willmottiae*, *Ceratostigma*

Sissinghurst is the most frequently visited garden in England.

~~

willmottianum and a host of cultivars such as a pink verbena and a phlox, both named 'Ellen Willmott.' Among those dubbed 'Miss Willmott' are a campanula, a dahlia, a delphinium, a dianthus, an iris, a narcissus, a nerine, a parahebe, a phlox and a scabiosa. E.H. Wilson wrote to tell her how pleased he was that she would allow her name to be given to the Chinese lily (*Lilium willmottiae*). And *Eryngium giganteum* earned the sobriquet

"Miss Willmott's ghost" from her habit of spreading its seed in the gardens she visited. Unfortunately, her garden itself now deserves that name. As her fortunes dwindled, Willmott watched Warley Place fall victim to weeds and disrepair.

Sissinghurst, however, the garden of Vita Sackville-West, survives in splendour and is now England's most visited garden. Sackville-West was born in 1892, the only daughter of Lionel and Victoria Sackville-West, and lived until her marriage at the ancestral Sackville palace, Knole, which "has been a garden for four hundred years," she wrote. She loved Knole, which she described as resembling "a mediaeval village" with 50 servants, but could not inherit it because of her sex. After her marriage to Harold Nicolson, the couple moved "downscale" to Long Barn in Kent, where they began to acquire a taste for gardening. Then they bought the property next door—Sissinghurst Castle—seven acres of weedy wilderness surrounding a complex of ruins. Sackville-West wrote, "The amount of old bedsteads, ploughshares, old cabbage-stalks, old broken-down earth closets, old matted wire and mountains of sardine tins, all muddled up in a tangle of bindweed, nettles and ground elder, should have sufficed to daunt anybody.

"Yet the place, when I first saw it on a spring day in 1930, caught instantly at my heart and my imagination. I saw what might be made of it. It was Sleeping Beauty's Garden: but a garden crying out for rescue. It was easy to foresee, even then, what struggle we should have to redeem it." Here, Sackville-West had a place to exercise the horticultural skills she had first practised at Long Barn. Between 1930 and 1932, the couple—she the plantswoman, he the designer—made a complete plan of the garden, which has remained much the same to this day. Enclosed on two sides by what remained of an old moat, the garden was virtually finished by 1939 and included, most impressively, areas devoted to only one or a few colours of flowers—one a garden with a purple theme and another mostly yellow and orange. Her tastes were sometimes expensive, always exacting. Just before the war, she told her husband, "Let us plant and be merry, for next autumn we may all be ruined." She estimated that in 1939, she had bought at least 11,000 Dutch bulbs. Two to four gardeners were always required to keep the place looking its best.

Only the famous white garden was still to be created. Sackville-West wrote in the *Observer*, "For my own part, I am trying to make a grey, green and white garden. This is an experiment which I ardently hope may be successful, though I doubt it. One's best ideas seldom play up in practice to one's expectations, especially in gardening, where everything looks so well on paper and in the catalogues but fails so lamentably in fulfilment after you have tucked your plants into the soil. Still, one hopes.

"I love colour and rejoice in it, but white is lovely to me forever. The ice-green shades that it can take on in certain lights, by twilight or by moonlight, perhaps by moonlight especially, make a dream of the garden, an unreal vision, yet one knows that it isn't unreal at all because one has planted it all for effect."

After the white garden was complete, she wrote of it: "There is an under-planting of various artemisias, including the old aromatic Southernwood; the silvery *Cineraria maritima*; the grey santolina, or Cotton Lavender; and the creeping *Achillea ageratifolia*. Dozens of the white Regale lily (grown from seed) come up through these. There are white delphiniums of the Pacific strain; white eremurus; white foxgloves in a shady place on the north side of a wall; the foam of gypsophila; the white shrubby *Hydrangea grandiflora*; white cistus; white tree peonies; *Buddleia nivea*; white campanulas; and the white form of *Platycodon mariessii*, the Chinese bell-flower."

Like Josephine and Ellen Willmott, Sackville-West was a flower lover, but she was less eclectic than the others. Indeed, she had the common touch, and although her standing in the horticultural world helped bring her many relatively new species, which she sometimes described to readers of her weekly garden articles in the *Observer*—*Jasminum polyanthum*, for instance, "a fairly recent introduction from China"—she said, "As a rule, I try to be practical, recommending only such plants as can be grown with some hope of success by the amateur gardener."

Her *Observer* column, "In Your Garden," which appeared from 1947 until 1961, a year before her death, was so popular—because she was not only a knowledgeable gardener but also a fine writer—that it was anthologized four times in her lifetime and again after her death. She preferred to write poetry, however, and was a close friend of members of the Bloomsbury group, especially Virginia Woolf, and won the Heinemann prize for "The Garden," a long, poetic expression not only of her sensitive, somewhat melancholy temperament but also of her identification with her garden:

The weeds in my garden remain as green,
And I cannot tell if I bring you pleasure,
But the one little patch I have cleared for you
That one small patch of my soul is clean.

Sissinghurst today is an extraordinary place, where a geometric order confines a delicate scheme of colour, shape and succession of bloom; clearly, the garden is the harmonious result of the work of two minds. If Sackville-West, like the other privileged women gardeners, had truly been incarcerated with her flowers, she would no doubt have agreed with Dylan Thomas, who "sang in my chains like the sea."

XI

"A Partnership With Nature"

Women and the business of horticulture

When pleasure becomes business,
women often become uncomfortable. There are
many reasons for this. Some are external—
women in business are often seen as less
competent than men and are excluded
from male networks—and some originate in
women themselves, who are justifiably wary of
competition and exploitation. When
plants are involved in profit, however, business
seems more benign, more pleasant and
more acceptable; its rough edges are rounded
like the curves of a petal. The story
of women in business, especially its early
chapters, has an interesting affiliation with the
overall story of women and plants.

～

Plant-oriented businesses of various sorts
have long kept at least a few women in a little
cash: selling herbs and medicines, pulling
weeds, making floral laces, embroidering.
In fact, women have been so closely involved
with plants that it has been natural

The silent partnership between women and plants can be profitable.

～

to use the relationship to pecuniary advantage. Turning a very modest profit became possible for countless rural women who advertised garden seeds and plants in magazines and American market bulletins in the last century and the early decades of this one. In the market bulletins, which consisted entirely of classified advertisements, farmers sold grains, livestock and farm wares, while women offered flower and herb seeds, usually for 10 or 15 cents, sometimes for the price of a stamp.

Many a woman would sell "native plants of her neighbourhood," according to Louise Beebe Wilder, who named several women as reputable sources of wildflower seeds. Laura Blanchard Dawson, in her 1910 lecture "Horticulture as a Profession for Women," described another instance of a woman-plant relationship that led naturally to moneymaking: a woman with a flower garden "that attracted so much notice that those walking by were accustomed to stop and admire it. To these visitors, she often presented bunches of flowers, and soon they came to her to buy

them, although at first, she had not thought of selling them." In 1909, she earned $270 and, a year later, had built a small greenhouse to further her enterprise.

In Victorian England, some of the most visible and numerous self-employed plantswomen, if so grand a phrase can be used to describe so humble an enterprise, were flower girls, fictionalized as Eliza Doolittle in George Bernard Shaw's *Pygmalion* and described factually in 1889 in *Toilers in London; or Inquiries Concerning Female Labour in the Metropolis* as "such a familiar sight to Londoners that few of us realize what the streets of the metropolis would miss if she were banished." At least 2,000 of these women existed at the time, including the poorest of the lot: old women selling watercress. Flower girls sold simple cottage-garden specimens in season: snowdrops, violets and crocuses in spring; daisies, roses, carnations, geraniums and mignonettes in summer; and "foreign flowers and ferns from the Continent" when local supplies dwindled. Their trade appeared to be a cheery one, but in a time when social services were desperately lacking, these women were barely able to keep their heads—and those of their children—above the murky street waters. Those who sold by day earned about 10 shillings a week—half a pound, or roughly $2. In winter, their hardest time, they sold oranges and matches and simply tried to survive.

At the same time, flower shops were proving attractive and more profitable propositions for well-bred ladies who desired or needed an income or who simply wanted an escape from the home. Eliza Doolittle expressed a desire "to be a lady in a flower shop 'stead of sellin' at the corner of Tottenham Court Road." As late as 1986, with virtually all professions accessible to women, Canadian statistics showed that still, more than twice as many women as men were involved in the florist and lawn-and-garden industries.

～

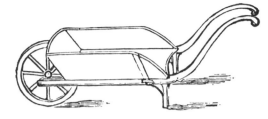

Special tools for women include this "ladies' wheelbarrow."

～

As the 20th century approached, a variety of paying opportunities became available to women in landscape design, flower-shop ownership and floral design, teaching, writing, gardening professionally, illustrating, selling seeds, plant breeding and the like. More than just a few women could now make a decent living instead of the subsistence income of the lace makers and flower girls or the pin money the farm women earned through their classified ads. The number of college-educated women rose rapidly, redefining their professional opportunities. By 1916, according to Myrtle Shepherd Francis, women who entered the horticultural professions "must remember that they are entering into a partnership with Nature, that experiments are costly. . . . If they put capital and good business judgement into it, they will reap the rewards that accrue from them."

If rural housewives and Victorian flower girls represent one end of the scale of self-employed plantswomen, the other end can best be represented by Gertrude Jekyll, whose artistic sensibility and horticultural knowledge have made a lasting impression on Western landscape design. When flower girls were selling their wares in Covent Garden and formal bedding styles predominated in gardens, Jekyll, a woman of independent means, proposed natural-looking arrangements of plants, mostly perennials, chosen according to colour, shape, height and habit alone. She

also did some plant breeding, introduced some of her own selections and wrote a series of books that have become classics of the genre. Jekyll's type of woman—innovative, talented and hardworking—had certainly been seen before, but she was very much a modern woman in her unequivocal maintenance of a position at the forefront of a male-dominated profession.

Born in England in 1843, Jekyll seemed set on the course of her career almost from birth. She wrote that, as a child, "I was very much alone and nearly always in my playtime found my own amusements in garden and shrubbery." She came to know plants "intimately by sight and handling, and keenly inquisitive smelling," and when she was 4, she "had already made friends with the daisies in the Berkeley Square Garden and with the dandelions in the Green Park . . . one Andromeda I used almost to worship; it was a bush, with the flowers on a level with my head. I did not know its name then, but to myself, I used to call it the Snowdrop-tree."

Jekyll studied art in her late teens and pursued an artistic career in her 20s and 30s. When her eyesight began to fail, the garden provided a palette for her aesthetic and experimental talents, as described in chapter nine. By the 1880s, she had already accepted some small landscape-design commissions. She might not have progressed much beyond that stage had it not been for a fortuitous meeting with the architect Edwin Lutyens in 1889, when he was just 20 and she 45. Lutyens had similar design and aesthetic priorities, and the two established a business partnership that launched Lutyens' career and dissolved Jekyll's self-imposed amateur status. Together, they produced more than a hundred house-and-garden marriages that are still celebrated throughout England. Working alone or with an architect, usually Lutyens, Jekyll eventually completed almost 350 design commissions.

～

Jane Loudon's Gardening for Ladies *includes an illustration of a "ladies' gauntlet invented by Miss Perry."*

～

Her business interests did not stop there, however. She also sold plants, some of which were her own developments, such as 'Munstead' primroses and the enduringly popular lavender of the same name. And she wrote books, for which she had a flair. "If my books have any merit," she said not long before she died in 1932, "it is because I have never written a word that was not a record of work actually done and because I have had some early training in the fine arts." Jekyll published more than a dozen, including *Home and Garden, Gardens for Small Country Houses* and *Flower Decoration in the House. Wood and Garden* alone went through six printings in its first year of publication, 1899. While Jekyll was fortunate enough to have an independent income, she could undoubtedly have supported herself had she needed to. Designer, author, plant breeder and artist, she was an amazingly talented and successful person. Unfortunately, few of her gardens survive.

People seem unable to talk about women for more than a few sentences without including a physical description, and this was certainly the case with the shy, likable and intelligent but very plain Jekyll. Her appearance is worth consideration here too, only because it is an indication of how seriously she took her work. Jekyll's clothing did little to flatter her but a great deal to help her in the garden—her priorities were obvious. Lutyens' wife wrote that Jekyll "dresses rather like a man," and the architect himself reported that although the first time he met her, she was dressed in her "Go-to-Meeting Frock," the second time, her dress showed her ankles, a faux pas of the day, and had a pocket "full of horticultural impedimenta." Her heavy leather boots were distinctive enough to be commemorated in a painting, now at Britain's National Portrait Gallery, by Sir William Nicholson, who said, "I would rather paint Gertrude Jekyll's boots than the most beautiful woman alive." The painting is, in one sense, a portrait of the spirit of Jekyll herself, and in a larger sense, it represents the spirit of any woman who works close to the earth in a serious way.

The move toward sensible clothing for garden work—and thus toward a businesslike attitude—had an early proponent in Louisa Johnson, who said that a pair of "Indian rubber shoes, or the wooden high-heeled shoes called 'sabots' by the French" was "indispensable" for women gardeners. Twenty years later, in 1865, Jane Loudon, almost as successful a writer as Jekyll, urged her readers to "be provided with clogs" as well as "a pair of stiff thick leathern gloves, or gauntlets." By 1885, Sophia Orne Johnson, who had the unfortunate pen name of Daisy Everbright, advocated that for her American readership, "a woolen bathing dress makes an excellent garden costume—for skirts are always in the way." (A contemporary wrote, "What would some of our small-waisted city belles, so tightly corsetted, so unnaturally attired, so enfeebled by irrational modes of dress that

*Schools for professional women gardeners filled
employment gaps when men went to war.*

a few minutes' brisk walk or the climbing of a flight of stairs throws them into palpitations, think of their sturdy sisters in the far West who plough, sow, pitch, cart . . . ?" And wear woollen bathing dresses in the garden, one might wonder.)

The torch was picked up by Viscountess Frances Wolseley, who started a school for professional women gardeners in Sussex in 1904. The students were expected to read all of Jekyll's books—and to dress sensibly. Wolseley's *Gardening for Women* includes a chapter devoted to "Dress for Lady Gardeners," in which she, like Loudon, recommended "thick leather gloves" and, like Jekyll,

believed that "boots are better than shoes, but they must be good." While Wolseley did not endorse woollen bathing dresses for the students, she concurred that "wool should be worn next to the skin, both in winter and summer. . . . A plain fitting flannel belt to cover the waist and abdomen is advisable. This is worn next to the skin, whether the usual underwear be merino or not. Knickerbockers, and not petticoats, should be worn. For winter wear, ready-made blue or black stockinette ones are best. Cheap ready-made cotton ones are useful for summer; or they can be obtained in khaki drill, should that material be preferred." Her students, she

Beth Chatto's company "brings out the whole meaning of the word 'nursery.' "

~

wrote, required "business habits and powers of organization and forethought . . . each year . . . removes us further from Jane Austen's heroines, that type of helpless charm." Gertrude Jekyll would have agreed.

Equipped with sensible woollens and organized habits of thought, professional gardeners, who would carry on in increasing multitudes the singular example set by Jekyll, were turned out by horticultural schools for women in England, Germany and Denmark early in the 20th century. This was part of a slow process of acceptance: although women were admitted to the course at the Royal Horticultural School in Germany, Laura Blanchard Dawson noted in 1910 that they were not allowed to take the state examinations. Meanwhile, the course at the gardens at Kew was out of bounds, because a woman "of culture and refinement" could not be expected

to "push a barrow and spade and fork by the side of a man for 11 hours a day."

The establishment of horticulture courses strictly for women was an important step, especially during World War I, when, wrote Frances Wolseley, "small incomes will be so reduced that women who formerly had not to earn a living will now have to do so," and many paid positions were newly vacated by men. "Until recently, many looked down upon the profession of gardencraft, for they imagined it to be a narrow life, restricted as regards its intellectual possibilities; others considered that women were unsuited to it." Now, however, gardeners of any shape or size were desperately required. Wolseley lamented that if only "those many hundred owners of large gardens . . . writing pitiful letters to Horticultural Colleges" had supported women gardeners in the past, "their wants could now be readily supplied."

In the United States, the Pennsylvania School of Horticulture for Women at Ambler, established in 1911 and described as "the first of its kind in America," followed closely along the lines of the European schools. A newspaper published at the school observed that "many interesting opportunities have opened up for women who have been trained for horticultural work, and the field seems to be a constantly widening one." Each student had her own flower garden and vegetable plot and her own section of the rose garden, where she was responsible for cultivation, spraying and pruning and keeping notes on the progress of the plants.

The June 1926 issue of *Home Acres*, the Women's National Farm and Garden Association magazine, features a retrospective about the school's beginning. The magazine is a fascinating document, overflowing with the enthusiasm that accompanied so many women's professional adventures in the 1920s but faded in the following decades (as Betty Friedan noted in *The Feminine Mys-*

tique). The magazine includes an article by Clara M. Boltz entitled "Native Plants for Our Gardens"; an advertisement for Bass true moccasins "for the outdoor woman who needs durable, strong, comfortable footwear"; and a photograph of "Mrs. Theodore Roosevelt Jr., an ardent garden fan, in her tulip garden at Oyster Bay." In the same issue, the American Landscape School in Newark, New York, advertises: "Become a landscape architect. Dignified, exclusive profession not overrun with competitors." Among the guest speakers at the opening of the school were Martha Gibbons Lear, talking about "Twenty-Four Years Experience of Nursery Work"; Miss M.V. Landmann on "Outdoor Work for Delinquent Girls"; and Mrs. Max Farrand, speaking on "Landscape Gardening for Women."

Farrand was an outstanding landscape architect whose attempts to become known professionally as "Beatrix Farrand without any qualifying Mr. or Mrs. or Miss, as I regard Beatrix Farrand as a sort of trade name," were consistently thwarted (even in a women's magazine). She was, however, the only woman among the 11 founders of the American Association of Landscape Architects in 1899 when she was just 27, and she eventually completed scores of demanding and prestigious contracts, such as those for university grounds, at a time when, she wrote, "the work of women in the profession consists almost entirely of what may be called the domestic branch. By this is meant the laying out and management of private places as opposed to public parks or land development or town planning."

Beatrix Farrand helped to bring Jekyll's landscaping style to America. Farrand managed to visit Munstead Wood in 1895 when she was 23 and was so impressed that all of Jekyll's books later found a home in her library of more than 2,700 volumes on horticulture and related subjects. Like Jekyll, Far-

Felicitas Svejda believes that women plant breeders will become more common.

rand thought that landscaping combined all arts: "With this grand art of mine, I do not envy the greatest painter or sculptor or poet that lived." She began to accept her own commissions a year later. Farrand, who described herself as a "landscape gardener" rather than the more prestigious "landscape architect," had three female assistants as well as an office staff and, by the 1920s, was earning the then handsome sum of $100 a day. Her greatest achievement, in her own opinion, was the garden at Dumbarton Oaks in Washington, D.C., begun in 1921 and completed about 20 years later. There, she and her client Mildred Bliss transformed what had been a farm into an exceptional acreage of varying mood and design.

It was a time of professional encouragement, and *Home Acres* noted that in 1914, the Women's National Farm and Garden Association (WNFGA) was established at Ambler on the model of the English Women's Farm and Garden Association "to create for all women a clearinghouse of information in farming and gardening" and "to develop opportunities for the trained woman in farming and gardening." Its first president was Louisa (Mrs. Francis) King, another woman who earned her living from plants and one whose enthusiasm was perfectly suited to the enterprising spirit of the time. Well known then as a lecturer and author of gardening articles and books, including *The Well-Considered Garden*, *The Little Garden* and *Chronicles of the Garden*, King did in the United States what her friend Jekyll had done in England: communicated her ideas of colour and design in a manner that could be understood easily by the amateur. She was a tireless promoter of women's gardening and was one of 24 women, including another popular author, Helena Rutherford Ely, who assembled in Philadelphia to form the Garden Club of America in 1913.

The early "female botanical societies" of the 19th century and later associations were important to the advancement of women in horticulture because, as the WNFGA stated, they created "a clearinghouse of information" that enhanced mutual support and increased the opportunities available to women. For example, Mrs. H.W. Wolcott, an early member of the WNFGA and a skilled horticulturist, established a very successful business in Jackson, Michigan, because of encouragement from Louisa King. King wrote in the WNFGA newsletter that when Wolcott asked if she could succeed in the business of selling rare rock-garden plants, "I replied that I knew such a plan would be successful, that we were then on the verge of a great awakening of garden interest and whoever could see this far enough in advance and plan accordingly would have a wonderful chance to create a good business in such things."

About 15 years later, in 1926, King visited Wolcott Nurseries, which had become a thriving business with a dozen people employed in shipping alpine plants and primroses all over the country. King wrote, "It

The bookplate of Isabella Preston indicates a plant lover.

may be that, as in the case of Mrs. Wolcott, women are more sensitive to the possible needs of gardeners than men — most men — seem to be. Therefore, with her very important position now in nursery work, her fine and unusual catalogue, she may be said not only to have arrived but to be an example and an encouragement to all women who may be considering some such work."

Similar inspiration arose from the example set by Theodosia Burr Shepherd, born in 1845, also an early member of the WNFGA and one of a long line of female amateur plant breeders. Her California business began in a very modest way in 1881, when, as a devoted but penniless hobby gardener married to a man whose investments were foundering, she traded plant material native to the state for items advertised in the exchange column of a children's magazine.

Shepherd's seeds and bulbs were so popular that she began to grow her own, some of which she offered to an eastern commercial seed house. The owner, Peter Henderson, advised her that "California, before 50 years have passed, will be the greatest seed- and bulb-growing country in the world. I advise you, if possible, to get into the business at once." (By 1978, Ventura County's agricultural income had reached $460 million, and close to 9,000 licensed flower growers and nursery people existed statewide.) Shepherd and her husband bought two acres of California land, and she began to grow bulbs and seeds to sell.

In a biography of Shepherd, her eldest daughter, Myrtle Shepherd Francis, wrote: "Thus Theodosia Burr Shepherd entered the field of horticulture, a delicate woman without previous knowledge, little children clinging to her skirts and poverty knocking at the door. Her only assets were an overwhelming love for plants, boundless enthusiasm and courage and abiding confidence in herself." Each season, Theodosia Shepherd's orders outstripped her supplies. She paid her children and their friends five cents for every tin mug they filled with smilax seeds, received $10 a pound for the seeds and made $75 for every thousand large calla bulbs she sent to her eastern contacts. Along the way, she was sent a sample of cosmos seeds by a Mexican friend, who wrote that the plant was "*muy grande*" but the flower "*chiquita.*" By the time Shepherd introduced North American gardeners to cosmos, the flower, too, was *grande*.

Hardworking and gifted with an ability to notice improved plants within a field of average ones, Shepherd also selected and multiplied a particularly large-flowered strain of California poppy, 'Golden West.' She became a specialist in begonias and was the first person to popularize the petunia by introducing the 'California Giants,' the most outstanding development of the species in half a century. She published her first seed and plant catalogue in 1889—"Theodosia B. Shepherd Co., Ventura-by-the-Sea, California"—only eight

Preston wrote bulletins characterized by "clear, unadorned, workmanlike prose."

years after the birth of her business in the barter columns.

Encouraged by her own success, Shepherd advised as many women as possible to enter the business of raising bulbs and seeds. "Above all else," wrote her daughter, "was her desire to see many women emancipated from the drudgery of housework and engaged in raising flower seeds, growing plants or entering the cut-flower business." Theodosia spoke to local women's clubs and involved her three daughters in the business, hoping to establish the Women's Flower Seed Company. But some of her grand plans were never realized. She reinvested in her business to such an extent that although she made a very good income, $1,000 a year in the 1880s, she was never far out of debt. And by the time she died in 1906, the entire California seed business had become extremely competitive and eastern firms, backed by considerable resources, were establishing their own acreages in the state.

Another Western story is that of Florence Bellis. Bellis moved to Gresham, Oregon, in the 1930s when, without a background in horticulture and with little more than a wood stove, two paraffin lamps, orange-crate furniture, two pianos and $5 for seeds from England, she set about establishing a nursery business. In "a ghastly dung-coloured cow barn," she worked with primroses — Gertrude Jekyll's 'Munstead' strains of yellows and whites among them — selecting the best seedlings and pollinating them by hand, something that had never been done before with primroses.

In 1939, she published her first list of what she called 'Barnhaven' strains. By 1944, she had won fame throughout the United States and Europe, and her catalogue included the first true blue primroses, the 'Barnhaven Marine Blues.' She would develop many more cultivars, including true pinks and, by a process of elaborate backcrossing, doubles. Always resistant to commercial pressures, she eventually donated her life's work to England, "whence it sprang and where it belongs." Soon after publishing a book about her gentle conservationist philosophy, *Gardening and Beyond*, Florence Bellis died in Oregon in 1988. Although I never met her, we exchanged letters that revealed her to be a woman who truly loved her work close to the earth. "For me," she wrote, "this work has been the very subsoil of happiness."

Today, Beth Chatto of Essex, England, continues the tradition of the self-educated, self-employed seedswoman. Her company, Unusual Plants, is respected worldwide, while her flower arrangements and her gardens, which are open to the public, have earned her fame in her own country. Chatto's philosophy — "I select plants that are by nature adapted to the kind of environment in which they will grow; ignoring a plant's natural environment leads to failure in performance as well as design" — grew naturally out of her own love of gardening, plant propagation and flower arranging, combined with her husband's interest in the natural association of plant communities. When his health began to suffer in the late 1960s, Chatto's hobby became, of necessity, a business. Her four-acre garden was now a place to grow, multiply and demonstrate the plants that would be sold at her nursery. "I think of my garden as a living catalogue," she says.

Chatto now employs a staff of about 14 and says she does not want her business to expand much — "double staff means double problems." When I talked with her in 1985, she had just returned from lecturing at the International Plant Propagation Society, some of whose members sell "about a million different plants. We sell only 1,500. We are more like a jeweller's shop, like a craft shop, so we bring out the whole meaning of the word 'nursery.' It's more difficult and more rewarding. Some of our plants take seven or eight years to grow, and for most nurseries, the profit margin would be too low — they wouldn't do it. Many I take care of myself. I look upon it as my future, the raising of rare plants and encouraging others to grow them."

Chatto, like Jekyll, Wolseley, King and Bellis, has published several books: *The Dry Garden*, *The Damp Garden*, *Beth Chatto's Garden Notebook* and *Plant Portraits*, an expanded version of her weekly column for the *Telegraph Sunday Magazine*. Communicating their gardening experiences has been a labour of love for these and many other women, especially in the 20th century, but more to the point of this chapter, it has also been a good way to make money and is a natural adjunct to the expository side of horticulture, just as teaching has often combined harmoniously with authorship.

Teaching was, along with nursing, one of the few respectable jobs for women in the 19th century and most of the 20th. Laura Blanchard Dawson said in 1910 that for women who have studied gardening, "the best-paid positions are those of horticultural

*Maud Grieve published the first herbal written in
English since the 17th century.*

teachers at the sanatoriums where horticultural work is part of the cure." Audrey Harkness O'Connor, author of *Herb Gardening* and designer of the Robuson herb garden at Cornell University, informed me that in 1935 when she graduated from Cornell, where she studied horticulture, "women who were successful in finding jobs after graduation were prepared to teach or trained as dietitians or home demonstration agents. Some women in my class married, had children and turned to careers later. A few went on to graduate or professional schools. If you were destitute, some interesting alternatives became possible through writers' and artists' federally funded projects. I worked for a year as a bookkeeper (six days a week, on call on Sundays, all for $7 a week). Through those years, I kept in touch with horticulture by doing freelance and ghost writing."

Among the most outstanding of scores of horticulturally inclined teacher-authors was Almira Hart Lincoln, who, as vice principal of her sister's Troy Female Seminary in New York, endeavoured to put more science into women's curricula. After she was widowed in the 1820s, she began to write textbooks such as *Familiar Lectures on Botany*, first published in 1829, illustrated by Thirza Lee, "teacher of drawing at the seminary," and destined to appear in at least 17 editions. The book helped make her a wealthy woman. More than a century later, Dorothy Hewer, who had a degree in science, started her own school, a herb farm in Kent, England, where she enrolled about a dozen pupils at a time. She published *Practical Herb Growing* (1941), which became the most popular English book on the subject and the first book written entirely about herbs for amateurs. Her successor at the school, Margaret Brownlow, published *Herbs and the Scented Garden* in 1957; it is still a valued reference book.

The best-known female authors are those who have written popular books, but many other women made a living that included publishing technical bulletins and books. Isabella Preston, for instance, was author of *Lilies for Every Garden* as well as several government bulletins and magazine articles. Her work, according to her biographer, Edwinna von Baeyer, was "characterized by clear, unadorned, workmanlike prose. No rhetorical flourishes or fancy metaphors cluttered the information she was so happy to impart."

But no example is as impressive as that of Maud Grieve, who was hired by the British government to organize the collection of information about "vegetable drugs" in 1914, when the war caused a shortage of imported herbs for medicine. Grieve prepared a series of leaflets to educate herbal growers and collectors, chiefly women and children, and eventually gathered the leaflets together into the two-volume *A Modern Herbal*, the first herbal written in English since John Parkinson's 1629 *Paradisi in sole* and still a valuable reference. Grieve also gave courses in growing and preparing herbs for the chemists' market and, in 1918, was the founder and first president of the British Guild of Herb Growers. To honour its first anniversary, she and Eleanor Rohde designed a herb garden for the Chelsea flower show, its first such display. Rohde managed a commercial nursery that was an extension of her own herb garden in England and wrote a series of classic books about herbs and garden history.

The government departments of horticulture employed many women, who generally entered at the level of the lowest-paying technical positions with titles such as "scientific assistant" and, if they were good, gradually worked their way upward over a series of obstacles. In 1863, a list of 28 employees in one branch of the United States Department of Agriculture (USDA) indicated that none were women, although Gladys Baker wrote, "It is probable that there were around 20 women in one of the back rooms packaging seed for distribution." Flora Patterson, eventually a noted mycologist for the USDA's Bureau of Plant Industry, was hired in 1895 only because a suitable man could not be found for the position. Even by 1973, when women constituted 22 percent of graduate students in horticulture in 43 Land Grant Institutions in the United States, they held just over 1 percent of USDA positions. Dr. Felicitas Svejda of Agriculture Canada says there are not many woman plant breeders "but there will be many more."

The struggle to find employment has been overcome by a few women like Shepherd, Bellis and Chatto, who have created their own businesses. In my job as garden editor of *Harrowsmith* magazine in Canada, I receive the catalogues of more than 100 seed companies and nurseries every year. The few run by women are conspicuous in their personal approach. Magda Van Gelder, who runs Happy Herbs in Ontario, sells the seeds of plants gathered on her own organic farm. Renée Shepherd began her California business, Shepherd's Garden Seeds, to bring to American gardeners the vegetable varieties preferred by Europeans, "who traditionally place high value on freshly prepared cuisine."

Jan Blüm of Seeds Blüm in Idaho runs an impressive seed network. She sells about 1,000 different open-pollinated vegetables, many of whose seeds are grown by home gardeners, and writes, "Doing this business has brought us in touch with some pretty wonderful people and has rekindled our hope that we, as common folk working together, can make some positive changes."

The profit in woman's partnership with plants has not been in terms of money so much as pleasure.

XII

"The Liberation of Nature"

A new look at the earth goddess

"I know I am made from this earth, as my
mother's hands were made from this earth, as
her dreams came from this earth, and all that
I know, I know in this earth . . . all that I know
speaks to me through this earth, and I
long to tell you, you who are earth too, and
listen as we speak to each other
of what we know: the light is in us."
—*Susan Griffin, 1978*

~

As I worked on this book, my intention had
always been that the final chapter would
deal with women and plants in the present day,
the end of the 20th century. But as
I researched the past, I began to anticipate a
blank chapter twelve. Until recently,
plants could be related to the status of women,
whether they were healers, cooks,
midwives, witches, "flowers of the church,"
embroiderers, botanists, writers or
even Nobel-prize winners. Plants had helped
women reach prominence in the arts and

sciences and business and had been, indeed, their silent partners in most areas of life. That is less true today, in a technical, urban age of increasing sexual equality, when there is no real need for women of the developed countries to be tied to either kitchen or garden. Floral names are out of fashion, as is botany. Three percent of Americans now grow the food for the remainder; the average family eats in a restaurant at least once a week. Medicine is almost entirely the province of doctors and pharmacists. And those things, many women would say, are very good – and liberating. Being an earth goddess had its shortcomings. In a Ms. magazine reader survey in 1990, gardening ranked third among subjects *not* wanted within its covers.

Indeed, in her essay "The Myth of Matriarchy: Why Men Rule in Primitive Society," Joan Bamberger writes that "as long as [woman] is content to remain either goddess or child, she cannot be expected to shoulder her share of community burdens as the co-equal of man." Betty Friedan argued in her 1963 best-seller *The Feminine Mystique* that the notion of femininity as "mysterious and intuitive and close to the creation and origin of life" is not a liberation but a trap for women, who, in being perceived as passive and nurturing, are discounted for more active roles in society. If the Earth Mother had a powerful role to play thousands of years ago and if the woman at the hearth worked closely with plants for centuries thereafter, the average housewife today is seen by advertisers, rightly or wrongly, as a quintessential consumer. Woman has, perhaps, finally broken her peculiar sympathetic bond with nature.

So has the story of women and plants come to an end with the conclusion of the second millennium? The relationship is surely too fundamental in humanity's mythical and subconscious life to have disappeared entirely, but how is it now manifested? Certainly, women are involved in many plant-oriented occupations – their numbers in some of them, such as floral design, are still disproportionately large – and flowers continue to be somehow connected with women, whether on clothing or in a gift box. About 90 percent of cut flowers are bought by or for women. "Mother Nature" continues to be part of the vernacular.

Various tantalizing thoughts occurred to me as I worked on the previous 11 chapters. Merlin Stone's book about the earth goddess, *When God Was a Woman*, had attracted an enthusiastic following and spawned a string of workshops and similar publications. Women were taught how to find the goddess within themselves – Gaia was a favourite. But I doubted that the average woman was touched by such publications and events.

It was not until I looked at the environmental movement that I saw the association between women and plants – "mother" and "nature" – in my own day. As prehistoric people intuitively recognized the danger and creativity of the earth as a duality bound to their own fates, so do scientists at the end of the 20th century. Gaia, the force of life that is both nurturing and destructive, is again receiving her due. The environmental movement – I use the term in its broadest sense, encompassing not only societies and publications but also individuals working in small, mostly unnoticed ways – has a femaleness of outlook that recalls the worship of the earth goddess. The movement is based on the science of ecology, which studies the interrelationships of living things with one another and with their surroundings. The word "ecology," Carolyn Merchant points out, "derives from the Greek word *oikos*, meaning house. Ecology, then, is the science of household – the Earth's household. The connection between the Earth and the house has historically been mediated by woman." The changes in the environment, however, affect

Rachel Carson alerted the world to the dangers of agricultural chemicals.

~~~

everyone. Perhaps Susun Weed's thought is most apt: "This planetary transformation is in the hands of woman, not just the woman that is in woman but the woman that is in men. It is the female spirit that is being called forth now for healing."

Nature has been so altered during the past century that all of its aspects, including plants, animals, weather and the patterns and incidence of human diseases, have been affected. The atmosphere's carbon-dioxide content has risen enormously since the Industrial Revolution (between 1958 and 1987, it increased almost as much as it did in the previous two centuries), changing world weather patterns. Acid rain, caused by air pollution, is having a measurable impact on the land in and near industrialized areas. A sample of rain tested in British Columbia had a pH of 4.2, about 50 times more acidic than normal. Hillsides in the Adirondack Mountains are turning brown as the trees die, the most sensitive species going first. Maple-syrup production is dropping. Songbird popula-

tions dwindle as pesticides accumulate in their surroundings and the rainforests where they overwinter are clear-cut. Even Antarctic penguins show traces of pesticides. Entire species of plants and animals are being eradicated at the rate of three per day at the beginning of the 1990s, according to the World Wildlife Fund. Garbage dumps overflow, pollutants contaminate wells, lakes, ocean bays and the air. Deserts are becoming larger, and in North America's best farming country, soil fertility and the soil itself are lost far more quickly than they can be replaced. The United Nations considers 20 million square kilometres of land to be on the brink of desertification. Every year, at least 3,000 square kilometres of prime farmland disappear under buildings and roads in developed countries alone.

A group of 200 scientists at a United Nations Educational, Scientific, and Cultural Organization (UNESCO) conference in 1968 determined that if modern technology were allowed to continue on its present course, it "may produce an extremely critical situation that could seriously harm the present and future welfare of mankind and become irreversible unless appropriate actions be taken . . . ." The environmental movement seeks to define, control and correct some of those alterations.

The movement is often said to have begun in 1962 with the publication of Rachel Carson's book, *Silent Spring.* Evidence of the dangerous side effects of certain pesticides such as DDT had been accumulating for more than a decade, but the book was the first popular one to point out, in dismaying detail, the widespread environmental damage caused by the chemical approach to farming. She wrote, "The 'control of nature' is a phrase conceived in arrogance, born of the Neanderthal age of biology and philosophy, when it was supposed that nature exists for the convenience of man."

~~~

As the mood of alarm spread, the environmental movement became identified with the "flower power" of the mid-to-late 1960s, a turning away from the industrial bureaucratic world of "the establishment." Some of the manifestations of that curious time were distinctly female. Young men grew long hair and wore jewellery; women, too, had long hair and long dresses. Low wages and menial work became socially acceptable. War, the military and the police, as well as corporate power and government (all largely male-oriented), were eschewed in favour of pacifism, small business enterprises, social work, local organization and a back-to-the-land movement. Suddenly, men were wearing pink with impunity. A daisy thrust into a gun barrel became the symbol of a decade, while other plants—herbal teas, herbal medicines, marijuana, vegetarian cuisine, wood as a building material, natural fibres, organic gardens—became important facets of a life style described as alternative, although in many ways, it was simply the traditional life style of peasant women. In the same decade, the first photographs of Earth were taken from space—the breathtaking image of a brilliant globe floating in space appeared everywhere—and the word "ecosystem" was born.

It was an era whose repercussions continue to be felt, although the 1960s are long gone, the era's hippies having disappeared into the hinterlands of Oregon or the canyons of Wall Street. Since then, there has been an increasing interest in business, government and consumer goods among young people; yet the pressing reality is that, with or without love beads, humanity must become aware of and able to work with the natural environment or our lives will surely change in ways we do not want them to.

"Our attitude toward plants is a singularly narrow one," Rachel Carson writes in *Silent Spring*. "If we see any immediate utility in a plant, we foster it. If for any reason we find its presence undesirable or merely a matter of indifference, we may condemn it to destruction forthwith." On the other hand, when we see plants as undergoing many of the same life processes people do, we begin to perceive the world in a new way. Annie Dillard's books, such as *Pilgrim at Tinker Creek*, a hymn of praise to nature, are manifestations of that point of view.

Margaret Mee came to love the rainforests of Brazil, where she painted endangered botanical specimens for almost 40 years. Her husband, she said, became "rather fed up when I go away to the jungle for two or three months at a time." After she died in 1989, a trust fund was established in her honour to further the studies of Brazilian botanists interested in the rainforest.

Some years ago, I met Dorothy Maclean, another lover of nature. She is one of the founders of Findhorn, a spiritual gardening community in Scotland. Maclean claims to be sensitive to the messages of the spirits of plants and other natural things, entities which she calls "devas" (a Sanskrit word meaning "shining one"), for lack of a more appropriate term for something quite indescribable. By meditating upon certain plants, for instance, she has, she says, received messages of a sort. Maclean herself is a down-to-earth, unpretentious, middle-aged woman— "I sometimes think I was chosen to do this work because I'm so practical," she says. With the aid of instructional messages from the devas, she and two friends were able, without any horticultural experience, to garden wisely and organically, raising sometimes spectacular crops on a windswept oceanside plot. Maclean says, "The devas, who at first seemed to be far-off beings, through a joyous communication, grew into close companions until eventually, they made me realize that they, like the kingdom of heaven, are within."

Another person with an unusual sensitiv-

*Margaret Mee's love of the rainforest, where she
painted for decades, is remembered in a trust fund
to aid Brazilian botanists.*

～～

ity to the natural world is James Lovelock, a physician and biologist and author of *Gaia: A New Look at Life on Earth* (1979) and *The Ages of Gaia: A Biography of Our Living Earth* (1988). I met him at his home in Dorset, England, where he continues to do the same measurement and assessment of changes in the environment that gave Rachel Carson her base data. He has come up with the hypothesis that life is self-regulating and self-sustaining. Lovelock points out, for instance, that the atmosphere of Earth is made up of a highly unstable mixture of gases and that the only way such a mixture, necessary for life, can be maintained is if life itself does it to perfection: "Earth's living matter, air, oceans and land surface form a complex system which can be seen as a single organism."

Lovelock calls this self-regulating system

Gaia, because the goddess was "very like most of the early earth goddesses: at once kind of gentle and nurturing and all the rest of it and at the same time a stern and unforgiving bringer of death to all that transgress. This fits exceedingly well with the scientific picture, actually, which is of a balancing system which is quite ruthless about species that don't obey the rules. They are just eliminated. And that's how the system keeps the environment constant, I think. Those that keep the environment fit are fit to survive, and those that don't are not.

"In the ordinary course of events," continues Lovelock, "any species that fouled up the environment to the point we have done would be doomed without question, but there are two other options that come into question for humans. One, we're sentient and

155
～～

can discover we're doing it and stop it perhaps, which I hope we will be able to do, and secondly, there may be a rapid change of global climate and composition to a new state which will be quite unfavourable for us. Now, that's the normal way for the system to get rid of unwanted species. But I think we're tough enough to survive it.

"We'll proceed to foul the new state too," he laughs. "But it will take time."

Lovelock's first option, that "we're sentient and can discover we're doing it and stop it," depends, in part, upon our ability to become more "green," to use an adjective employed in the 14th-century poem *The Floure and the Leafe* quoted in the first chapter, in which members of the green party, followers of the goddess Flora, were lazy and irresponsible but loved life and nature, while the white party was upstanding, highly principled and goal-oriented. The whites were evidently the more admirable models. Six centuries later—with no reference to that poem—Stephen Toulmin writes in *The Return to Cosmology*:

"The white philosophy has roots in psychotherapy. The green philosophy, by contrast . . . has roots, most typically, in the theories of ecology and the practices of 'natural living.' It encourages us, both as individuals and in our collective affairs, to pursue harmony with nature. Our primary responsibility is to deepen our understanding of the interdependence that binds humanity and nature." If the greens appear unproductive, they are beginning to be recognized as better planetary citizens in the long run.

Not everyone needs to be able to communicate with plants as Dorothy Maclean does, but a trusting, courageous relationship with other living things is needed if humanity is to learn to live in harmony with its surroundings. In the same way that plants are seldom recognized as fully alive beings—defaced, broken and cut down without a second thought—so is quiescence in people a quality easily overlooked and undervalued in the rush and noise of more active life. William Leiss writes, "The task of mastering nature ought to be understood as a matter of bringing under control the irrational and destructive aspects of human desires. Success in this endeavour would be the liberation of nature—that is, the liberation of human nature: a human species free to enjoy in peace the fruits of its productive intelligence."

This process naturally assumes mutual respect between the sexes and a recognition of women as full participants in spiritual, scientific and creative matters. According to the final statement from the Women and Environment workshops at the United Nations Decade for Women conference, "The growth of women's power and the sustainability of development are ecologically tied." Carolyn Merchant finds parallels between ecology and feminism in that both promote equality, both value the caretaking of the home, both assume that energy is required and expended and both recognize that there is "no free lunch," that reciprocity and cooperation are required.

This attitude may hark back to the era between 6500 and 3500 B.C., which Marija Gimbutas describes in *The Goddesses and Gods of Old Europe* as a time when "all resources of human nature, feminine and masculine, were utilized to the full as a creative force."

We cannot really know, though, how people thought and acted more than 8,000 years ago. Tonight, an evening in May, as I finally complete this book, I look out the window over my computer at a fading blue sky behind silhouetted pines. Out there, the blackflies bite, the meteors fall, the bats fly, the moon rises. It is a world the devotees of the earth goddesses might have imagined.

I try to think ahead 8,000 years. I try to imagine the pines, the blackflies.

My imagination conjures only the earth and the moon.

Bibliography

Chapter I

Bachofen, Johann Jakob, *Myth, Religion and Mother Right*, trans. Ralph Manheim, Princeton University Press, Princeton, N.J., 1967.

Branston, Brian, *The Lost Gods of England*, Thames & Hudson, London, 1957.

Campbell, Joseph, *The Hero With a Thousand Faces*, Princeton University Press, Princeton, N.J., 1949.

Cato, Marcus Porcius, *On Agriculture*; Varro, Marcus Terentius, *On Agriculture*, trans. William Davis Hooper, Heinemann, London, 1934.

Chaucer, Geoffrey(?), *The Floure and the Leafe and the Assembly of Ladies*, ed. D.A. Pearsall, Thomas Nelson & Sons, Edinburgh, 1962.

Cook, Roger, *The Tree of Life: Symbol of the Centre*, Thames & Hudson, London, 1974.

Coxwell, C. Fillingham, *Siberian and Other Folk Tales*, C.W. Daniel, London, 1925.

Diamond, Jared, "The Worst Mistake in Human History," *Discover*, May 1987, pp. 64-66.

Eberhard, Wolfram, *Folktales of China*, University of Chicago Press, Chicago, 1965.

Frazer, James George, *The Worship of Nature*, Macmillan, London, 1926.

Gimbutas, Marija, *The Goddesses and*

Gods of Old Europe, 6500-3500 B.C.: Myths and Cult Images, 2nd ed., Thames & Hudson, London, 1982.

Gray, Louis Herbert (ed.), Mythology of all Races, Marshall Jones, Boston, 1916.

Harding, M. Esther, Woman's Mysteries Ancient and Modern, Putnam, New York, 1971.

Harlan, Jack, Crops and Man, American Society of Agronomy, Madison, Wisc., 1975.

Hatt, Gudmund, "The Corn Mother in America and in Indonesia," Anthropos, vol. 46, 1951, pp. 853-914.

Heiser, Charles B., Jr., Of Plants and People, University of Oklahoma Press, Norman, 1985.

------, Seed to Civilization, Freeman, San Francisco, 1973.

Held, Julius S., "Flora, Goddess and Courtesan," in De Artibus Opuscula: Essays in Honour of Erwin Panofsky, New York University Press, New York, 1961, pp. 201-218.

Hill, Thomas, The Gardener's Labyrinth, Oxford University Press, Oxford, 1987 (first published in 1577).

Huxley, Anthony, An Illustrated History of Gardening, Paddington, New York, 1978.

James, E.O., The Cult of the Mother-Goddess, Thames & Hudson, London, 1959.

------, The Tree of Life: An Archaeological Study, Brill, Leiden, Netherlands, 1966.

Kahn, E.J., Jr., "The Staffs of Life I: The Golden Thread," The New Yorker, June 18, 1984, pp. 67-72.

Lao Tsu, Tao Te Ching, trans. Gia Fu Feng and Jane English, Vintage, New York, 1972.

Lederer, Wolfgang, The Fear of Women, Grune & Stratton, New York, 1968.

Love Poems of Ancient Egypt, trans. Ezra Pound and Noel Stock, New Directions, New York, 1962.

Magic and Medicine of Plants, Readers Digest, Pleasantville, N.Y., 1986.

McLeod, Enid, The Order of the Rose: The Life and Ideas of Christine de Pizan, Rowman and Littlefield, Totowa, N.J., 1976.

Merchant, Carolyn, The Death of Nature: Women, Ecology and the Scientific Revolution, Harper & Row, San Francisco, 1980.

Moffat, Mary Jane and Charlotte Painter (eds.), Revelations: Diaries of Women, Random House, New York, 1974.

Murphy, Dervla, Eight Feet in the Andes, Century, New York, 1983.

Neumann, Erich, The Great Mother, Pantheon, New York, 1954.

Parrinder, Geoffrey (ed.), World Religions From Ancient History to the Present, Facts on File, New York, 1971.

Paulson, Ivar, The Old Estonian Folk

Religion, Indiana University Publications, Bloomington, 1971.

Pizan, Christine de, *The Book of the City of Ladies*, trans. Earl Jeffrey Richards, Persea, New York, 1982.

Pliny the Elder (Caius Plinius Secundus), *Natural History*, trans. H. Rackham, Harvard University Press, Cambridge, Mass., 1945.

Reed, Charles A., *Origins of Agriculture*, Mouton, The Hague, 1977.

"Religion and the New Science," *Ideas*, Canadian Broadcasting Corporation (CBC), Montreal, 1985.

"Return of the Goddess," *Ideas*, CBC, Montreal, 1986.

Reuther, Rosemary Radford, *New Woman, New Earth*, Seabury, New York, 1975.

Robinson, Trevor, "An Introduction to the Chemistry of Herbs, Spices and Medicinal Plants," *The Herb, Spice and Medicinal Plant Digest*, fall 1988, pp. 1-4, 10.

Rohde, Eleanor Sinclair, *The Old English Herbals*, Longmans, Green, London, 1922.

Schwab, Gustav, *Die shonsten Sagen des klassischen Altertums*, 5th ed., Carl Ueberreuter, Wien, 1952.

Stone, Merlin, *When God Was a Woman*, Harcourt, Brace, Jovanovich, San Diego, 1976.

Traill, Catharine Parr, *Pearls and Pebbles*, or Notes of an Old Naturalist, W. Briggs, Toronto, 1894.

Virgil, *The Georgics*, trans. C. Day Lewis, Jonathan Cape, London, 1940.

Von Cles-Reden, Sibylle, *The Realm of the Great Goddess*, Prentice-Hall, Englewood Cliffs, N.J., 1962.

Chapter II

Amherst, Alicia, *A History of Gardening in England*, Bernard Quaritch, London, 1896.

Bradley, Richard, *The Country Housewife and Lady's Director*, Prospect, London, 1980 (first published in London in 1736).

Caldwell, Joseph R., "Cultural Evolution in the Old World and the New," in *Origins of Agriculture*, Mouton, The Hague, 1977.

Cato, Marcus Porcius, *On Agriculture*; Varro, Marcus Terentius, *On Agriculture*, trans. William Davis Hooper, Heinemann, London, 1934.

Clarkson, Rosetta E., *The Golden Age of Herbs & Herbalists*, Dover, New York, 1972.

Coke, Mary, *The Letters and Journals of Lady Mary Coke*, Lonsdale & Bartholomew, Bath, 1970.

Coleman, M. Clare, *Downham-in-the-Isle: A Study of an Ecclesiastical Manor in the 13th and 14th Centuries*, Boydell, Woodbridge, Suffolk, 1984.

Coles, William, *The Art of Simpling*, by

J.G. for Nath: Brook at the Angell in Cornhill, London, 1656.

Columella, Lucius Junius Moderatus, *On Agriculture*, trans. Harrison Boyd Ash, Harvard University Press, Cambridge, Mass., 1960.

Dahlberg, Frances (ed.), *Woman the Gatherer*, Yale University Press, New Haven, Conn., 1981.

Digby, George Wingfield, *Elizabethan Embroidery*, Faber & Faber, London, 1963.

Evelyn, Charles, *The Lady's Recreation, or The Art of Gardening Farther Improved*, London, 1718.

Farb, Peter, *Man's Rise to Civilization as Shown by the Indians of North America from Primeval Times to the Coming of the Industrial State*, Dutton, New York, 1968.

Fiennes, Celia, *Through England on a Side Saddle*, Field & Tuer, London, 1888.

Fitzherbert, Anthony, *The Boke of Husbandry*, London, 1534.

"From the Craftsman, Number II," *The Universal Magazine of Knowledge and Pleasure*, June 1756, pp. 268-269.

Fussel, G.E., *Farming Technique from Prehistoric to Modern Times*, Crofts, New York, 1925.

Gimbutas, Marija, *The Goddesses and Gods of Old Europe, 6500-3500 B.C.: Myths and Cult Images*, 2nd ed., Thames & Hudson, London, 1982.

Grampp, Christopher, "Social Meanings of Residential Gardens," in *Meanings of the Garden*, Center for Design Research, University of California at Davis, 1987.

Gras, Norman Scott Brien, *A History of Agriculture*, Crofts, New York, 1925.

Harlan, Jack R., *Crops and Man*, American Society of Agronomy, Madison, Wisc., 1975.

Hill, Thomas, *The Gardener's Labyrinth*, Oxford University Press, Oxford, 1987 (first published in London in 1577).

Lawson, William, *The Country House-Wives Garden*, W. Wilson for E. Brewster, London, 1653.

Lederer, Wolfgang, *The Fear of Women*, Grune & Stratton, New York, 1968.

Lees-Milne, Avilde and Rosemary Verey (eds.), *The Englishman's Garden*, Penguin, London, 1982.

Leighton, Ann, *Early American Gardens: For Meate or Medicine*, Houghton Mifflin, Boston, 1970.

Loyd, Bonnie, "Armchair Gardening: The Pleasure of Garden Catalogs," in *Meanings of the Garden*, Center for Design Research, University of California at Davis, 1987.

Lucas, Angela M., *Women in the Middle Ages: Religion, Marriage and Letters*, Harvester, Brighton, 1983.

Malinowski, Bronislaw, *The Sexual Life of Savages in North-Western Melanesia*, Routledge and Kegan Paul, London, 1932.

Markham, Gervase, *A Way to Get Wealth*, George Sawbridge, London, 1678.

Mason, Ronald J., *Great Lakes Archaeology*, Academic Press, New York, 1981.

McLean, Teresa, *Medieval English Gardens*, Viking, New York, 1980.

Le Ménagier de Paris, Slatkine, Genève-Paris, 1982 (first published in 1393).

Modern Curiosities of Art and Nature, Sieur Lemery, London, 1685.

More, Hannah, *Coelebs in Search of a Wife*, T. Cadell & W. Davies, London, 1809.

Parkinson, John, *Paradisi in sole, paradisus terrestris*, London, 1629.

Partridge, John, *The Treasurie of Commodious Conceits*, Richard Jones, London, 1573.

Perényi, Eleanor, *Green Thoughts*, Vintage, New York, 1981.

Platt, Hugh, *Delightes for Ladies, to Adorn Their Persons, Tables, Closets & Distillatories*, Robert Young, London, 1636.

Pliny the Elder (Caius Plinius Secundus), *Natural History*, trans. H. Rackham, Harvard University Press, Cambridge, Mass., 1945.

Reed, Howard S., *A Short History of the Plant Sciences*, Chronic Botanica, Waltham, Mass., 1942.

Rohde, Eleanor Sinclair, *The Story of the Garden*, The Medici Society, London, 1932.

Sauer, Carl Ortwin, *Land and Life*, University of California Press, Berkeley, 1963.

Seager, Elizabeth, *Gardens and Gardeners*, Oxford University Press, Oxford, 1984.

Strachey, William, *Travaile into Virginia*, Hakluyt Society Publications, v, vi, London, 1849, p. 111.

Struever, Stuart (ed.), *Prehistoric Agriculture*, Natural History Press, Garden City, N.Y., 1971.

Tiffany, Sharon W., *Women, Work and Motherhood*, Prentice-Hall, Englewood Cliffs, N.J., 1982.

Trigger, Bruce E., *The Huron, Farmers of the North*, Holt Rinehart Winston, New York, 1969.

Trusler, John (?), *The Garden-Companion for Gentlemen & Ladies*, Library Press, London, 1795.

Tusser, Thomas, *A Hundreth Good Pointes of Husbandrie*, R. Tottell, London, 1557.

------, *Five Hundred Pointes of Good Husbandrie*, The English Dialect Society, Trubner, Ludgate Hill, 1878 (edition of 1580 collated with those of 1573 and 1577).

Wilson, Gilbert L., *Buffalo Bird Woman's Garden*, Minnesota Historical Society Press, St. Paul, 1987 (first published as *Agriculture of the Hidatsa Indians*, 1917).

Chapter III

Anderson, Frank J., *An Illustrated History of the Herbals*, Columbia University Press, New York, 1977.

Arcana Fairfaxiana, Mawson, Swan & Morgan, Newcastle-on-Tyne, 1890.

Barrow, Mark V., "A Civil War Period 'Home Remedy for the Treatment of Dropsy,'" *Bulletin of the History of Medicine*, vol. 40, 1966, pp. 376-378.

Bashkirtseff, Marie, *The Journal of Marie Bashkirtseff*, trans. Mathilde Blind, Cassell, London, 1890.

Beeton, Isabella, *The Book of Household Management*, S.O. Beeton, London, 1861.

Blackwell, Elizabeth, *A Curious Herbal*, for Samuel Harding, London, 1737.

Blake, John B., "The Compleat Housewife," *Bulletin of the History of Medicine*, vol. 49, 1975, pp. 30-42.

Blencowe, Ann, *The Receipt Book of Mrs. Ann Blencowe, A.D. 1694*, Adelphi, London, 1925.

Bradley, Richard, *The Country Housewife and Lady's Director*, Prospect, London, 1980 (first published in London in 1736).

Brooks, Stewart, "The Mysterious Ways of Digitalis," *MD*, December 1985, pp. 15-16.

Bruynswyke, Jherom, *The Vertuous Boke of Distyllacyon of the waters of all maner of Herbes*, L. Andrews, London, 1527.

Burton, Robert, *The Anatomy of Melancholy*, Tudor, New York, 1955 (first published 1621).

Camden, Caroll, *The Elizabethan Woman*, Elsevier, Houston, 1942.

Clarkson, Rosetta E., *The Golden Age of Herbs and Herbalists*, Dover, New York, 1972 (first published as *Green Enchantment*, 1940).

La Claviere, R. de Maulde, *The Women of the Renaissance*, Swan Sonnenschein, London, 1900.

Coles, William, *The Art of Simpling*, by J.G. for Nath: Brook at the Angell in Cornhill, London, 1656.

The Cook Not Mad, James Macfarlane, Kingston, Upper Canada, 1831 (reprinted by Cherry Tree Press, Toronto, 1972).

Culpeper, Nicholas, *Culpeper's Complete Herbal*, W. Foulsham, London (reprinted from *The English Physician* and *The English Physician Enlarged*, 1652 and 1653).

Debus, Allen G., *Man and Nature in the Renaissance*, Cambridge University Press, Cambridge, 1978.

Eagle, Robert, *Herbs, Useful Plants*, British Broadcasting Corporation, London, 1981.

Forbes, R.J., *A Short History of the Art of Distillation*, Brill, Leiden, Netherlands, 1970.

Fraser, Antonia, *The Weaker Vessel*, Knopf, New York, 1984.

Freud, Sigmund, *The Origins of Psychoanalysis*, trans. Eric Mosbacher and James Strachey, Doubleday, Garden City, N.Y., 1957.

Gerard, John, *Gerard's Herbal: the History of Plants*, ed. Marcus Woodward, Bracken, London, 1985 (from the edition of Th. Johnson, 1636).

Graedon, Joe, "16 Home Remedies You Can Trust," *Family Circle*, March 25, 1986, pp. 44-49.

Grieve, Mrs. M., *A Modern Herbal*, Jonathan Cape, London, 1931.

Griggs, Barbara, *Green Pharmacy: A History of Herbal Medicine*, Methuen, Toronto, 1982.

Hale, Sara Josepha, *The Good Housekeeper*, 2nd ed., Weeks, Jordan, Boston, 1839.

Hamarneh, Sami K., "The First Known Independent Treatise on Cosmetology in Spain," *Bulletin of the History of Medicine*, vol. 39, 1965, pp. 309-312.

Hill, Albert F., *Economic Botany*, McGraw Hill, New York, 1952.

Hill, John, *Virtues of the British Herbs*, for R. Baldwin, London, 1770.

The Illustrated Annual Register of Rural Affairs for 1874, Luther Tucker & Son, Albany, N.Y., 1874.

Jackson-Stops, Gervase, "Dressing Rooms, Cabinets and Closets," *House & Garden*, February 1986, p. 147.

The Ladies Cabinet Opened; Wherein is Found Hidden Severall Experiments in Preserving and Conserving, Physicke, Surgery, Cookery and Huswifery, Richard Meighen, 1639.

The Ladies Dispensatory, or Every Woman her own Physician, James Hodges, London.

The Ladies Dressing-Room Unlock'd, Joseph Wild, London, 1700.

Lawrence, Elizabeth, *Gardening for Love: The Market Bulletins*, Duke University Press, Durham, N.C., 1987.

Lee, Sarah Wallis Bowdich, *Trees, Plants and Flowers: Their Beauties, Uses and Influences*, Grant & Griffith, London, 1854.

Lewis, Walter H. and Memory P. Elvin-Lewis, *Medical Botany*, Wiley, New York, 1977.

Lindsay, J. Seymour, *Iron and Brass Implements of the English House*, The Medici Society, London, 1927.

Lyly, John, *Euphues and His England*, London, 1617.

Makheja, A.N. and J.M. Bailey, "The Active Principle in Feverfew," *Lancet*, 1981, p. 1054.

Markham, Gervase, *A Way to Get Wealth* (includes *The English Housewife* and *The English Husbandman*), George Sawbridge, London, 1678.

McIntosh, Charles, *The Practical Gardener*, Thomas Kelly, London, 1828.

McLean, Teresa, *Medieval English*

Gardens, Viking, New York, 1980.

A New Dispensatory of Fourty Physicall Receipts, Salvator Winter, London, 1649.

Ordish, George, The Living Garden, Bodley Head, London, 1985.

Parkinson, John, Theatrum Botanicum: The Theater of Plantes, Thomas Coles, London, 1640.

Pierrepont, Robert, The French Gardiner, trans. John Evelyn, by J.M. for John Crooke, London, 1669.

Platt, Hugh, Delightes for Ladies, to Adorne Their Persons, Tables, Closets & Distillatories, H. Lownes, London, 1609.

Pliny the Elder (Caius Plinius Secundus), Natural History, trans. H. Rackham, Harvard University Press, Cambridge, Mass., 1945.

Precious Treasury of Twenty Rare Secrets, La Fountaine, London, 1649.

Pugh, W.J., in British Medical Journal, March 23, 1985, p. 925.

Rohde, Eleanor Sinclair, The Old English Herbals, Longmans, Green, London, 1922.

------, The Story of the Garden, The Medici Society, London, 1932.

Rowland, Beryl, Medieval Woman's Guide to Health, Kent State University Press, Kent, Ohio, 1981.

Smith, Keith Vincent, The Illustrated Earth Garden Herbal, Elm Tree,

London, 1979.

"Sophia," Woman Not Inferior to Man, John Hawkins, London, 1739.

Stacey, Sarah, "God's Own Drug Store," BBC Wildlife, July 1988, pp. 378-381.

Stevenson, Allan, Catalogue of Botanical Books in the Collection of Rachel McMasters Miller Hunt, Pittsburgh, 1961.

Talbot, Elizabeth, Countess of Kent, A Choice Manuall of Rare and Select Secrets in Physick and Chirurgery . . . , 14th ed., Gartrude Dawson, London, 1663.

The Treasury of Hidden Secrets Commonly Called The Good-Huswives Closet of Provision, for the Health of Her Houshold, Jane Bell, London, 1653.

Trew, Christoph Jakob, The Herbal of the Count Palatine, Harrap, London, 1984.

A True Gentlewoman's Delight, Wherein Is Contained All Manner of Cookery Together With Preserving, Conserving, Drying and Candying, W.G. Gent, London, 1663.

Turner, William, A New Herball, J. Gybken, London, 1551.

Tusser, Thomas, Five Hundred Pointes of Good Husbandrie, The English Dialect Society, Trubner, Ludgate Hill, 1878 (the edition of 1580 collated with those of 1573 and 1577).

Weintraub, Pamela, "Scentimental Journeys," Omni, April 1986, pp. 52, 114-116.

Chapter IV

Arcana Fairfaxiana, Mawson, Swan & Morgan, Newcastle-on-Tyne, 1890.

Benedeck, Thomas G., "The Changing Relationship Between Midwives and Physicians During the Renaissance," *Bulletin of the History of Medicine*, vol. 51, 1977, pp. 550-564.

Boguet, Henri, *Discours exécrable des sorciers*, Jean Osmont, Rouen, 1606 (translated as *An Examin of Witches* by E. Allen Ashwin, John Rodker, Great Britain, 1929).

Burton, Robert, *An Anatomy of Melancholy*, Tudor, New York, 1955 (first published 1621).

Caporael, Linnda R., "Ergotism: The Satan Loosed in Salem?" *Science*, April 2, 1976, pp. 21-26.

Castaneda, Carlos, *The Teachings of Don Juan: A Yaqui Way of Knowledge*, University of California Press, Berkeley, 1968.

Chambers Information for the People, W. & R. Chambers, London, 1874.

Clark, Alfred J., "Flying Ointments," in Margaret Murray, *The Witch-Cult in Western Europe*, Oxford University Press, London, 1921.

Coles, William, *The Art of Simpling*, by J.G. for Nath: Brook at the Angell in Cornhill, London, 1656.

A Collection of Rare and Curious Tracts relating to Witchcraft, John Russell Smith, London, 1838.

Conklin, George N., "Alkaloids and the Witches' Sabbat," *American Journal of Pharmacy*, May 1958, pp. 171-174.

Culpeper, Nicholas, *Culpeper's Complete Herbal*, W. Foulsham, London (reprint of *The English Physician* and *The English Physician Enlarged*, 1652 and 1653).

Ehrenreich, Barbara and Deirdre English, *Witches, Midwives and Nurses: A History of Women Healers*, Feminist Press, Old Westbury, N.Y., 1973.

Gerard, John, *Gerard's Herbal: The History of Plants*, ed. Marcus Woodward, Bracken, London, 1985 (from the edition of Th. Johnson, 1636).

Grollman, Arthur, *Pharmacology and Therapeutics*, Lea & Febiger, Philadelphia, 1962.

Hansen, Chadwick, *Witchcraft at Salem*, Braziller, New York, 1969.

Hansen, Harold A., *The Witch's Garden*, Unity Press, Santa Cruz, 1978.

Hardin, James W. and Jay M. Arena, *Human Poisoning From Native and Cultivated Plants*, Duke University Press, Durham, N.C., 1974.

Harner, Michael J. (ed.), *Hallucinogens and Shamanism*, Oxford University Press, New York, 1973.

Heiser, Charles B., Jr., *Nightshades, the Paradoxical Plants*, Freeman, San Francisco, 1969.

Hoyt, Charles Alva, *Witchcraft*, Southern Illinois University Press, Carbondale, 1981.

Huff, Barbara B. (ed.), *Physicians' Desk Reference*, Litton, Oradell, N.J., 1976.

Hughes, Pennethorne, *Witchcraft*, Longmans, Green, London, 1952.

Lea, Henry Charles, *Materials Toward a History of Witchcraft*, Yoseloff, New York, 1957.

Lee, Sarah Wallis Bowdich, *Trees, Plants and Flowers: Their Beauties, Uses and Influences*, Grant and Griffith, London, 1854.

Mather, Cotton, *On Witchcraft, Being the Wonders of the Invisible World*, Peter Pauper Press, Mount Vernon, N.Y., 1950 (first published in Boston, 1692).

Neumann, Erich, *The Great Mother*, Pantheon, New York, 1954.

Norman, H.J., "Witch Ointments," in Montagu Summers' *The Werewolf*, Kegan Paul, Trench, Trübner, London, 1933.

O'Connor, Audrey H., *An Herb Garden Compendium*, Cornell University Press, Ithaca, N.Y., 1984.

Pliny the Elder (Caius Plinius Secundus), *Natural History*, trans. H. Rackham, Harvard University Press, Cambridge, Mass., 1945.

Rohde, Eleanor Sinclair, *The Old English Herbals*, Longmans, Green, London, 1922.

Rothman, Theodore, "De Laguna's Commentaries on Hallucinogenic Drugs and Witchcraft in Dioscorides' *Materia Medica*," *Bulletin of the History of Medicine*, vol. 46, 1972, pp. 562-567.

Schleiffer, Hedwig (ed.), *Narcotic Plants of the Old World*, Lubrecht & Cramer, Monticello, N.Y., 1979.

Scot, Reginald, *The Discoverie of Witchcraft*, William Brome, London, 1584 (reprinted by Southern Illinois University Press, Carbondale, 1964).

Spanos, Nicholas P. and Jack Gottleib, "Ergotism and the Salem Village Witch Trials," *Science*, December 1976, pp. 1390-1394.

Starkey, M.L., *The Devil in Massachusetts*, Knopf, New York, 1949.

Stuart, Malcolm (ed.), *The Encyclopedia of Herbs and Herbalism*, Orbis, London, 1979.

Thompson, C.J.S., *The Mystic Mandrake*, Rider, London, 1934.

Tuvil, Daniel, *Asylum veneris, or a Sanctuary for Ladies*, E. Griffin for Laurence L'Isle, 1616.

Tyler, Varro E., *The Honest Herbal*, Stickley, Philadelphia, 1981.

Wassén, S. Henry, "The Anthropological Outlook for Amerindian Medicinal Plants," in *Plants in the Development of Modern Medicine*, Harvard University Press, Cambridge, Mass., 1972.

Chapter V

Axon, William E.A., *A Fifteenth-Century Life of St. Dorothea*, 1901.

Clarkson, Rosetta E., *The Golden Age of*

Herbs and Herbalists, Dover, New York, 1972 (first published as *Green Enchantment*, 1940).

Comito, Terry, *The Idea of the Garden in the Renaissance*, Rutgers University Press, New Brunswick, N.J., 1978.

D'Ancona, Mirella Levi, *The Garden of the Renaissance: Botanical Symbolism in Italian Painting*, Leo S. Olschki, Firenze, 1976.

De Turk, Phillip Eugene, "Medieval Monastic Gardens," in *An Introductory History of Medieval Castle Gardens*, Master's of Landscape Architecture thesis, University of Illinois, Urbana, 1961.

Eckenstein, Lina, *Woman Under Monasticism*, Russell & Russell, New York, 1896.

Gasquet, Abbot, *English Monastic Life*, Methuen, London, 1904.

Hawkins, Henry, *Parthenia sacra*, John Cousturier, 1633.

Herrad of Hohenbourg, *Hortus deliciarum*, Brill, Leiden, Netherlands, 1979.

The Loughborough Echo, January 8, 1954.

McLean, Teresa, *Medieval English Gardens*, Viking, New York, 1980.

McLeod, Enid, *The Order of the Rose: The Life and Ideas of Christine de Pizan*, Rowman & Littlefield, Totowa, N.J., 1976.

The Myroure of Oure Ladye, Richard Fawkes, 1530 (reprinted by the Early English Text Society, London, 1873).

Nichols, John, *The History and Antiquities of the County of Leicester*, vol. III, part II, S. R. Publishers, London, 1971 (first published by John Nichols, London, 1804).

O'Connor, Audrey H., *An Herb Garden Companion*, Cornell University Press, Ithaca, N.Y., 1984.

Pizan, Christine de, *Oeuvres Poétiques de Christine de Pizan*, ed. Maurice Roy, Didot, Paris, 1891.

Power, Eileen, *Medieval English Nunneries c. 1275 to 1535*, Cambridge University Press, London, 1922.

Putnam, Emily James, *The Lady*, University of Chicago Press, Chicago, 1970.

Singer, Charles, "The Scientific Views and Visions of Saint Hildegard (1098-1180)," in *Studies in the History and Method of Science*, Oxford University Press, London, 1917.

Smith, A.W., *A Gardener's Dictionary of Plant Names*, St. Martin's, New York, 1963.

The Song of Solomon, *The Holy Bible*, Cambridge University Press, Cambridge.

Tasso, Torquato, *The Householders Philosophie*, by J.C. for Thomas Hackett, London, 1588.

Victoria County History, Hampshire, vol. 2.

Victoria County History, Lincolnshire, vol. 2.

The Voyages and Travels of Sir John Mandeville, London, 1722.

Wilkins, Eithne, *The Rose-Garden Game*, Gollancz, London, 1969.

Chapter VI

Blake, John B., "Women and Medicine in Ante-Bellum America," *Bulletin of the History of Medicine*, vol. 39, 1965, pp. 99-123.

Borowski, M.L., *Plants From Ukraine in Canada*, Ukrainian Free Academy of Sciences, Winnipeg, Man., 1975.

Bowsfield, Hartwell, *Fort Victoria Letters*, Hudson's Bay Record Society, Winnipeg, Man., 1979.

Burr, Esther Edwards, *The Journals of Esther Edwards Burr*, eds. Carol F. Karlsen and Laurie Crumpacker, Yale University Press, New Haven, Conn., 1984.

Colden, Jane, *Botanic Manuscript of Jane Colden*, Chanticleer, New York, 1963.

Cuthell, Edith, *My Garden in the City of Gardens*, John Lane, London, 1905.

Darlington, William, *Memorials of John Bartram and Humphrey Marshall*, Lindsay & Blakeston, Philadelphia, 1849.

Downie, Mary Alice and Mary Hamilton, "*And Some Brought Flowers*," University of Toronto Press, Toronto, 1980.

Drury, Clifford Merrill (ed.), *First White Woman Over the Rockies*, Arthur H. Clarke, Glendale, Calif., 1963.

Duchaussois, P., *The Grey Nuns in the Far North (1867-1917)*, McClelland and Stewart, Toronto, 1919.

Eager, Samuel W., *An Outline History of Orange County*, S.T. Callahan, Newburgh, 1846-47.

Earle, Alice Morse, *Colonial Dames and Good Wives*, Houghton Mifflin, Boston, 1895.

Erichsen-Brown, Charlotte, *Use of Plants for the Past 500 Years*, Breezy Creeks, Aurora, Ont., 1979.

Ewanchuk, Michael, *Pioneer Profiles: Ukrainian Settlers in Manitoba*, Michael Ewanchuk, Winnipeg, Man., 1981.

Faragher, John Mack, *Women and Men on the Overland Trail*, Yale University Press, New Haven, Conn., 1979.

Fletcher, Stevenson Whitcomb, *Pennsylvania Agriculture and Country Life 1640-1840*, Pennsylvania Historical & Museum Commission, Harrisburg, 1950.

Grant, Anne, *Memoirs of an American Lady*, Wells, Wait and Hastings, Etheredge and Bliss, Boston, 1809.

Hale, John (ed.), *Settlers*, Faber & Faber, London, 1950.

Heaton, Claude Edwin, "Medicine in New Amsterdam," *Bulletin of the History of Medicine*, 1941, pp. 125-143.

Hennepin, Louis, *Description of Louisiana*, trans. Mario E. Cross, University of Minnesota Press, 1938.

Hobbs, Christoper, "Sarsaparilla: A Literature Review," *Herbalgram*, summer 1988.

Hollingsworth, Buckner, *Her Garden Was Her Delight*, Macmillan, New York, 1962.

Kalm, Pehr, *Travels into North America*, trans. John Reinhold Foster, for T. Lownes, London, 1772.

Leighton, Ann, *American Gardens in the Eighteenth Century: For Use or Delight*, Houghton Mifflin, Boston, 1976.

Megquier, Mary Jane, *Apron of Gold: The Letters of Mary Jane Megquier from San Francisco 1849-1856*, Huntington Library, San Marino, Calif., 1949.

Prior, Mary Barber, "Letters of Martha Logan to John Bartram," *The South Carolina Historical Magazine*, January 1958, pp. 38-46.

Traill, Catharine Parr, *Backwoods of Canada*, McClelland and Stewart, Toronto, 1929 (first published by Charles Knight, London, 1836).

------, *The Canadian Settler's Guide*, McClelland and Stewart, Toronto, 1969 (first published as *The Female Emigrant's Guide*, Maclear, Toronto, 1854).

------, *Studies of Plant Life in Canada*, A.S. Woodburn, Ottawa, 1885.

Van Rensselaer, May, *The Goede Vrouw of Mana-ha-ta 1609-1760*, Scribner's, 1898.

Wiser, Vivan (ed.), *Two Centuries of American Agriculture*, Agricultural History Society, Washington, 1976.

Wright, Richardson, *The Winter Diversions of a Gardener*, Lippincott, Philadelphia, 1934.

Chapter VII

Bashkirtseff, Marie, *The Journal of Marie Bashkirtseff*, trans. Mathilde Blind, Cassell, London, 1890.

Benn, June Wedgewood (ed.), *The Woman's View*, Routledge and Kegan Paul, London, 1967.

Bloomer, Amelia (ed.), *The Lily*, Seneca Falls, New York, 1852.

British Weekly Commissioners, *Toilers in London, or Inquiries Concerning Female Labour in the Metropolis*, Hodder and Stoughton, London, 1889.

Caulfield, S.F.A. and Blanche C. Saward, *Encyclopedia of Victorian Needle-Work*, Dover, New York, 1922 (reprint of *The Dictionary of Needlework*, 1882).

Coats, Peter, *Flowers in History*, Weidenfeld and Nicolson, London, 1970.

Croly, Jane Cunningham, *Talks on Women's Topics*, Lee and Shepard, Boston, 1864.

Dudden, Faye E., *Serving Women*, Wesleyan University Press, Middletown, Conn., 1983.

Dumas, Alexandre, *Camille: The Lady of the Camellias*, trans. Henriette Metcalf, Samuel French, New York, 1931.

Embolden, William A., *Bizarre Plants: Magical, Monstrous, Mythical*, Macmillan, New York, 1974.

An Essay in Defence of the Female Sex, for S. Butler, London, 1721.

Flora and Thalia, or Gems of Flowers and Poetry, Henry Washbourne, London, 1835.

The Floral Knitting Book, Groombridge & Sons, London, 1847.

Flower Lore, McCaw, Stevenson & Orr, Belfast, 1879.

Fox, Caroline, *Memories of Old Friends: Extracts from the Journals and Letters of Caroline Fox, 1835-1871*, ed. Horace N. Pym, Smith, Elder, London, 1882.

Fuller, Margaret, *The Letters of Margaret Fuller*, ed. Robert N. Hudspeth, Cornell University Press, Ithaca, N.Y., 1983.

Gordon, Leslie, *Green Magic*, Viking, New York, 1977.

Grandville, J.J., *Les Fleurs Animées*, translated as *The Flowers Personified* by N. Cleaveland, Johnson, Fry, New York, 1847.

Grounds, Miss, *Crochet Chenille Flowers from Nature*, Simpkin, Marshall, London.

Hale, Sarah Josepha, *Flora's Interpreter and Fortuna Flora*, Mussey, Boston, 1850.

The Hand-Book of Useful and Ornamental Amusements and Accomplishments, Smith, Elder, London, 1845.

Hassard, Annie, *Floral Decorations for the Dwelling House*, Macmillan, London, 1876.

Heineman, Helen, *Restless Angels: The Friendship of Six Victorian Women*, Ohio University Press, Athens, Ohio, 1983.

Hodgins, John George, *Her Majesty the Queen*, John Lovell, Montreal, 1868.

Johnson, Edwin A., *Winter Greeneries at Home*, Orange Judd, New York, 1878.

Johnson, S.O., *Every Woman Her Own Flower Garden*, Ladies Floral Cabinet, New York, 1885.

Mangles, James, "On the Means of Improving the View From the Window of a Back Parlour in a Suburban Villa," *The Ladies' Magazine of Gardening*, William Smith, London, 1842.

Montagu, Mary Wortley, *The Complete Letters of Lady Mary Wortley Montagu*, ed. Robert Hansband, Oxford University Press, London, 1965.

O'Connor, Audrey H., *An Herb Garden Companion*, Cornell University Press, Ithaca, N.Y., 1984.

Parrish, Edward, *The Phantom Bouquet*, Lippincott, Philadelphia, 1865.

Phantom Leaves: A Treatise on the Art of Producing Skeleton Leaves, Tilton, Boston, 1864.

Pickston, Margaret, *The Language of Flowers*, Michael Joseph, London, 1968.

Pratt, Anne, *The Field, the Garden and the Woodland*, Charles Knight, London,

1838.

Putnam, Emily James, *The Lady*, University of Chicago Press, Chicago, 1970.

Rand, Edward S., Jr., *The Window Gardener*, Shepard and Gil, Boston, 1872.

Randolph, Cornelia J., *The Parlor Garden*, Lee and Shepard, Boston, 1884.

Reader, W.J., *Life in Victorian England*, · Batsford, London, 1964.

Russell, Mary, Countess von Arnim, *Elizabeth and Her German Garden*, W.B. Conkey, Chicago, 1901.

Seager, Elizabeth, *Gardens and Gardeners*, Oxford University Press, London, 1984.

Seaton, Beverly, "This Modern Mythology of Flowers: French Flower Books of the Early Nineteenth Century," presented at the National Convention of the Popular Culture Association, Pittsburgh, April 27, 1979.

Talbot, Elizabeth, Countess of Kent, *Flora Domestica, or The Portable Flower-Garden*, Taylor and Hessey, London, 1823.

Verey, Rosemary, *The Scented Garden*, Van Nostrand Reinhold, New York, 1981.

Warner, Anna, *Gardening by Myself*, Anson D.F. Randolph, New York, 1872.

The Wax Bouquet, W. Kent, London, 1855.

Withycombe, Elizabeth Gidley, *The Oxford Dictionary of English Christian Names*, Clarendon, Oxford, 1948.

Wollstonecraft, Mary, *A Vindication of the Rights of Women*, Humboldt, New York, 1792.

Wright, Richardson, *Another Gardener's Bed Book*, Lippincott, Philadelphia, 1933.

------, *The Winter Diversions of a Gardener*, Lippincott, Philadelphia, 1934.

Chapter VIII

Adams, J.F.A., "Is Botany a Suitable Subject for Young Men?" *Science*, February 4, 1887, pp. 116-117.

Amherst, Alicia, *A History of Gardening in England*, Bernard Quaritch, London, 1896.

Barber, Lynn, *The Heyday of Natural History, 1820-1870*, Jonathan Cape, London, 1980.

Bayne, Peter, *Life and Letters of Hugh Miller*, Gould & Lincoln, Boston, 1871.

Blackwell, Antoinette Brown, *The Sexes Throughout Nature*, G.P. Putnam's Sons, New York, 1875.

Catlow, Agnes, *Popular Field Botany*, Reeve, Benham and Reeve, London, 1848.

------, *Popular Garden Botany*, Lovell Reeve, London, 1855.

Coats, Alice M., *The Treasury of Flowers*, Phaedon, London, 1975.

Colden, Jane, *Botanic Manuscript of Jane Colden*, eds. H.W. Rickett and Elizabeth C. Hall, Garden Club of Orange and Duchess Counties, New York, 1963.

Conversations on Vegetable Physiology, Longman, Rees, Orme, Brown and Green, London, 1829.

Darlington, William, *Memorials of John Bartram and Humphrey Marshall*, Lindsay & Blakeston, Philadelphia, 1849.

Every-Day Things, or Useful Knowledge Respecting the Principal Animal, Vegetable and Mineral Substances in Common Use, Grant & Griffiths, London, 1850.

Every Lady's Guide to Her Own Greenhouse, Wm. S. Orr, London, 1851.

A Familiar Account of Trees, George East, London, 1837.

Farquharson, Mrs., "Work of Women in the Biological Sciences," in *International Congress of Women of 1899*, Unwin, London, 1900.

Fiennes, Celia, *Through England on a Side Saddle*, Field & Tuer, London, 1888.

Fitton, Sarah Mary, *Conversations on Botany*, Longman, Hurst, Rees, Orme and Brown, London, 1817.

Flora and Thalia, or Gems of Flowers and Poetry, Henry Washbourne, London, 1835.

Handbook of Town Gardening, James McGlashen, Dublin, 1847.

Hobbs, Christopher, "Sarsaparilla: A Literature Review," *Herbalgram*, summer 1988.

Hollingsworth, Buckner, *Her Garden Was Her Delight*, Macmillan, New York, 1962.

Howe, Bea, *Lady with Green Fingers: The Life of Jane Loudon*, Country Life, London, 1961.

The International Congress of Women of 1899, ed. Countess of Aberdeen, Unwin, London, 1900.

Jackson, Maria E., *Botanical Dialogues Between Hortensia and Her Four Children*, J. Johnson, London, 1797.

Johnson, Louisa, *Every Lady Her Own Flower Garden*, William S. Orr, London, 1845.

The Juvenile Gardener, Harvey and Darton, London, 1824.

Keeler, Harriet L., *The Wildflowers of Early Spring*, The Book Shop, Cleveland, 1894.

Lee, Sarah Wallis Bowdich, *Trees, Plants and Flowers: Their Beauties, Uses and Influences*, Grant & Griffith, London, 1854.

Lincoln, Almira, *Familiar Lectures on Botany*, H. & F. Huntington, Hartford, 1831.

Lindley, John, *Ladies' Botany*, James Ridgway, London, 1834.

Loudon, Jane, *Botany for Ladies*, John Murray, London, 1842.

------, *The Ladies' Flower Garden of Ornamental Annuals*, William S. Orr, London, 1849.

------, *The Ladies' Flower Garden of Ornamental Bulbous Plants*, William Smith, London, 1841.

------, *The Ladies' Flower Garden of Ornamental Perennials*, William S. Orr, London, 1849.

Marcet, Jane, *Conversations on Vegetable Physiology*, Longman, Rees, Orme, Brown and Green, London, 1829.

Murray, Charlotte, *The British Garden*, S. Hazard, London, 1799.

Phantom Leaves: A Treatise on the Art of Producing Skeleton Leaves, Tilton, Boston, 1864.

Pratt, Anne, *The Field, the Garden and the Woodland*, Charles Knight, London, 1838.

------, *The Flowering Plants, Grasses, Sedges and Ferns of Great Britain*, Frederick Warne, London.

Pringle, James S., "Anne Mary Perceval (1790-1876): An Early Botanical Collector in Lower Canada," *Canadian Horticultural History*, 1985, pp. 7-13.

Rossiter, Margaret, *Women Scientists in America: Struggles and Strategies to 1940*, Johns Hopkins University Press, Baltimore, 1982.

Rudolph, Emanuel D., "Women in Nineteenth Century American Botany: A Generally Unrecognized Constituency," *American Journal of Botany*, vol. 69, no. 8, 1982, pp. 1346-1355.

Sargant, Ethel, "Women in Botanical Science," in *International Congress of Women of 1899*, Unwin, London, 1900.

Siegel, Patricia Joan and Kay Thomas Finley, *Women in the Scientific Search*, Scarecrow Press, Metuchen, N.J., 1985.

Simpson, Beryl, "Women in Botany," *Plant Science Bulletin*, June 1973, pp. 22-24.

Smith, A.W., *A Gardener's Dictionary of Plant Names*, St. Martin's, New York, 1963.

Stearns, Raymond Phineas, *Science in the British Colonies of America*, University of Illinois Press, Urbana, 1970.

Talbot, Elizabeth, Countess of Kent, *Sylvan Sketches*, Taylor and Hessey, London, 1825.

Taylor, Gordon Rattray, *The Science of Life*, Thames & Hudson, London, 1963.

Traill, Catharine Parr, *Studies of Plant Life in Canada*, A.S. Woodburn, Ottawa, 1885.

Wakefield, Priscilla, *An Introduction to Botany*, Thomas Burnside, Dublin, 1796.

------, *An Introduction to the Natural History and Classification of Insects*, Darton, Harvey & Darton, London, 1816.

Williams, Greg and Pat, Review of

Collecting and Preserving Plants for Science and Pleasure, by Ruth B. McFarlane, HortIdeas, February 1986.

Wollstonecraft, Mary, A Vindication of the Rights of Women, Humboldt, New York, 1792.

Wright, Richardson, The Winter Diversions of a Gardener, Lippincott, Philadelphia, 1934.

Chapter IX

Beck, Thomasina, Embroidered Gardens, Viking, New York, 1979.

Blackwell, Elizabeth, A Curious Herbal, for Samuel Harding, London, 1737.

Blunt, Wilfred, The Art of Botanical Illustration, Collins, London, 1950.

Bookshaw, George, A New Treatise on Flower Painting, or Every Lady Her Own Drawing Master, Longman, Hurst, Rees, Orme and Brown, London, 1816.

Chicago, Judy, Embroidering Our Heritage: The Dinner Party Needlework, Anchor Books, Garden City, N.Y., 1980.

Christie, Mrs. Archibald H., Embroidery and Tapestry Weaving, Pitman & Sons, London, 1924.

Coats, Alice M., The Treasury of Flowers, Phaedon, London, 1975.

Cunningham, Anne S., "Crewel Gardens," Threads, August/September 1986, pp. 48-50.

------, "Joanna Reed's Crewel Seasons," The Green Scene, January 1987, pp. 24-27.

Daniels, Gilbert, Artists from the Royal Botanic Gardens, Kew, Hunt Institute, Pittsburgh, 1974.

Delany, Mary, A Catalogue of Plants Copyed from Nature in Paper Mosaick, 1778.

Digby, George Wingfield, Elizabethan Embroidery, Faber & Faber, London, 1963.

Edwards, Joan, Crewel Embroidery in England, William Morrow, New York, 1975.

Flora Portrayed: Classics of Botanical Art from the Hunt Institute Collection, Hunt Institute for Botanical Documentation, Pittsburgh, 1985.

The Flower-Garden Display'd, R. Montagu, London, 1734.

Green, J. Reynolds, A History of Botany in the United Kingdom From the Earliest Times to the End of the 19th Century, Dent & Sons, London, 1914.

Greene, Edward Lee, Landmarks of Botanical History, Stanford University Press, Stanford, Calif., 1983.

Hatton, Richard G., Handbook of Plant and Floral Ornament, Dover, New York, 1960 (first published as The Craftsman's Plant-Book, 1909).

Hayden, Ruth, Mrs. Delany: Her Life and Her Flowers, British Museums Publications, 1980.

Hollingsworth, Buckner, Her Garden Was

Her Delight, Macmillan, New York, 1962.

Hunt, P. Francis, *Orchidaceae*, Baunton, Hunt, Rachel McMasters Miller, *Catalogue of Botanical Books in the Collection of Rachel McMasters Miller Hunt*, Hunt Botanical Library, Pittsburgh, 1958.

Jekyll, Francis, *Gertude Jekyll: A Memoir*, Jonathan Cape, London, 1934.

Jekyll, Gertrude, *A Gardener's Testament*, Country Life, London, 1937.

------, *Colour in the Flower Garden*, Newnes/Country Life, London, 1908.

Jones, Mary Eirwen, *English Crewel Designs*, Macdonald, London, 1974.

Kendrick, A.F., *English Needlework*, A. & C. Black, London, 1933.

Kiger, Robert (ed.), *Kate Greenaway: Catalogue of an Exhibition*, Hunt Institute, Pittsburgh, 1980.

King, Ronald, *Botanical Illustration*, Clarkson N. Potter, New York, 1978.

Korach, Karen A., *Third International Exhibition of Botanical Art and Illustration*, Hunt Institute, Pittsburgh, 1972.

Lawrence, George M., *Second International Exhibition of Botanical Art and Illustration*, Hunt Institute, Pittsburgh, 1968.

Llanover, Lady (ed.), *Life and Correspondence of Mrs. Delany*.

Lounsberry, Alice, *A Guide to the Wild Flowers*, William Briggs, Toronto, 1899.

Marianne North 1830-1890, Trustees of the Royal Botanic Gardens, Kew.

Mescent, Jean, *Embroidery and Nature*, Charles T. Branford, Watertown, Mass., 1980.

Miller, Heather S., *A Needleworker's Botany*, New Hampshire Publishing, Somersworth, 1978. *Mrs. Delany's Flower Collages from the British Museum*, The Pierpont Morgan Library, New York, 1986.

Mullins, Edwin, "Saying It with Flowers," London, *Telegraph Sunday Magazine*, September 29, 1985, pp. 62-65.

North, Marianne, *Recollections of a Happy Life: The Autobiography of Marianne North*, Macmillan, London, 1893.

------, *Some Further Recollections of a Happy Life*, Macmillan, London, 1893.

------, *A Vision of Eden: the Life and Work of Marianne North*, Royal Botanic Gardens, Kew and Webb & Bower, Exeter, 1980.

Palliser, Mrs. Bury, *History of Lace*, Sampson Low, Marston, London, 1910.

Paviere, Sydney H., *Floral Art*, F. Lewis, Leigh-on-Sea, 1965.

Potter, Beatrix, *The Journal of Beatrix Potter from 1881-1897*, transcribed from her code writing by Leslie Linder, Frederick Warne, London, 1966.

Ruh, Glen B., "How Petals From the Sea

Form These Fragile Blossoms," *Smithsonian*, January 1987, pp. 107-110.

Sanecki, Kay, "The Formal Herb Garden," *The Garden*, vol. 112, part 6, June 1987, pp. 291-296.

A Schole-House for the Needle, R. Shoreleyker, London, 1627.

Seligman, G. Saville and Talbot Hughes, *Domestic Needlework*, Country Life, London, 1926.

Siegel, Patricia Joan and Kay Thomas Finley, *Women in the Scientific Search*, Scarecrow Press, Metuchen, N.J., 1985.

Tooley, Michael J. (ed.), *Gertrude Jekyll*, Michaelmas Books, Witton-le-Wear, 1984.

Verlet, Florisoone and Tabard Hoffmeister, *Great Tapestries*, Edita S.A., Lausanne, 1965.

Victoria and Albert Museum, *Flowers in English Embroidery*, 2nd ed., Her Majesty's Stationery Office, London, 1963.

White, James J. and Donald E. Wendel, *Fifth International Exhibition of Botanical Art and Illustration*, Hunt Institute, Pittsburgh, 1983.

Wright, Richardson, *The Winter Diversions of a Gardener*, Lippincott, Philadelphia, 1934.

Chapter X

Brown, Jane, *Vita's Other World*, Viking, London, 1985.

Cartwright, Julia, *Italian Gardens of the Renaissance*, Smith, Elder, London, 1914.

Coats, Peter, *Flowers in History*, Weidenfield and Nicolson, London, 1970.

Coke, Mary, *The Letters and Journals of Lady Mary Coke*, Lonsdale & Bartholomew, Bath, 1970.

Cowell, F.R., *The Garden as a Fine Art*, Houghton Mifflin, Boston, 1978.

Dawson, Laura Blanchard, "Horticulture as a Profession for Women," *Transactions of the Massachusetts Horticulture Society*, vol. 1, 1910, pp. 68-78.

Ely, Helena Rutherford, *A Woman's Hardy Garden*, Grosset & Dunlap, New York, 1908.

Epton, Nina, *Josephine and Her Children*, Weidenfeld & Nicolson, London, 1975.

Evelyn, Charles, *The Lady's Recreation, or The Art of Gardening Farther Improved*, London, 1718.

Fessenden, Thomas, G., *The New American Gardener*, Otis, Broaders, Boston, 1843.

Festing, Sally, "The Duchess of Portland and Her Plants," *The Garden*, August 1987, pp. 361-365.

------, "The Second Duchess of Portland and Her Rose," *The Journal of the Garden History Society*, autumn 1986, pp. 194-196.

Glendenning, Victoria, *Vita: The Life of V. Sackville-West*, Knopf, New York, 1983.

Greatheed, Bertie, *An Englishman in Paris, 1803: The Journals of Bertie Greatheed*, Geoffrey Bles, London, 1953.

Grimaldi, Grace, *My Book of Flowers*, Doubleday, Garden City, N.Y., 1980.

Harlan, Jack R., *Crops and Man*, American Society of Agronomy, Madison, Wisc., 1975.

Johnson, Louisa, *Every Lady Her Own Flower Garden*, William S. Orr, London, 1845.

Knapton, Ernest John, *Empress Josephine*, Harvard University Press, Cambridge, Mass., 1964.

Langdon, Carolyn S., "Eight Great Women in the Garden World," *Home Garden*," May 1967, pp. 59-60.

Le Lievre, Audrey, *Miss Willmott of Warley Place*, Faber & Faber, London, 1980.

Lees-Milne, Avilde and Rosemary Verey, *The Englishwoman's Garden*, Chatto & Windus, London, 1983.

McDouall, Robin, "An Excursion From London: Sissinghurst and the Three Chimneys," *Gourmet*, July 1981, pp. 16-17, 79-81.

Memoirs Illustrative of the Life and Writings of John Evelyn Esq., 1641-1705, ed. William Bray, for Henry Colburn, London, 1818.

Netherlands Flowerbulb Information Centre, "Plant Dahlias in Spring to Enjoy Flowers Through Fall," Toronto, 1988.

Perényi, Eleanor, *Green Thoughts*, Vintage, New York, 1981.

Putnam, Emily James, *The Lady*, University of Chicago Press, Chicago, 1970.

Russell, Mary, Countess von Arnim, *Elizabeth and Her German Garden*, W.B. Conkey, Chicago, 1901.

Sackville-West, Vita, *Collected Poems*, vol. 1, Hogarth, London, 1933.

------, *A Joy of Gardening*, Harper & Row, New York, 1958.

------, *Vita Sackville-West's Garden Book*, Michael Joseph, London, 1968.

Scott-James, Anne, *Sissinghurst: The Making of a Garden*, Michael Joseph, London, 1974.

Seager, Elizabeth, *Gardens and Gardeners*, Oxford University Press, London, 1984.

Chapter XI

Austin, Principal, *Woman: Her Character, Culture and Calling*, Book & Bible House, Brantford, Ont., 1890.

Balmori, D., D.K. McGuire and E.M. McPeck, *Beatrix Farrand's American Landscapes: Her Gardens and Campuses*, Sagapress, Sagaponack, New York, 1985.

Barnhaven Seeds catalogue, no. 8,

Kendal, Cumbria, 1985.

Bellis, Florence, *Gardening and Beyond*, Timber Press, Beaverton, Oreg., 1986.

Bolzau, Emma Lydia, *Almira Hart Lincoln Phelps: Her Life and Work*, Philadelphia, 1936.

British Weekly Commissioners, *Toilers in London, or Inquiries Concerning Female Labour in the Metropolis*, Hodder and Stoughton, London, 1889.

Chatto, Beth, *Beth Chatto's Garden Notebook*, Dent, London, 1988.

------, *The Dry Garden*, Dent, London, 1978.

------, *Plant Portraits*, Dent, London, 1985.

Cobb, Shirley, "With Upright Piano Box, She Parlayed Survival Needs Into Seed Industry," *News-Chronicle*, Thousand Oaks, Calif., August 23, 1979, p. 8.

Cole, John, "The Woman Behind the Wildflower That Stopped a Dam," *Horticulture*, December 1977, pp. 30-35.

Dawson, Laura Blanchard, "Horticulture as a Profession for Women," *Transactions of the Massachusetts Historical Society*, vol. 1, 1910, pp. 68-78.

Every Lady's Guide to Her Own Greenhouse, Wm.S. Orr, London, 1851.

Far North Gardens catalogue, Wisconsin, 1982.

Francis, Myrtle S., "Opportunities for Profit in Horticulture," *The Monthly Bulletin*, December 1916, pp. 434-437.

------, "Theodosia Burr Shepherd, California's Pioneer Floriculturalist," *The Ventura Historical Society Quarterly*, August 1963, pp. 3-20.

Fraser, Marian, "Bluestockings: Wicked Virgins and Hyenas in Petticoats," *Ideas*, Canadian Broadcasting Corporation, Montreal, 1984.

Friedan, Betty, *The Feminine Mystique*, Norton, New York, 1963.

Galloway, B.T., "Flora W. Patterson 1847-1928," *Phytopathology*, vol. 18, 1928, pp. 877-879.

Grieve, Maud, *A Modern Herbal*, Jonathan Cape, 1931.

Grout, A.J., "Elizabeth Gertrude (Knight) Britton," *Bryologist*, vol. 38, 1935, pp. 1-3.

Haas, Violet B. and Carolyn C. Perrucci (eds.), *Women in Scientific and Engineering Professions*, University of Michigan Press, Ann Arbor, 1984.

Hollingsworth, Buckner, *Her Garden Was Her Delight*, Macmillan, New York, 1962.

Home Acres (formerly *Farm and Garden*), vol. 14, nos. 1, 2 (1926), 3, 5, 6 (1927).

Jekyll, Francis, *Gertrude Jekyll: A Memoir*, Jonathan Cape, London, 1934.

Jekyll, Gertrude, *Flower Decoration for the House*, Newnes/Country Life, London, 1907.

------, *A Gardener's Testament*, Country Life, London, 1937.

------, *Home and Garden*, Longmans, Green, London, 1900.

------, *Wood and Garden*, Longmans, Green, London, 1899.

------ and Lawrence Weaver, *Gardens for Small Country Houses*, Newnes/Country Life, London, 1912.

Johnson, Louisa, *Every Lady Her Own Flower Garden*, Orr, London, 1845.

Lawrence, Elizabeth, *Gardening for Love: The Market Bulletins*, Duke University Press, Durham, N.C., 1987.

Lincoln, Almira, *Familiar Lectures on Botany*, Huntington, Hartford, 1831.

Log House Plants catalogue, Cottage Grove, Oreg., 1986.

Loudon, Jane, *Gardening for Ladies and Companion to the Flower Garden*, Wiley, New York, 1865.

MacPhail, Elizabeth C., *Kate Sessions: Pioneer Horticulturist*, San Diego Historical Society, San Diego, Calif., 1976.

Massingham, Betty, *A Century of Gardeners*, Faber & Faber, London, 1982.

Morris, Karen S.C., "Profiles: Important Contributors to the Study of Herbs: Eleanor Sinclair Rhode," *The Herb, Spice and Medicinal Plants Digest*, summer 1990, p.6.

Perry, Frances, *The Woman Gardener*, Farrar, Straus & Cudahy, New York, 1955.

Raver, Anne, "Beatrix Farrand," *Horticulture*, February 1985, pp. 32-45.

Rion, Hanna (Verbeck), *Let's Make a Flower Garden*, McBride, Nast, New York, 1912.

Rossiter, Margaret, *Women Scientists in America: Struggles and Strategies to 1940*, Johns Hopkins University Press, Baltimore, 1982.

Sanecki, Kay, "The Formal Herb Garden," *The Garden*, June 1987, pp. 291-296.

Shaw, George Bernard, *Pygmalion: A Romance in Five Acts*, Penguin, Edinburgh, 1941.

Siegel, Patricia Joan and Kay Thomas Finley, *Women in the Scientific Search*, Scarecrow, Metuchen, N.J., 1985.

Svejda, Felicitas, *New Winter-Hardy Roses and Other Flowering Shrubs*, Publication 1727, Agriculture Canada, Ottawa, 1984.

Theodosia B. Shepherd Co. catalogues, Ventura, Calif., 1906, 1913.

Thompson, Maxine M., "Women in Horticulture," *HortScience*, April 1973, pp. 77-78.

Tozer, Eliot, "Gertrude Jekyll's Great Vision," *Horticulture*, November 1984, pp. 30-39.

Usborne, H.M. (ed.), *Women's Work in*

War Time, T. Werner Laurie, London, 1917.

Verey, Rosemary and Ellen Samuels, *The American Woman's Garden*, Little, Brown, Boston, 1984.

Von Baeyer, Edwinna, "The Horticultural Odyssey of Isabella Preston," *Canadian Horticultural History*, vol. 1, no. 3, 1987, pp. 25-175.

------, *Rhetoric and Roses: A History of Canadian Gardening 1900-1930*, Fitzhenry & Whiteside, Toronto, 1984.

Wilder, Lousie Beebe, *Adventures in My Garden and Rock Garden*, Doubleday, Garden City, N.Y., 1926.

Wilson, Carol Green, *Alice Eastwood's Wonderland*, California Academy of Sciences, San Francisco, 1955.

Wiser, Vivian (ed.), *Two Centuries of American Agriculture*, Agricultural History Society, Washington, 1976.

Wolseley, Frances, *Gardening for Women*, Cassell, London, 1908.

------, *Women and the Land*, Chatto & Windus, London, 1916.

Chapter XII

Bamberger, Joan, "The Myth of Matriarchy: Why Men Rule in Primitive Society," in *Woman, Culture and Society*, Stanford University Press, Stanford, Calif., 1974.

Bateson, Gregory, *Steps to an Ecology of Mind*, Ballantine Books, New York, 1972.

Berman, Morris, *The Reenchantment of the World*, Cornell University Press, Ithaca, N.Y., 1981.

Berry, Thomas, *The Dream of the Earth*, Sierra Club, San Francisco, 1988.

Black, John, *The Dominion of Man: The Search for Ecological Responsibility*, University Press, Edinburgh, 1970.

Carson, Rachel, *Silent Spring*, Houghton Mifflin, New York, 1962.

Chaucer, Geoffrey (?), *The Floure and the Leafe and the Assembly of Ladies*, ed. D.A. Pearsall, Thomas Nelson & Sons, Edinburgh, 1962.

Currie, Jo, "Earth on the Edge," *Canadian Living*, January 1989, pp. 39-49.

Dillard, Annie, *Pilgrim at Tinker Creek*, Harper's Magazine Press, New York, 1974.

Duncan, Muriel, "Animal Rights," *The United Church Observer*, August 1988, pp. 27-35.

Ferguson, Marilyn, *The Aquarian Conspiracy*, Tarcher, Los Angeles, 1980.

Findhorn Community, *The Findhorn Garden*, Harper & Row, New York, 1975.

Friedan, Betty, *The Feminine Mystique*, Norton, New York, 1963.

Gimbutas, Marija, *The Goddesses and Gods of Old Europe, 6500-3500 B.C.: Myths and Cult Images*, 2nd ed., Thames & Hudson, London, 1982.

Griffin, Susan, *Woman and Nature*, Harper & Row, New York, 1978.

Leiss, William, *The Domination of Nature*, Braziller, New York, 1972.

Lovelock, James E., *The Ages of Gaia*, Norton, New York, 1988.

------, *Gaia: A New Look at Life on Earth*, Oxford University Press, Oxford, 1979.

Meaning of the Garden: Proceedings of a Working Conference to Explore the Social, Psychological and Cultural Dimensions of Gardens, University of California at Davis, 1987.

Merchant, Carolyn, "Earthcare: Women and the Environmental Movement," *Environment*, June 1981, pp. 6-13, 38-40.

Nasr, Seyyed Hossein, *Science and Civilization in Islam*, Harvard University Press, Cambridge, Mass., 1968.

Ornstein, Holly, "A Quiet Boom in Blooms," *The New York Times*, June 13, 1986, p. 10F.

Ortner, Sherry B., "Is Female to Male as Nature Is to Culture?" in *Woman, Culture and Society*, Stanford University Press, Stanford, Calif., 1974.

Paul, Gerald Walton, "Letters from Paul: Earthquake and Camel-Bells," The Kingston *Whig-Standard*, December 3, 1988, p. 7.

Peterson, Rebecca, "Ten Active Years: A Review of Women and Environments Research," *Women and Environments*, fall 1986, pp. 9-11.

Reich, Charles A., *The Greening of America*, Random House, New York, 1968.

"Religion and the New Science," *Ideas*, Canadian Broadcasting Corporation, Montreal, 1985.

Reuther, Rosemary Radford, *New Woman, New Earth*, Seabury, New York, 1975.

Roszak, Theodore, *The Making of a Counter Culture*, Doubleday, New York, 1968.

Stone, Merlin, *When God Was a Woman*, Harcourt, Brace, Jovanovich, San Diego, 1976.

Thibodeau, Francis R. and Hermann H. Field (eds.), *Sustaining Tomorrow: A Strategy for World Conservation and Development*, University Press of New England, Hanover, 1984.

Toulmin, Stephen, *The Return to Cosmology: Postmodern Science and the Theology of Nature*, University of California Press, Berkeley, 1982.

White, Lynn, Jr., *Machina ex Deo: Essays in the Dynamics of Western Culture*, MIT Press, Cambridge, Mass., 1968.

Index

Credits